Philosophies of Science/
Feminist Theories

Philosophies of Science/ Feminist Theories

JANE DURAN

UNIVERSITY OF CALIFORNIA–
SANTA BARBARA

 WestviewPress

A Division of HarperCollins*Publishers*

Copyright © 1998 by Westview Press, A Division of HarperCollins Publishers, Inc.

Published in 1998 in the United States of America by Westview Press, 5500 Central Avenue, Boulder, Colorado 80301-2877, and in the United Kingdom by Westview Press, 12 Hid's Copse Road, Cumnor Hill, Oxford OX2 9JJ

A CIP catalog record for this book is available from the Library of Congress.
ISBN 0-8133-3299-0 (hc).—ISBN 0-8133-3325-3 (pbk)

The paper used in this publication meets the requirements of the American National Standard for Permanence of Paper for Printed Library Materials Z39.48-1984.

10   9   8   7   6   5   4   3   2   1

*For the feminist philosophers of science
and radical critics of science who
have altered our views*

Contents

Preface

Science studies has taken on an extraordinary life in recent years, and contemporary debates surrounding such disparate phenomena as the Sokal hoax, the AIDS virus (or nonvirus), and the existence of life on Mars take on added salience when we consider the proximity of much of the current research in science to our daily lives.

The philosopher of science, however, may feel somewhat cut off from such debates, because the rigorous training provided by most programs in philosophy of science may appear, superficially at least, to be at odds with much of the material in the popular press or, indeed, even in the academic press that is relevant to science studies. This work aims to fill in the gaps for those whose training is primarily in philosophy, but at the same time it attempts to be accessible to readers trained in other disciplines, including the social sciences and women's studies. If the greatest impetus for the growth of work revolving around the cultural status of science has come from feminist theory, any explanation of what might be involved in finding the intersection of philosophy of science and contemporary feminism is timely. In this book I have tried to acquaint the philosopher of science with feminist theory and the feminist with at least a minimal amount of philosophy of science, and to provide as well some overview of other crucial relevant areas, such as the radical critique of science and sociology of science.

The first part of the book is probably the most directly philosophical and no doubt the most difficult for those who do not originally have training in philosophy. Because so much is written about positivism and the work springing from it, it is important to be precise about the original positivist project and its offspring. An overview of the entire project and a closer look at positivism, the Vienna Circle, and movements in philosophy of science allied with it comprise the first section.

Few revolutions have had the impact of the Kuhnian revolution, and so an explanation of it and its relation to the work that historically preceded it begins the second section. The importance of sociology of science, particularly the Edinburgh school, is the topic of Chapter 5 of this work, and

Chapter 6 is devoted exclusively to feminist theory and the feminist critique of science. Although feminist theory is touched on throughout the work, it is Chapter 6 that tries to provide an overview of it in terms of its relationship to current science studies.

Because the radical critique of science is closely allied to lines of criticism that originated in feminist thought, this critique constitutes Chapter 7. In both Chapters 7 and 8 I not only underscore the Marxist, and hence materialist, origins of the radical critique but also show how recent work in naturalized epistemology and epistemic justification theory might be tied to new work on the notion of scientific justification. The concluding section, Chapter 9, provides an overview of the entire work.

Philosophy of science began as something of a stepchild to work in that more traditional area of philosophizing, epistemology, and because of my previous work in epistemology I was intrigued by the early work in the feminist critique of science. I quickly saw that many issues were closely related, even if the lines had not always been clearly drawn. Feminist epistemology asks us to see what might count as androcentrism in epistemic theorizing and to develop new lines of theory based on other cognitive styles. The feminist and radical critiques of science are asking us to look at how the social structure of science informs its projects, its participants, and their results. Feminists can have few more valuable areas of endeavor than those that encourage us to consider how the social production of knowledge impinges on the rest of our lives.

It should be possible to read most of this text, except for the first three chapters, without the benefit of technical training in philosophy of science. And even in the first three chapters, the careful nonspecialist reader will probably be able to follow most of the argument. If the work can be used in both departments of philosophy (of whatever stripe) and women's studies programs, it will have fulfilled its intended purpose.

Jane Duran

Acknowledgments

The philosopher of science is bound to be struck these days by the number of projects that fall under the currently popular rubric "science studies." The explosion of work in recent years has made for a much richer dialogue with respect to science and science-related disciplines than was previously available, and the University of California at Santa Barbara is extremely fortunate to have on its faculty a number of workers in these fields. For a varied and steady diet of science studies colloquia and get-togethers, I thank the Science, Technology, and Culture Research Focus Group at UCSB, led by Chuck Bazerman. Special thanks also go to Michael Osborne and Patrick Sharp.

I also owe a continuing debt of gratitude to the Social Networks Seminar of the UCSB Sociology Department, where I have for some years been able to pursue scintillating discussions in philosophy of science as it impacts on contemporary research in the social sciences with such colleagues as John Sonquist, John Mohr, and Eugene Johnsen. In addition to work that is actually part of philosophy of science, I have benefited greatly from watching the instantiation of a number of critical thinking projects in the elementary schools of the Goleta Valley Unified School District in conjunction with research projects directed by the UCSB Graduate School of Education.

It has been particularly exciting to teach these issues to UCSB undergraduates in conjunction with work in the Women's Studies Department. Special thanks are due to my class in contemporary feminist theory during the spring quarter of 1996, whose students engaged me tirelessly in discussions of the work of Evelyn Fox Keller and Sandra Harding. Also valuable was the discussion of Freud's *Dora* as it relates to issues in justification in another UCSB women's studies class, "Feminist Perspectives on Western Thought," during the fall quarter of 1996.

I first began to think about issues in philosophy of science, and epistemic issues in general, as a graduate student at Rutgers in the late 1970s, and seminars on topics in philosophy of science there were particularly helpful, as were discussions with members of informal meeting groups in the Princeton area. I also thank Giles Gunn, whose invitation asking me to speak to his English Department seminar on topics relating to American pragmatism forced me to look at the contemporary critics of analytic philosophy of science in a new way.

As always, I owe a significant debt of gratitude to Ruth Doell, whose work with me on two papers, one of which was published in *Dialectica* in 1993, forced me to try to look at issues in philosophy of science and sociology of science through the eyes of a practicing scientist. Ruth's encouragement has not only been extremely important to my academic endeavors but has been greatly beneficial in establishing a network of California colleagues. I owe another debt to Armen Marsoobian, editor of *Metaphilosophy* (where I published on the question of explanation and reference in 1996), for whom reviewing has been a pleasure, as it has allowed me to peruse an enormous amount of contemporary work.

Finally, my thanks as always go to my husband, Richard Duran, who shows exemplary patience in being married to a philosopher; to Greg Kelly and Anita Guerrini, who also have a strong interest in science studies; and to other colleagues. The warm climate and beauty of the Santa Barbara area make scholarly research there all the more enjoyable, and have resulted, I hope, in an interdisciplinary work reflective, at least to some extent, of the range of talent that UCSB has to offer.

J. D.

Part One

The Growth of Philosophy of Science

1

Philosophy of Science: An Overview

It is a commonplace of contemporary feminist theorizing that, within the traditional divisions of philosophy, some of the strongest progress has been made in epistemology and philosophy of science. Yet this important claim overlooks the differences between work that might more properly be labeled "epistemological" and that which might be thought to fall under the rubric "philosophy of science," and also frequently ignores the controversial but exciting theorizing in allied fields such as the sociology of science and the history of science.[1]

Philosophy of science as such, and as practiced at many professional venues within philosophy, has itself not been the subject of as much critique as some seem to believe. Rather, the critique that is usually referred to as "feminist" has often been aimed at the practice of science or at allied fields such as those mentioned above. And yet philosophy of science, in its purest form and in the form that poses such traditional questions as those regarding the nature of a theory, the strength and importance of the realist/instrumentalist controversy, the relevance of the unity thesis, and so forth, may of course be the target of directed feminist criticism.

Insofar as such criticism has yet been established, an additional lacuna involves the provision of an overview that might allow the novice a chance to peruse at least some of the relevant areas at one go. The work of Evelyn Fox Keller, for example, although it might indeed be called feminist philosophy of science, presumes a certain sophistication with regard to the practice of science and assumes a certain level of knowledge with respect to theorization, hypothesis formation, and so forth. The works of other theorists, such as Hilary Rose, allude comparatively little to traditional theorizing, and so one might be forgiven for failing to learn of certain theoretical problems and areas if one reads largely the more radical critiques of science, much of which is also feminist.[2]

In this work I plan to provide an overview of various areas in philosophy of science—or philosophies of science, as they might more accurately be called—and various filaments of feminist theorizing that might be adduced to support criticism of these philosophies or to provide an area of contrast. Part of my aim is to provide sufficiently ample scope for each area (both philosophies of science and feminist theories) so that a reader who knew relatively little about either area could learn enough profitably to read more. Thus I will presuppose little acquaintance with either area, particularly in the case of the various philosophies of science and their offspring. Understanding what philosophy of science amounts to as an intellectual enterprise is obviously related to the history of philosophy, analytic philosophy in particular, in the twentieth century, and it is to this area that I now turn.

Philosophy of Science and Its Origins

The area of study now called "philosophy of science" began as something of a stepchild of that classical division within philosophy, epistemology. It might be tempting to think that the growth of science as an international intellectual endeavor alone gave rise to a demarcated area, philosophy of science, but this might not have been the case had not epistemology itself grown and altered drastically during the early years of this century.

The simultaneous developments of epistemology and philosophy of science may be traced to the growth and emergence of analytic philosophy, the rise of the Vienna Circle, and, somewhat nonphilosophically, the emergence of scientists with European training in the United States during World War II and immediately afterward. Each of these alterations in the structure of intellectual life gave rise to trends that strengthened and formalized the type of theorizing under review.[3] The Russellian attempts at logical atomism and the Wittgensteinian moves in the *Tractatus* provided a structure, based on the growth and development of logic since Gottlob Frege's nineteenth-century theorizing, that allowed for the development of a rigorous epistemology. Such an epistemology, predicated on notions of privileged access, could establish a degree of certainty with respect to hedged claims about particulars, and as Russell himself noted, the statements were founded on the sense experience of qualia of short duration.[4] This rigidly foundationalist epistemology had an influence on theorizing in contemporary analytic philosophy that cannot be overestimated, since it itself became tied to the correspondence rules of positivism.

The work of the Vienna Circle in at least some of its formulations is, of course, directly responsible for the emergence of what we now call philosophy of science. Interestingly, although one might be inclined to regard the circle's theorizing as an exercise in comparative philosophical purity, there is as much disagreement, historically, about the work of some members of the circle as there is with respect to any other area of philosophy. The contemporary realist/instrumentalist controversy, for example, might be deemed to have its origins in the work of at least some members of the circle, and yet commentators have difficulty in deciding whether one can discern realist or instrumentalist trends in the work of Moritz Schlick, for instance.[5]

What is remarkable about the Received View of positivism, at least insofar as it can be tied to the growth of the circle, is that it provides, again, a rigorously formal method of codifying a foundationalist approach to scientific confirmation. The language of observation becomes tied to the language of theory via a series of correspondence rules, and the linkage to privileged-access epistemic verification provides a degree of certitude that comes as close to deductive certainty, according to the argument, as one can get. Finally, the arrival in the United States of trained scientists, many of whom came from the cultural milieu of the circle and its discussants, furthered the debate on science, the nature of scientific theorizing, and its philosophical underpinnings. Each of these three factors was crucial in the development of philosophy of science, and without any one of them the various permutations in thinking that characterized the postwar period would not have occurred.

The Postwar Moves

Work that continued within the broad frame of the positivist tradition proceeded after the war and was perhaps most strikingly articulated by Carl Hempel. The Deductive-Nomological model, or "D-N" as it was usually known, attempted to codify within the framework of the first-order predicate logic the standards of confirmation reflective of scientific theorizing.

The notion that confirmation proceeded, logically speaking, along the lines of the move known as "denying the antecedent," a logically fallacious move, forwarded the notion that disconfirmation, rather than confirmation, was the crucial scientific notion.[6] Disconfirmation, or falsification, could be modeled in stringent logical fashion by the simple expedient of using the obvious pattern, *modus tollens*. But the paradox of induction—the notion that induction cannot stand, evidentially, as its own support, and the process of induction never tells us with certainty anything about the n + 1 case—has its analogue in the notion that there is no logically valid model for the process of confirmation.

Work by Karl Popper and others focused on the concept of falsification, but much of this work was shoved to one side, so to speak, by studies in the late 1950s and early 1960s that began to be more reflective of the manner in which scientists actually worked. With the publication of Thomas Kuhn's *The Structure of Scientific Revolutions* in 1962, philosophy of science took a turn from which it has not yet fully rebounded.[7] Although Kuhn does not himself regard his work as centrally located in sociology of science, its description of the ways in which paradigm shifts occur signaled a new awareness of the vast gulf between normative work in philosophy of science and work that was descriptively accurate.[8] This chasm itself was later to be reflected in the moves that distanced normative epistemologists from those who attempted to naturalize epistemic theory, but at the time Kuhn's work was noteworthy for its reliance on the actual rather than the idealized.

At the same time, work by Imre Lakatos, Norwood Hanson, and others forwarded new, less positivistic ways of viewing the procedures of science.[9] The upshot of this work was that respect for the Received View declined precipitously at the same time that few views with a comparable amount of epistemic rigor were being brought forward. This set the stage for an intense battle between views that were more realist and views that were less so, a battle that in some ways echoed the preceding wars in that stringent, instrumentalist empiricism that did not ask one to accept unobservables was frequently perceived as being not as rigorous or hard-core a position as the new realism.[10] Many versions of realism tended to rely on rigorous notions of reference so that the contention that the "success of science" could be explained only by the positing of the actual entities referred to became linked to a certain perception of the usage of many terms.[11]

Feminist Critique and Radical Critique

The feminist critique of science that now amounts to a virtual commonplace works in tandem with another, possibly less noticed critical construction, and that is the radical stance toward science and science-related activities. Both of these critiques take it as a given that the intellectual structure of science, its results, its effects on the culture, and its social network are positioned in ways that make science androcentric, class- and race-biased, insensitive to the needs of the oppressed, and hierarchical with respect to social indicators and markers.

The feminist critique might be thought to be in some sense the descendant of portions of the weltanschauungen stances, because it would not have been theoretically likely in former times to construct such a view without paying attention to the practice of science. Views focusing on the practice of science emphasized the divorce of its practice from anything resembling the idealized patterns of confirmation/disconfirmation posited by the more classically minded theoreticians, and focus on its practice also revealed statistics about the training of scientists, their gender and social-class origins, the hallmarks of strong and prestigious science networks, and so on. Such a focus inevitably came to rest on the lack of women practitioners, a result of which, as feminist theory became ever more sophisticated, was a concomitant observation of differences in types of cognitive styles and/or approaches.[12]

Science's androcentricity, so this approach goes, is located not so much in the absence of numbers but in matters of style. Keller, for one, labeled the masculinist bias of the vast majority of scientific researchers (whether male or female) "stylistic aggression,"[13] and the import of this notion resonates throughout contemporary critiques of science.

Science, qua purely intellectual endeavor, is of course the offspring of historical strands passing backward through the Enlightenment to figures such as Descartes, and ultimately to Aristotle and Plato. Keller, in her important essay "Love and Sex in Plato's Epistemology,"[14] reminds the reader of the strength of Plato's view that concepts attached to the highest degree of ontological structure are those concepts born of dialectic between two males. Thus from its outset in the Western tradition the notion that the rigorously intellectual was a purely male enterprise received great impetus, and nothing that took place in the succeeding centuries dislodged the importance of this early stance. Descartes's somewhat solipsistic meanderings in the *Meditations* have also been subjected to similar feminist criticism.[15] More importantly, perhaps, it is the overall task of science itself, particularly in the nineteenth and twentieth centuries, that has been the point of departure for much feminist criticism.

The tasks and projects of science are closely allied with the overview that Thomas Nagel has labeled the "view from nowhere."[16] Purporting to or alleging neutrality and empirically sanctified objectivity, the "facts" of science are the product of the work of males, almost all of whom are of European ancestry and the vast majority of whom come from at least middle-class backgrounds. The structure of these "facts," the manner in which they are uncovered, the social settings in which they are elucidated, and the styles or modes of training received by those who claim to be the uncoverers—all of these phenomena display the androcentric or masculinist bias of those doing the work, while claiming to be value neutral.[17]

Similarly, so the radical critique goes, science has been insensitive to the needs and/or social stations of persons and groups who might be deemed to be oppressed, and the uses to which scientific facts are often put belie the attempts to distance the discoverers from any sort of social bias. In the developed countries in particular, the history of much technological advance since World War II has been that the advances were often made, literally, at the expense of less-advantaged communities. A long list of citations could be assembled, but one of the most salient examples involves the use and construction of facilities involving nuclear waste, the employment of persons at those facilities, their geographical placement, and so forth.[18] Likewise, work in the social sciences has often resulted in the displacement or disruption of the lives of those marginalized by such work, as can readily be seen in the recent controversy over *The Bell Curve*.[19]

Thus a long examination of the various disciplines related to science—philosophy and history of science, sociology of science, rhetoric of science, and so forth—pushes us away from any kind of notion of science as engaged in largely deductive work that is to some extent beyond the need for contact with the world of the senses and toward a notion of science as indeed mired in the real world of politics and machinations. The upshot of the convergence of these lines of theory has been that the feminist critique of science has come to the fore at the same time that other attacks on science have also achieved prominence. One might wonder, then, what is left of the original forms of theorizing that came to light before the weltanschauungen-derived views of science just mentioned achieved hegemony.

New Disputes in Scientific Theorizing

The intensity of the realist/instrumentalist controversy in contemporary philosophy of science mirrors some of the older debates that had originally shaped the dialogue between the Received View and the Kuhnian views and is perhaps one of the areas least examined by feminist and radical critics of science.[20] The realists, on the one hand, want to claim that there is nothing that accounts for the "success of science" save the "epistemic access" to real entities that is granted by the use of referentially secure scientific terms in certain contexts.[21] The instrumentalists, or, as Bas Van Fraassen wants to call them, the "strict empiricists," hold that it is unnecessary and undesirable to engage in the intellectual self-deception involved in constructing a hard realism for science and that there is nothing in the use of scientific terms that entitles us to go beyond a warrant, or ticket of inference, about the predictive reliability of certain theoretical constructs.[22]

That this debate has the heat and excitement it does is testimony perhaps to an enduring legacy from positivism, whether acknowledged or not. Positivism at least had the merit of insisting, minimally, that theoretical constructs did entitle one to certain kinds of inferences, and the dispute in positivistic circles had more to do with whether or not one was entitled to go beyond the phenomena, as it were, than it did with whether science was a rational enterprise.[23] In more contemporary terms, the force of the antiscience side has now become such that the realist/instrumentalist controversy is noteworthy for the presuppositions it entails and not just because it happens to be a focal point of current scientific commentary.

Van Fraassen has argued very convincingly that nothing allows the theoretician to posit "real entities" behind the terms and that a refusal to acknowledge this amounts to an "epistemology for dinosaurs."[24] He is here talking about evolutionary epistemology, but the two controversies have sometimes been linked, since part of what supports realism, according to some, is the notion that if theoretical terms had not referred, humankind would not have been able to survive. Thus it is not going too far to speculate that beneath the surface of the acrimony between the strict empiricists and the rigid realists is a fear that the voices of the sociologists, historians, and so on who have claimed that science is a less-than-rational process are going to win out. Not, of course, that the social-science minded do not themselves have evidence on their side; it is merely the case that what was once taken for granted as a base or platform of support for disputes within philosophy of science itself is now up for grabs.

Sociology of Science and the New Theoreticians

Perhaps the greatest single move since the 1970s in the disciplines that investigate science as a whole, including philosophy of science, has come from the position now known as "relativism." Bruno Latour, Barry Barnes, David Bloor, and others are all to some extent identified with varieties of this position.[25]

Drawing on work in the sociology of science, those who have come to see the enterprise of science as simply one among many human intellectual enterprises—with no privileged epistemic status or with an allegedly, rather than actually, privileged status—have begun to have enormous influence in academic meetings and in the general public arena. What all of these programs have in common is a desire to demystify science and puncture its pretensions to some sort of special standing among intellectual enterprises.

Thus Latour's work, for example, not only tries to establish that science is entitled to no special status but goes to great pains to show that the notion of empirical confirmation is vacuous and that what passes for empirical confirmation in science is itself no more than a social construction. In a number of works, Latour argues that broad epistemic categorizations, themselves social products and the results of the times in which various actors live, help to determine the categories that are employed to theorize about phenomena, including categories that purport or allege to be scientific. Latour claims that modernism defined "what Nature is supposed to be" and that various other epistemic prescriptions flow socially from this, with no more regard for anything resembling actual empirical confirmation than can be achieved by pointing out the social relations among the persons involved.[26]

The desire to strip science and scientific activity of any pretension to a god's-eye view is forcefully articulated by such critics as Steve Fuller, whose writings are all the more powerful because combined training in both philosophy of science and sociological perspective informs them.[27]

In his *Social Epistemology*, Fuller argues that the kinds of epistemological views that supported the Received View of positivism at an earlier point in this century (views to which I have already alluded here) are themselves the product of the same kinds of social forces that we normally think of as constructing other, less hallowed stances, and are deserving of no special consideration. Drawing on Foucault and other French and Continental thinkers, Fuller claims that the leading *memes* of philosophy of science are in fact just that, and that they are deeply wedded to other, less intellectually oriented social phenomena. Finally, such French theorists as Jean Baudrillard have also been cited in this debate, because Baudrillard's attack on the possibility of any kind of meaningful reference has been used by some critics as further fuel for debates about science.[28]

One might be tempted to think that postmodern debates about truth would have little influence in American scientific or science-oriented communities, but this has not been the case. A long tradition in sociology, dating back to Émile Durkheim and certainly to Karl Mannheim, affords sociologists the tools to claim that intellectual constructions are on all fours with each other; and bringing this claim to the disciplines concerned with science, including philosophy of science, is merely the next step in the enterprise. A further tangle is that much of feminist theory has been at least moderately influenced by the portions of French theory closely allied to it; and the intersection of this thought itself becomes a further stimulus for attacking epistemic privilege, including areas that were previously beyond reproach such as hard foundationalism and the foundationalist epistemology that had originally supported positivism.

The upshot of all this inventive theorizing is that material is entering the domain of "philosophy of science" at a rapid clip. It is difficult to foresee what the long-term effects of this will be, but the short-term effects include the very great and obvious problem of trying to come to grips with what it is that constitutes "philosophy of science."

The Problem of Incommensurability

Incommensurability, as a problem for philosophy of science, might be thought of as exemplary of a number of current trends in that area, and the examination of it may yield several insights. It is indicative of the nature of much of what passes for current theorizing in philosophy of science that there seems to be little general agreement over what "incommensurability" amounts to or the uses to which it might be put qua theoretical rubric. Although we do not ordinarily think of Richard Rorty as a philosopher of science, he, along with many other thinkers, has appropriated this term and made use of it in his work, much in the same way that the Kuhnian notion of "paradigm shift" has now traveled outside of scientific circles.

At the bottom, the problem of incommensurability might originally have been articulated as the problem of trying to decide between rival theories that purport or allege to cover much the same area but that are not distinguishable on the same body of evidence.[29] Unfortunately, as is so often the case in philosophy, this relatively simplistic explanation does not do justice to the number of permutations that have appeared in the literature.

Fuller, citing Paul Feyerabend, gives us a gloss on the history of this problem that originally places it near the realist/instrumentalist controversy and that parallels much of what has rendered various stances in philosophy of science vulnerable to feminist criticism. If positivism may be thought of as largely instrumentalist (and even this idea is up for grabs), insofar as purely phenomenal constructs might be deemed to have largely predictive power, then the notion of incommensurability turns out to be something of a realist problem, since presumably evidence that will be used to decide between two theories has at least some relevance to the causal mechanisms invoked.[30] But having said as much, it is unclear what precisely is meant by a phrase as broad as "distinguishable on the same body of evidence." Fuller notes that, at least on one reading, which he associates with the Quinean tradition, any such lack of commensurability of rival theories is probably due to some semantic mishap, since "given the same evidence, and the same background knowledge, all rational individuals would license the same inferences."[31] But still another way of interpreting what the problem is amounts to fleshing it out more fully and yet still allowing for a sophisticated rendering of it. Clark Glymour and others who might be more realistically minded try to "make sense of the intuition that evidence bears only on parts of theories, and on different sized parts of different theories."[32] And yet Fuller has at least one more version of this problem ready at hand:

> Nevertheless, to say that the evidence does not bear on two theories equally is *not* to say that the two theories do not bear the burden of proof equally. In order to identify the condition necessary for the two theories not bearing the same burden of proof, imagine that one predicts that some event will happen (O) and the other predicts that the event will not happen (-O). The burden of proof would be different, then, only if the kind of evidence that is adequate for showing the truth of O is not also adequate for showing that -O is false. A typical case would involve proponents of one theory needing only to assert

"O" as evidence for O because the truth of O is so well entrenched that mere assertion commands assent, while advocates of an opposing theory need to go through a great many arguments and experiments in order to persuade the scientific community that -O is really the case: mere assertion of "-O" may command little more than incredulous looks.[33]

This take on the problem of incommensurability refines the problem and, more importantly, provides us with still one more twist on it. What is at stake here is not so much the problematic area itself, or any attempted resolution of it, but the nature of debate in contemporary philosophy of science. Humor about the incommensurability of rival versions of the problem of incommensurability may be misplaced, but the fact that a leading work by a contemporary philosopher of science acquaints us with so many variants of a single problem is indicative of the gravity of the situation. Just as the rise in prominence of history of science, along with the post-Kuhnian theorizing of those who have been influenced by the social structures of science, has shown us how far the actual practice of science has been from some of the more idealized extant versions of it, so a delineation of what counts as or what constitutes the articulation of various prominent "problems" in the philosophy of science heightens our awareness of the looseness and fluidity of the field. Incommensurability is but one such area in contemporary philosophy of science.

History of Science and Its Impact

One final area of theorizing to which one might allude is the history of science. The growth in the impact of this field since the 1970s has been nothing short of phenomenal, and it parallels much of the work in sociology of science and the more Kuhnian areas of philosophy of science to which we have already referred.

History of science has had an impact largely because of an awareness of the importance of contextualization for theorizing. Just as the feminist critique and the radical critique have furthered the notion that it does not make sense to think of a god's-eye view or to talk of an area of theorizing that is not subject to the dominance of one point of view, the history of any given area in the sciences, or of science as a whole, has furthered the notion that each area is subject to the constraints of localization under which it was initially formed. Many of the sciences have proceeded with physics as a paradigm or exemplar, a fact that has sometimes led the area in question into disputable terrain, since not every area of endeavor, particularly in the social sciences, is equally subject to quantification. The desire to quantify and to try to obtain still further rigorous and pure data has, at least in some areas of the social sciences, led to the kind of damage that has itself been the subject of the radical critique.

To take but one example, psychology has tried to gain increased credibility in the latter part of the twentieth century by modeling itself after the harder sciences. The upshot of this has been an increase in the tendency to quantify and employ statistical methods, frequently at the expense of the credibility of the discipline as a whole. Driven by a need to appear "scientific," psychologists have often essayed to theorize quantitatively at any cost. Writing in *Science in Context*, the historian of science Mitchell Ash has described this tendency of psychology in historical terms:

> By exaggerating certain scientistic preferences, in particular by relying heavily on machine metaphors to generate explanatory models, [and] by reifying certain conventions of method and measurement in a "cult of empiricism" . . . academic psychology holds up a distorting mirror to common conventions of the scientific enterprise. . . . Instead, as Roger Smith rightly argues, the meanings constituted by traditional psychological categories or discourses need to be reconstructed or understood in their own contexts, in their references to one another and to other discourses about nature, morals, society, and politics. . . . At first blush, the history of the discipline and profession called psychology would not seem like promising research territory. . . . The interest comes, first, in showing why and how psychology has been so permeable to ideological influences.[34]

In speaking of psychology's need to "exaggerate scientistic preferences" and of its "permeability to ideological influences," Ash simply strips away a veneer of pretension from psychology but, to be fair, it is a veneer that could be stripped from virtually each and every science. Indeed, if the trends in philosophy of science and allied disciplines have shown us anything in recent years, it is that science on the whole contains the same defects that Ash here attributes to the social sciences in general and specifically to psychology. The hard sciences are only marginally better off and only appear to be better off if they are not themselves subjected to the same withering critique.

Taken in toto, the advances in sociology of science, history of science, and that portion of philosophy of science that engages in sufficient introspection, lead us to see science as an enterprise on all fours with any other enterprise, filled with the contextualized and particularized material that is part and parcel of everyday life. Nevertheless, this does not mean that the more standard areas of philosophy of science are not worth pursuing, especially since science itself proceeds forward and requires philosophical investigation.

In this work my goal will be to articulate the currents in contemporary philosophy of science that genuinely seem to push the cause of conceptual analysis insofar as science is concerned, while still developing the notion of feminist criticism of science, among, of course, other lines of criticism. These two projects are not necessarily as disparate as they might seem, because a closer examination of science and scientific practice yields the notion that the best kind of philosophy of science is self-reflective. For example, a better account of the relationship between instrumentalism and early positivism relies on the notion that we can examine the pronouncements of positivism with an eye toward, in some instances, reading between the lines. That we can do so furthers philosophy of science, the allied disciplines, and feminist theory. This is the project that informs the present work.

2

Positivism and
the Vienna Circle

Philosophy of science is frequently spoken of, particularly by those laboring in disciplines other than philosophy, as if it consisted of little more than positivism and warmed-over versions of positivistic doctrines. It is particularly ironic that these labels are bandied about because in many cases they only refer to the crudest caricatures of positivism. Many currently working in such areas as rhetoric of science and history of science, for example, seem to regard positivism as little more than "verification."[1] What precisely could be meant by a notion so vague is never explained, but then again it is presumably not the task of those in other disciplinary areas to fill in the blanks in these sorts of conceptual problems.

Any delineation of the system known as "positivism" associated loosely with the Vienna Circle and work done at a much earlier point in the twentieth century must be clear on the relationship between the notion of verification and its concomitant epistemology, and also on the relationship between statements of the observation language ("protocol statements") and statements in the theoretical language. To fail to do so is to fail to come to grips even minimally with what positivism or the positivist legacy represents, and yet this sort of error is frequently made.

Positivism, or the Received View as it is sometimes referred to by critics and commentators, has been formally expounded by many and relies on work done in logic at an earlier point in this century.[2] Painting in broad strokes, statements produced in a scientific context were supposed to be reducible, at a bare minimum, to protocol or "observation" statements, which in turn could be reduced to sense-data statements. Sense-data statements (bare-bones expressions of the phenomena divorced from any putative attachment to referent) are frequently couched in terms constructed canonically by J. L. Austin and others, such as "I am appeared to redly" or "I seem to see a reddish patch before me."[3] Although Austin himself was concerned to argue against the epistemic incorrigibility of such statements since he was at least partly engaged in responding to the work of A. J. Ayer, the classical position with regard to such statements is that they are the strongest candidates for epistemic incorrigibility: Only I can know how I am "appeared to," and if I further hedge my claim with such qualifiers as "I seem . . . ," then I may very well have made a statement that is irrefutable under any circumstances—a statement that might be thought to be the empirical analogue of deductive certainty.

The crucial link between the V_o, or observation statements, and the V_t, or theoretical statements, in positivist doctrine is supposed to come from the biconditionals that link each epistemically incorrigible statement in the observation language to a statement in the language of theory, a statement that presumably would be deductive (relying, of course, on mathematical theory) and hence epistemically privileged in its own right.

Whatever the merits or demerits of this grandiose construction, a scientific theory established through the linkage of such statements would, according to the argument at hand, have extremely strong epistemic support. It is this aspect of positivism, frequently ignored by commentators who may not have training in the philosophy of science, that yields a special place for positivistic theory; and given the preeminence of physics as a science in the earlier part of the twentieth century, it is easy to see, historically, how this took place.

More importantly, however, once one has clarified the rough-and-ready view of positivism that is a necessary concomitant of further examination of twentieth-century philosophy of science, one comes to see the antecedents of many contemporary debates, some of which have been cast in feminist terms or are relevant to the feminist critique of science. Critics of positivism often write, for example, as if it were taken for granted that original positivist thought was largely instrumentalist, but this is by no means the case and is itself an area of contention. Given the importance of the current realist/instrumentalist controversy, and the fact that at least some feminist philosophers of science and feminist critics of science have seen instrumentalism as the view that is, in some sense, less androcentric, it might be worthwhile to establish the original positivist position on this issue.[4]

Early Positivistic Moves

Moritz Schlick, among others, wrote pieces that indicate that, although early versions of positivism seemed to emphasize tendencies that could be labeled instrumentalist, such tendencies may have been exaggerated and based on certain fundamental misunderstandings of material.[5] The characteristic core of the debate has to do with the notion that the purely phenomenal can be captured under some scheme of conceptualization that does not involve, or involves only minimally, the kind of general categorizing that is related to scientific projects. If an interpretation of positivist doctrine is given that emphasizes the phenomenal, then that interpretation tends toward an instrumentalist version of the doctrine. Insofar as interpretations can be given that de-emphasize the purely phenomenal or that make it appear that the purely phenomenal cannot be captured without advertence to the more-than-phenomenal, then positivism begins to take a more realist turn. Joia Lewis cites Schlick's response to Ernst Mach in an article that is important for our purposes, but also critical for an overview of the beginning moves in positivism is Schlick's essay "The Boundaries of Scientific and Philosophical Concept-Formation."[6]

In this essay, which is surely a key to much of what follows, Schlick wants to make a sharp distinction between the quantitative and that which is concomitant to qualities, with the former demarcating the sciences and the latter the philosophical, conceptual, and so on. What is important about this piece is not only the wedge that Schlick drives between these two realms, but his admission that the move to the spatiotemporal quantitative, which he sees as being the preserve of physics, is a difficult one to make. Here is a noteworthy passage:

> We saw that the peculiarity of concept formation in the exact sciences consists in eliminating qualities so far as possible, and in reducing all qualitative relations to purely quantitative, mathematically formulable relations. It is now a matter of investigating what areas of reality are accessible to, and can be mastered by, such a method of concept-formation.
>
> The answer to this question must undoubtedly be that *all natural processes,* as such, in whatever particular science they may currently be dealt with, can be exactly depicted in this mathematical, spatio-temporal formulation. . . . Is there, then, any other science possible beside it? . . . The answer to this is very easy. The mathematico-scientific concept formation, which reduces the whole world to a play of purely quantitative relations, is absolutely powerless in the place of pure qualities which are not further reducible.[7]

But the question is, of course, what are these "pure qualities"? Schlick goes on to specify the difficulty, in many cases, of moving beyond quality (he is especially concerned about the mental). More importantly, however, we might ask a separate but related question: Even in the cases where we can move beyond quality, how do we know when we have made such a move, and at what epistemic level is the move made?[8] He gives us rather little to go on here, but we are left with the distinct impression that the earlier conceptually the move can be made, the better.

This take on categorization, combined with arguments that have been made about the difficulty of divorcing the purely phenomenal from conceptualization at any point, underscores the nature of the problematic inherent in attempting to give a completely instrumentalist twist to positivism.[9] The instrumentalist take asks us to think that it makes conceptual sense, so to speak, to try to get at or pinpoint bare phenomena apart from the categorization that normally occurs as part of thought to those who have linguistic capacity. W. V. O. Quine has spent a great deal of time on this problem in a number of essays, and the extent to which even the most minimal noticing of phenomena involves some kind of conceptualization has been a large and important part of his theoretical apparatus. The small child learns the word "red," for example, as part and parcel of an intermixing process of language acquisition, ostensive definition, objectification, and so forth, in which no real demarcative boundaries can be drawn between, say, a purely phenomenal experience and one that already involves linguistic acquaintance. One might assert that this is merely part of what it means to be human, to be a biological being and an acquirer of language in the world in which we live.

But the correspondence rules of positivism, if taken with a minimalist view, demand that the observation sentences be as divorced from conceptualization as possible so that the kind of distinction needed between theoretical language and protocol language can be made. This presents a difficult area for the theoretician, and it is made no less difficult by the fact that, if the epistemic foundationalism that is necessary to support the observation statements is set up, then incorrigibility must be the aim of the claims, further reducing the extent to which they can rely on extensive categorization.

Still another version of this same problem that may prove instructive for the philosopher of science interested in a recapitulation of the early positivist material is Schlick's take on post-Kantian attempts to subsume Einsteinian theory in Kantian categories. The problem here has some parallel—if "space" and "time" are seen as Kantian "forms of pure intuition," then the Kantian theorist has difficulty accounting for the empirical uses to which they are put in twentieth-century physics. The quaintness of this endeavor qua philosophical problematic should not deter us from the advisability of addressing it, since the terms in which it is cast by Schlick are helpful in coming to grips with the correspondence debate.

In a 1921 essay, "Critical or Empirical Interpretation of Modern Physics?" Schlick provided an analysis of what it would mean to attempt to salvage something like the original Kantian forms of intuition and the conceptual uses made of them. Schlick is careful to note that there is little in the newer relativistic work in physics that supports anything like a Kantian reading, tempting though it may be to try to build such a view, especially for older theorists trained in the German tradition. He notes:

> [A]nyone who upholds the critical claim, must, if we are to accord him credence, also really set forth the a priori principles which must form the solid basis of all exact science. For transcendental philosophy, as Cassirer rightly says, space and time are not things, but 'sources of knowledge'. We therefore have to demand a statement of the cognitions of which space, for example, is the source.[10]

Crudely speaking, this is still another version of the conceptual difficulty examined above with respect to the Quinean problem of ostensive definition and the acquisition of language. It is one thing to try to claim that space and time are intimately related to modes of categorizing; it is another task altogether to try to articulate this claim in such a way as to make it consistent with the possibility of doing empirically grounded work in physics. Schlick was largely concerned to review a book by Ernst Cassirer in the cited piece, but it is interesting to note that Schlick concludes, even with respect to Cassirer, that "we are left with the impression that this standpoint already transcends the region of critical philosophy proper."[11]

A Carnapian Contrast

Material on positivism's past can push us in more than one direction—this is obvious from both the response to Schlick's work and the reply to other material that is essentially taken from Rudolf Carnap. A number of studies have tried to articulate what it was that Carnap was actually saying in the work he published before he had read Alfred Tarski. An examination of this debate will, I believe, move us in the direction of making more sense of the origins of the realist/instrumentalist controversy and its relationship to positivism.

J. Alberto Coffa has argued that the standard view is that Carnap underwent some sort of change of heart about the relationships between coherence and syntax, and correspondence and semantics, after becoming acquainted with material from Poland. The importance of understanding this matter involves notions of correspondence and semantics. It seems to be a given of the theoretical structure of the situation that to engage in a correspondence view is to attach a semantics to a term in question; the attachment of such a semantics would, of course, preclude interpreting phenomena at the most fundamental level in a nonconceptual way. This point is of paramount importance. Although some commentators, Coffa included, will decline to link this argument to realism, it clearly is an argument that moves beyond pure instrumentalism, and understanding Carnap's position on the question is urgent. Coffa tries to make the point in the following passage that Carnap had already staked out a claim in this territory before he had read Tarski:

Tarski came along. . . . What happened then—as I should now like to argue—was philosophically less momentous than is generally thought. It is widely believed that Tarski's theory led Carnap to alter his views on the relationship between language and reality. I believe that it is much closer to the truth to say that what it did was to allow him to realize that he could express his old philosophical convictions in correspondentist language, without being thereby committed to a metaphysics or an epistemology that he found intolerable.

There is for the pre-semanticist Carnap a connection which is mediated by rules for 'the learning of an original language.' These rules, however, can't be formulated in any useful way; not because they deal with the domain of the showable-but-unsayable (whatever that may be) but because one does not teach a baby its first language by handing it a grammar and a dictionary.[12]

The last phrase of the final sentence here reminds us of the fact that infants and young children learn language by a complicated process involving ostensive definition and the continual mediation of physical objects of varying shapes and sizes, as indicated earlier. Carnap is here, according to Coffa, trying to avoid the epistemological and metaphysical commitments that hypothesize a bare given independent of and prior to attempts at conceptualization. But an epistemic correspondence view, as has been indicated, does push one in the direction of purchasing an extralinguistic reality, and it is in this direction that Carnap appears to have been headed before 1936 (the opposing camp wants to claim that his position was more along the lines of coherentism). Insofar as the language of science is concerned, to claim that conceptualization is concomitant to phenomenal experience forwards one more in the direction of what will become known as realism.

Explanation seems to be the key here. The overall tone in early positivism that Schlick labeled "antiscientific" was the very tone that spoke of the bare phenomena without interpretation. Even if we try to force this notion to go along with an epistemic view, we can still see a role looming for explanation.

The Carnapian concern with language and reality to which I have just alluded (as Coffa remarked, a concern about "the learning of an original language") came about because the relevant distinctions between theory and observation cannot be made without addressing these problems. As Lindley Darden has noted, "[A discussion] of theory and observation [shows] . . . that the philosopher of science concerned with the growth of scientific knowledge must not lose sight of the distinction the positivists had viewed from their more static perspective of that which is to be accounted for and that which accounts for it."[13] We can think that one take on what "accounts for something" is that which explains it (indeed, it might be said that this is a very large part). Even though it might appear that prediction was the leading theme of the positivist project, it was clearly more than that. Darden also claims, in developing the notions of reduction and unity of science, the following:

> None of the positivistic analyses proves to be adequate in understanding actual cases in science. But an examination of these informative failures aids us in asking better questions that lead to new problems and categories that promise to yield a more adequate understanding of the scientific enterprise. In so doing we must not lose sight of the important goals of the positivists of

providing an understanding of the objectivity of science, the way in which science progresses and becomes unified. These constitute an important heritage from our philosophical predecessors.[14]

Darden's point here is that explanation was an integral part of the original project, even if it was not always labeled as such. The very "success" of science that is now the focus of much of the commentary in the new realism analyses is a theme of the original positivistic analysis of progress and of the reductionist unity of science.

The upshot of this analysis is that it is safe to say that there is a strong realist strain to early work in positivism that is not always identified. The concepts of acceptability of evidence and theoretical explanation assume, implicitly, that there is some kind of linkage between language and the world, a linkage about which Carnap had already shown himself to be concerned.

Finally, Frederick Suppe himself bolsters such a view when he recounts some of the moves made with regard to the status of correspondence rules and V_t terms in the Received View. To try to oppose the presence of realist strains undermines one's scientific credibility to some degree, according to Suppe.

> Maintaining an instrumentalist interpretation of the Received View poses a problem, however: Why are theoretical terms necessary? . . . Commitment to an instrumentalist interpretation [however] . . . does not call for the eliminability of theoretical terms. In fact, Hempel's dissolution of the theoretician's dilemma shows that theoretical terms generally are necessary under the instrumentalist interpretation of theories . . . Nonetheless to allow theoretical terms while holding an instrumentalism leaves one in the uncomfortable position of holding that theoretical terms are necessary, but they do not mean anything or refer to anything. Rather than maintain such a position, most people who accept the legitimacy of theoretical terms in scientific theorizing also commit themselves to the position that they have real referents in the world.[15]

Nineteenth-century moves in philosophy of science were made to account for the new physics—as was indicated earlier, the neo-Kantian philosophy did not allow room for such theoretical maneuvers. But the phenomena to be accounted for are subject to explanation—and the claim that theoretical terms must be tied in the logically rigorous fashion of the correspondence rules to observation terms does not, according to Suppe, entail that the results of the observation are purely instrumentalist.

Foundationalism and Protocol Sentences

One of the most important aspects of positivism in any account that would attempt to tie its history and influence to later developments in philosophy of science, including those informed by feminist theory, is the extent to which it was related to a foundationalist epistemology.

It is hard to overestimate the importance of this linkage, for it is the foundationalist epistemology and its later ties to still other philosophical views that might be deemed to be among the most androcentric portions of the theorizing. The aim of most epistemic views that receive the label "foundationalist" is usually to assert epistemic privilege to certain propositions or sentences on the basis of their place in a chain or pyramid of other propositions/sentences. Although some foundationalisms are more "modest" than others, particularly within contemporary theory,[16] the sort of foundationalism that was supposed to support the observation language terms of the Received View was, classically, that of incorrigibility. Despite some quibbling on this score in the writings of, for example, Otto Neurath and Carnap, it is clear from the formulation of protocol sentences that either they reduce immediately to the kinds of phenomenal sense-data statements that have often been held to be incorrigible or they could be so reduced.[17]

This problem is related to, but separate from, the difficulties mentioned in the preceding sections in that the kind of foundationalism necessary to undergird the protocol sentences can itself be the subject of commentary irrespective, at least to some extent, of the status of the terms in it.[18] What is important, especially insofar as later views are concerned, is the desire for incorrigibility as an epistemic analogue of deductive certainty. Carnap and later Ayer are driven to propose first-person phenomenalistic accounts, because they are the closest parallels to the primitives in the axiomatized system of the theoretical language that will hold together the other side of the formulation in correspondence rules.[19] Aside from inquiring what possible motivations of, as Evelyn Fox Keller has it, "stylistic aggression" might support the desire for such certainty, another line of inquiry revolves around the virtual complete divorce of the logic of the structure from anything actually accruing to scientific behavior. To be sure, numerous commentators, even members of the original Vienna Circle, made note of this disparity, but the purity of the original formulation necessitates strong comment on it.[20]

In any case, it is also clear that later, more Austinian objections to these kinds of formulations are philosophically crucial and also go a long way toward helping us understand the original positivist project. In *Sense and Sensibilia*, Austin objected to the notion that any such formulation (the first-person perception sentence) could be hedged sufficiently to provide for incorrigibility with a few rather flat, commonsense rejoinders, no less devastating because they were derived from ordinary experience. In a well-known passage, Austin remarked that "It appears to me as if I am seeing magenta now" is just as susceptible to later recantation and refutation as any one of a number of other utterances, at least partially, as Austin notes, because one can always claim that one meant to say something else, that one was mistaken in one's application of the color term, and so forth. A complete recapitulation of this passage is beyond the scope of this discussion, but Austin's dissolution of much of Ayer's original project is well known.

Nevertheless, even if it cannot be claimed that such sentences are incorrigible, they are in most cases strongly self-justifying, and their role in the formulation of the Received View should be recounted.[21] Neurath himself, while disagreeing to some extent with what he regards as a more phenomenalistically phrased take on protocol sentences, uses as sample protocol sentences such obvious candidates for putatively incorrigible foundationalism as "Otto now sees a red circle" or "Otto now joy."[22] When one considers the justificatory status of such sentences or propositions, one is immediately struck by the extent to which something close to sense-data material is already adverted to and the extent to which, although such statements might later be retracted, they are on much sounder epistemic footing than many other less-hedged, less-privileged statements would be.

It is this epistemic foundationalism, combined with the logically tight structure of the core components of positivism, that gives positivism both its initial appeal and later unappealingness, according to many. The biconditional formulation of the correspondence rules, taken in toto with the pure structure of the foundationalist epistemology, yields a view that is virtually completely divorced from scientific functioning. It is perhaps no accident that this view later gave rise to another marked swing of the pendulum.

The Motivation Behind Positivism

Although I have already alluded to the neo-Kantian philosophy that preceded the adoption of the Received View, the desire to provide a structure for theories deriving from and concomitant to the new physics at the turn of the century is perhaps the single greatest impetus behind the growth of positivism.

Frederick Suppe, in his *The Structure of Scientific Theories,* has provided an admirably detailed overview of the emergence of positivism from the detritus of three philosophical systems popular at the turn of the century. Suppe refers to these systems as the neo-Kantianism already mentioned, mechanistic materialism, and Machian neopositivism, respectively.[23] Although the latter might be deemed to be closest to what later became the

Received View, each view is noteworthy for its convergence and divergence from later important positivistic principles.

As we have seen, any kind of outlook derived from Kantian philosophy, with its emphasis on space and time as forms brought to sensation rather than having any empirical content taken from it, could not begin to cohere with the developments in physics at the turn of the century. Suppe admirably states the emergence of a new approach in philosophy when he describes the situation at the time of the publication of Einstein's early work:

> At [this] time, however, theoretical physics was coming into its own, and the physical sciences were developing much more theoretical and mathematical branches. In 1905 Einstein published his special theory of relativity, and shortly thereafter the old quantum theory was well on its way in development. Relativity theory and quantum theory were thought to be incompatible with all three of these philosophies of science, and acceptance of them seemed to require abandonment of these philosophical positions. In Germany the neo-Kantian and mechanistic materialistic schools of physics typically opposed the replacement of classical physics by relativity theory and quantum theory— largely on neo-Kantian or mechanistic materialistic grounds. Primary German support for the new physics came from those schools which were sympathetic to Machian positivism; but embracement of the new physics did require abandonment of a strict adherence to the new positivism.[24]

Thus positivism was born simultaneously from a desire to ground the new sciences in a structure that was sufficiently rigorous to provide them adequate support and to dismantle the pretensions to philosophical purity, or even relevance, of the old schools. The birth of positivism at the same time as the growth of what we now think of as contemporary science is not only no accident but helps to clarify elements of the theories that were later to become unattractive to feminist and other critics. If science requires a rigorous framework, particularly insofar as the logical structure of theories is concerned, then it is a corollary of such a motivation that its tendencies toward what one might call "Complete Accountism" will be exacerbated and the androcentricity of such theorizing will become quite pronounced.[25] It is not merely the stringency of the theorizing that is constitutive of androcentrism here, although the case for that could no doubt be made, but the desire to provide an overview of all phenomena and to encompass the phenomena under applicable scientific laws is, of course, the very sort of Baconian conquest of nature of which many feminist theorists have written.[26]

Developments in logic by Gottlob Frege, Bertrand Russell, and Alfred North Whitehead, combined with Russell's philosophy of logical atomism and the spirit of Wittgenstein's *Tractatus*, provided the impetus for the establishment of the Received View as articulated here in previous sections, particularly the biconditional linkage of the correspondence rules so that each observation or protocol sentence was tied to a sentence in the theoretical language.[27] Not only was the enterprise reminiscent of the motivations to establish a logically perfect language, but, more importantly, the logicism that underlay the *Principia* provided the framework for an axiomatized system of theoretical terms that would support the V_t sentences on the theoretical side of the correspondence rules.[28] All in all, the emergence of positivism was a phenomenon completely tied to the emergence of twentieth-century science and twentieth-century physics in particular. That this is the case may aid us in coming to understand how the various other projects of the later part of this century, including those critical of the dominance of the scientific power structure, achieved the status that they now enjoy.

The Vienna Circle and Its Discussants

As described in the preceding sections, part of the impetus behind the development of a positivist view was the desire to ground new work in science, particularly in physics. But another large part of the impetus was the influence of the work of Frege, Russell, and, in particular, Wittgenstein on the members of the Vienna Circle. These two trends—one the result of new developments in physics, especially the special theory of relativity, and one the result of new work in logic during the latter half of the nineteenth century—came together in a way that was remarkably fruitful, and the influence of Wittgenstein was crucial in the development of this merger.[29]

Oswald Hanfling reports, as is widely known, that the members of the circle—Moritz Schlick, Ernst Mach, Hans Reichenbach, and others—read Wittgenstein carefully and had meetings that were devoted to the study of the *Tractatus*. But it remains to be articulated what it is, precisely, from the *Tractatus* that is related to other portions of positivistic theory and in what, specifically, the influence lies. Recalling that the *Tractatus* is similar in many ways to much of Russell's philosophy of logical atomism, it is the value of the notion of correspondence and of an atomistic structure for propositions that provides the core of the catalytic material here.[30] For if propositions can be constructed atomically, and if the structure of, say, compound propositions mimics the structure of a sentence in sentential calculus along the lines of Fa v Gb, then individual constants have the function of picking out; and phenomena can be pinpointed, given logically proper names, and then placed in a structure of assertions of varying degrees of complexity.

As Hanfling notes, the logically atomistic take on language and the notion of an epistemology to support it are only a part of the story, although as we have seen from the discussion of the place of incorrigibility in positivism, they are an important part of the story. What is also important here is the notion that looking at phenomena in this way and building protocol statements in this manner supports the notion of the unity of science, one that Carnap himself was, of course, concerned to sustain.[31] Potentially, any statement in any discipline purporting or alleging to be a science could be handled in this manner, and the fact that advances in physics seemed to be taking place at a rapid clip during the time that members of the circle did their most important work helped to buttress this belief.

The *Tractatus*, Russell's logical atomism, and the nature of protocol statements themselves all are based on the assumption that language and experience can be linked together closely enough to more or less encapsulate some phenomenalistic moments. The sample protocol statement mentioned earlier, "Otto now joy," is indeed an exemplar of this type of statement, and the bone of contention here is perhaps not so much about the nature of the protocol statements as about what they can do.

It may well be the case that there are such things as protocol statements, especially with regard to visual phenomena, that serve the purpose for which they were intended insofar as they provide support for other small claims, or insofar as they come closer than many types of statements to irrefutability or incorrigibility. But the original point of the correspondence rules was, of course, to establish something far more ambitious: The protocol statements on one side were to serve as an observational link to theoretical statements on the other that themselves were to be supported epistemically by material axiomatically derived. Thus something approaching airtight epistemic foundationalism is the objective on both sides of the correspondence rules—on one side through pure deduction and on the other, through its empirical analogue, phenomenal incorrigibility. Science, then, is supported by such a foundation, insofar as it encompasses the structure of scientific theories themselves.

As Hanfling notes, the Wittgenstein of the *Investigations* is not only divorcing himself from his early work, but from the work of others to which it is related as well. The stylistic aggression of the attempt to encompass all of scientific knowledge within the bounds of the justificatory logic of positivism is intellectually off-putting, perhaps most of all to the person who was one of the system's initial formulators.

The Place of Value

Perhaps one of the greatest caricatures of the work of the positivists, particularly insofar as it stretches up to our time, is the notion that all the positivists held something like an emotive view of ethical statements, or that members of the Vienna Circle routinely held that no cognitive import of any kind could be attributed to statements of value.

Part of this belief no doubt stems from the work of many who were not actually members of the circle but whose work is widely regarded as carrying on the positivist tradition, such as A. J. Ayer.[32] But, like most caricatures, this one is not entirely accurate. Michael Scriven, in an interesting essay titled "Logical Positivism and the Behavioral Sciences," makes the point that much of what the positivists did might be thought of as a reaction to the notion of *Verstehen*, a commonplace of nineteenth-century theorizing.[33] But as Scriven notes, the situation is more complicated than constituting merely a flat-footed rejection of this concept.

> The topic of special interest for us here is the nature of our understanding of people. On this issue the positivists reacted against the school of historians proposing the "*Verstehen* theory", that is, the doctrine that empathic insight was a special and valuable tool in the study of human behavior which was without counterpart in the physical sciences. This view did not die with them, for it is explicit in Collingwood's philosophy of history and implicit in the practice of many other historians.
>
> The positivists argued that empathy was not a reliable tool at all, and that the methods of obtaining knowledge, especially knowledge in history, were just the same as those used in the physical sciences. In particular, understanding was possible via subsumption only under established laws.[34]

While acknowledging the importance of this take on *Verstehen* for the growth and development of positivism, however, Scriven makes the argument that, even though it attempts to be consistent with other formulations by the positivists, this particular stance need not be seen as the only stance. I cannot recapitulate Scriven's position here, but the rest of his paper is devoted to showing that *Verstehen,* if properly used, is not necessarily inconsistent with the notion of gaining knowledge from context and also is not necessarily inconsistent with the notion of subsuming such knowledge under some kind of law.[35] More importantly for our purposes, the fact that Scriven can recapitulate such an argument indicates that even a close reconstruction of some parts of the positivist position on this matter yields a different analysis.

Hanfling, in providing an overview of the opinions of members of the circle on this issue, is also able to show that an oversimplification results if the foci of disagreements between members of the circle are not given. One such focus is whether or not value statements have any cognitive import whatsoever. Hanfling is quick to make a sharp distinction here between the work of Reichenbach, for example, and that of Schlick. He notes:

With these views [that the statement that something is desirable, for example, is meaningless] Reichenbach would not disagree. But whereas he (like many others) sees the purport, or the main purport, of moral statements as being that of imperatives rather than statements, this is not so in the case of Schlick. According to him, moral statements, no less than others, are objects of knowledge and verification. Being about human desires, they are, he maintains, part of the subject matter of psychology. The main task of ethics is to examine the causes of these desires and ethics is thus a branch of psychology; the latter, in turn, being part of a single, unified science.[36]

In this short excision, Hanfling is easily able to show us that we err when we attempt to place all of the statements and beliefs of the positivists about value under one rubric. Although their position might generally be best summed up as emotive, Schlick's work alone indicates that there is a great deal of complexity here.[37] Perhaps more contentious than any single utterance of the positivists with regard to value is Schlick's position as cited above, that value statements themselves can reduce to concomitants of psychology and that these can then be investigated under the unity of science.

Reductionism and the Unity of Science

Ultimately, the positivist project encompassed all possible avenues of human knowledge, since it was the stated aim of Carnap, Neurath, and others in the *International Encyclopedia of Unified Science* to delineate the conditions for the possible reduction of physical-thing statements and statements in the social sciences.[38] Although this project may have been somewhat misunderstood—in his essay in Hanfling's anthology, Carnap states at more than one juncture, "We do not, of course, know whether it [this aim] ever will be reached"[39]—there can be no doubt that its goal was simply the outcome of the various positions on syntax, semantics, and the relations between theoretical and observational vocabulary that have been articulated earlier here.

Given a materialist interpretation of the world, and given the atmosphere of progress and forward-looking achievement that characterized the period in which the circle members worked, it is not difficult to account for the ambition and scope of what positivism originally encompassed. What is striking, however, is the comparative naïveté of some of the original statements, which seem to want to claim that fairly easy reductions into theoretical statements of physics could be made for any given statement in the physical-thing language or in some other, not-yet-reduced science.[40]

Carnap notes:

> [T]here is a unity of language in science, viz., a common reduction basis for the terms of all branches of science, this basis consisting of a very narrow and homogeneous class of terms of the physical-thing language. This unity of terms is indeed less far-reaching and effective than the unity of laws would be, but it is a necessary and preliminary condition for the unity of laws.[41]

What is striking today about such formulations is the Complete Accounts nature of the goal and the comparative optimism about the possibility of reaching that goal. The unity-of-science thesis and the goal of reduction assumes (wrongly) that the nature of physics itself as a discipline will not change in unrecognizable ways, that further work in given scientific areas will yield results that mesh or cohere with results that we already possess, and so forth.

It is this sort of hope and the somewhat arrogant foundation on which it rests that give rise, at a much later and perhaps more diluted point, to the feminist criticisms of science that I now examine. For more than mere stylistic aggression is at work here—this system represents an objectification of the nature and the substance of science that makes the original Baconian scheme look vapid by comparison.

The feminist commentary on this sort of orientation, much of it driven by psychoanalytic object-relations theory or, in the case of some of Keller's work, by a recapitulation of the erotic underpinnings of early Platonic theory, makes a great deal of sense when one thinks of male goals or drives, their sublimation, and the Platonic union-of-essences outlook that informs the earliest notions of epistemology in the Western tradition.[42] The desire to give a Complete Account is, perforce, the desire to master all things and have all things subject to a given overview. That this is related to what are essentially male drives toward dominance, mastery, and will is obvious; what is not so obvious is how these drives, mutated though they might be in a highly intellectualized culture, could have gone unrecognized for what they were for so long.

Feminist Criticisms

One feature of the positivist legacy that has been relatively ignored in this section is the tendency toward operationalism in the social sciences that has resulted from an overall behaviorist influence traceable to positivist antecedents.[43] Part of what this has meant is that many of the constructs of the social sciences—constructs that have more importance in everyday life than might at first be obvious—are cast in heavily operationalist terms or have a history of operationalist influence such that no immediate possibility of divorce from this history is apparent. Intelligence quotient (IQ), as a measurable construct, is the legacy of the notion that "intelligence" is what intelligence tests define, and the damage done by this notion is so patent that, were it not for its ubiquitousness in social science circles, one could scarcely imagine how the construct could continue to be employed.[44]

This portion of the positivist legacy is indeed ripe for feminist and other sorts of criticism, and it itself invites commentary in terms now familiar to those who have followed the rise of feminist theory. As indicated earlier, the desire to objectify and quantify is related to a certain position that can be labeled as "male objectification," and it is also clearly linked historically to the overview of the Vienna Circle, which emphasized correspondence rules, deductive certainty, empirical tightness, and so forth. But culturally speaking, this rise can also be traced as but one in a series of movements beginning with the Enlightenment and carrying through to the present day. The growth of knowledge in the nineteenth century alone virtually guaranteed the views that we now associate with modernism, views that demanded that we accept the idea of constant progress and greater unification of knowledge.

If, as Susan Bordo has argued, we can accept a sociohistorical account of the origin of, for example, Descartes's project, then we can also accept, on the level of individuation, the notion that male thinkers experience the psychoanalytic and developmental stages posited by those psychologists who have been influenced by Freudian theory.[45] When viewed in this light, an account of the origins of androcentric theory on a personal level might prove extremely useful to the feminist theorist who wants to know how it is that a given thinker came to demonstrate the goal of dominance and mastery associated with not only the scientific enterprise as a whole but with the specific, extremely rigid projects that I have examined in this chapter.

Without attempting to provide a psychoanalytic analysis of any of the thinkers involved, I can hypothesize that the combination of the growth in the power of the bourgeoisie, the culmination of post-Enlightenment notions of progress, and the extremely patriarchal and distanced child-rearing patterns of late nineteenth-century Europe probably serve to partially explain the development of early twentieth-century philosophy of science. Nevertheless, the power of the positivistic pattern remains, and its influence has been such that it is by no means easy to discard the view of science that it provides for us.

A more important focus for critique then becomes the lack of allusion within the model to any functioning of actual scientists or to the patterns employed in the thinking of actual scientific practitioners. Although, as we have seen, members of the circle were careful, at least in their later work, to note the extent to which the Received View, for example, is intended to be entirely nondescriptive,[46] there is no interest in the circle's written corpus in providing any account that smacks of actual practice.

These two strands then—the developmental strand that asks us to investigate motivations for androcentric views of quest and dominance in science, and the more naturalized strand that asks us to think of what the actual practice of scientists might be—push us in the direction of a critique that will later become of overwhelming importance in the philosophy of science.

It is perhaps ironic that some of the most influential voices in the critique come from later investigators with formal training in the area who discarded remnants of the Received View on their own. But this did not take place until positivistic thinking had influenced all of the science-related disciplines. I must now investigate how this level of influence was achieved.

3

Positivist Influences

Perhaps the largest portion of the legacy of the positivists was the portion that attempted to provide a logical apparatus for scientific thinking. Although it might be the case that the foundationalist line of argument underlying positivist claims—a line that I examined in the preceding chapter—was rather easily attacked and dismantled, the desire to provide a "logic of justification" for the enterprise of science was one that did not die easily.

The work of Carl Hempel may be thought of as an offshoot of the positivist enterprise not only because of its structure of logic for the process of justification but also, more flat-footedly, because of the rigor and precision of its overall argument. If the notion of correspondence rules had tried to show how theoretical structure could be tied to the observable world, Hempel's work on explanation attempted to be specific about that theoretical structure and its explanatory relationship to data.

These two enterprises are clearly related but not identical. The original Received View merely articulates a translation device for the observable and the theoretical; Hempel's work attempts to set out a logic of explanation.[1]

The importance of Hempel's work was such that only the weltanschauungen views have had, in the period since World War II, as great an impact. Hempel noted that in most of the instances of what we cite as explanation, there are general "covering laws" at work and then more specific instantiating conditions that can be articulated. This valuable insight makes it easy to distinguish the cases in which new laws are discovered or adverted to from the multitude of cases in which the alleged new material is more or less simply an explanation of particular conditions.

Hempel notes:

> The explanations . . . may be conceived, then, as deductive arguments whose
> conclusion is the explanandum sentence, E, and whose premiss-set, the ex-
> planans, consists of general laws. L1, L2, . . . , Lr, and of other statements, C1,
> C2, . . . , Ck, which make assertions about particular facts. . . . Explanatory
> accounts of this kind will be called explanations by deductive subsumption
> under general laws, or *nomological deductive explanations*. (The root of the
> word 'nomological' is the Greek word 'nomos', for law.) The laws invoked in
> a scientific explanation will also be called covering laws for the explanan-
> dum phenomenon, and the explanatory argument will be said to subsume
> the explanandum under those laws.[2]

The virtue of the precision of Hempel's analysis here is that it allows
one to be specific about what notion is being invoked at a given stage in
the proceedings—either a law or a specific set of conditions that describe
an event that might be subsumed under a law. The latter notion is crucial
because, as indicated previously, there might be a tendency to think that
conditions that are actually instantiating are themselves to be thought of
as laws. Hempel is clear about this when he asserts that "corresponding
general laws are always presupposed by an explanatory statement to the
effect that a particular event of a certain kind G . . . was *caused* by an event
of another kind F."[3] Any regularity that may be subsumed under the notion of causation is itself lawlike, and this accounts for a good deal of the
import of the structure of Hempel's model.

A classic case of an incident of scientific discovery work that corre-
sponds closely to the pattern of the model was the discovery of the planet
Neptune. Hempel describes this particular instance as follows:

> [T]ake the celebrated explanation, propounded by Leverrier (and indepen-
> dently by Adams), of peculiar irregularities in the motion of the planet
> Uranus, which on the current Newtonian theory could not be accounted for
> by the gravitational attraction of the other planets then known. Leverrier
> conjectured that they resulted from the gravitational pull of an as yet unde-
> tected outer planet, and he computed the position, mass, and other charac-
> teristics which that planet would have to possess to account in quantitative
> detail for the observed irregularities. His explanation was strikingly con-
> firmed by the discovery, at the predicted location, of a new planet, Neptune.[4]

Hempel's covering law, or D-N model, is an excellent tool for attempting to theorize about such instances of fulfilled predictions, and the structure of the positivistic views that preceded it is manifested in the logical
articulation of the view itself. But positivism is also associated with other
theoretical tendencies deemed by some to be more deleterious, among
them operationalism.

The Operationalist Conundrum

Operationalism has been closely allied with the Received View, but has fallen into disrepute in some of the more contemporary literature, especially with regard to the attempt to maintain operationalist definitions of such constructs from the social sciences as IQ.[5] Part of the difficulty may be addressed by citing Hempel's opening definition of operationalism in the relevant chapter of his *Aspects of Scientific Explanation*, since the example he picks is readily illustrative of the difficulty:

> An operational definition of a term is conceived as a rule to the effect that the term is to apply to a particular case if the performance of specified operations in that case yields a certain characteristic result. For example, the term 'harder than' might be operationally defined by the rule that a piece of mineral, x, is to be called harder than another piece of mineral, y, if the operation of drawing a sharp point of x across the surface of y results in a scratch mark on the latter. Similarly, the differing numerical values of a quantity such as length are thought of as operationally definable by reference to the outcomes of specified measuring operations.[6]

These conceptually easy examples of operationalism do not address the difficulties associated with the use of the construct in the social sciences or the difficulties with the notion in the literature of positivism, yet it is precisely these areas that make the concept so controversial. To say, for example, that "intelligence" is what "intelligence tests measure" begs the question on any independent definition of the term in question and throws the meaning of such assertions open to debate.[7]

Operationalism is, of course, the semantically precise component of positivism; as Hempel remarks, "Hypotheses incapable of operational test or, rather, questions involving untestable formulations, are rejected as meaningless."[8] But part of the problem for operationalism has involved its very condition of stipulation, for it is easy to stipulate operationally under specified conditions, but once the notion of specified conditions is done away with, operationalism loses much of its theoretical punch. According to its explicators,

> [There is] the question whether it is not possible to conceive of methods more general and flexible than definition for the introduction of scientific terms on the basis of the observational vocabulary. One such method has been developed by Carnap. It makes use of so-called reduction sentences, which constitute a considerably generalized version of definition sentences and are especially well suited for a precise reformulation of the intent of operational definitions. As we noted earlier, an operational definition of the simplest kind stipulates that the concept it introduces, say C, is to apply to those and only those cases which, under specified test conditions S, show a certain characteristic response R.[9]

But this rather simplistic beginning for stipulations of the use of operationalism runs into the difficulty that, even within a given "interpretative
system,"[10] there are gradations of experiential import.[11]

In *Aspects of Scientific Explanation*, Hempel goes on to fill in the blanks on
the ways in which these gradations might be categorized formally, but
more interesting for our purposes are the uses to which operationalist definitions of social constructs have been put in the social sciences.

In an important article originally published in *Philosophy and Public Affairs* in the mid-1970s, "IQ: Heritability and Inequality," Ned Block and
Gerald Dworkin write about what they term "operationalism" and the
absurdities to which it commits proponents of, for example, the notion
that intelligence is what IQ tests measure. Lines of argument developed
by Arthur Jensen and subjected to a critique in this article are related to issues having to do with today's *Bell Curve* controversy; therefore, understanding what operationalism amounts to in this context is important.
Hearkening back to the tone of Hempel's argument, Block and Dworkin
note that there is even a conceptual twist involved in the simple claim
that temperature is what thermometers measure, let alone any claim more
sophisticated than that. After having cited both Jensen and the noted psy-
chologist Edwin Boring on the notion that intelligence can be measured,[12]
Block and Dworkin assert that "the operationalist claim that temperature
is by definition what thermometers measure commits its proponents to
absurdities."[13] Using standard philosophical counterarguments, Block
and Dworkin point out that some of what is involved in this basic claim is
the notion that thermometers cannot be improved; or that even if all thermometers malfunctioned simultaneously and in the same way, the result-
ing measurement would still be a measurement of temperature.[14]

The point of the foregoing is, of course, the notion that if operationalist
definitions can be problematic for simple devices that purport to relate
causally straightforward phenomena, then any device purporting or alleging to measure more complex phenomena subject to social definition
and construction is in grave trouble. The Block and Dworkin essay is
lengthy and complex, but its flavor and the strength of its argument can
be sampled in the following excerpt:

> There is, however, an obvious alternative sense of "what thermometers mea-
> sure," namely, what thermometers are *supposed* to read or say. In this second
> sense of the phrase, defining "temperature" as what thermometers measure
> is harmless enough, though the definition would perhaps be more useful as
> a definition of "thermometer" than of "temperature." But notice that it is the
> first sense [that it is simply what a thermometer measures] of "what IQ tests
> measure" that Jensen and Herrnstein require, not the second sense. For in the
> second sense, even if one accepts the definition of "intelligence" as what IQ
> tests measure, one can reasonably ask whether IQ tests *do* say what they are
> supposed to say. But this was just the sort of question the "operational defi-

nition" was intended to forestall. The operationalist dilemma here is that one of the interpretations of Boring's definition is *absurd* while the other is *useless* for their purposes.[15] (Emphasis in original)

As we can see from the Block and Dworkin attack on IQ as an operationalist construct, operationalism has achieved an importance in the social sciences that might never have been intended by its original proponents. The desire to try to tighten the social sciences, psychology in particular, to achieve the level of precision that the original Vienna Circle theorists had categorized as characteristic of physics and the physical sciences was, of course, a driving force behind the behaviorist and operationalist motivations at work in psychology. But, as we shall see at a later point, the feminist and radical critique of these enterprises is by no means misplaced, and it is helpful in attempting to lay the groundwork for such a critique to examine its antecedents. The importance of operationalism as a positivist-influenced construct can hardly be overestimated.

The Work of Popper

Part of the legacy of the Received View of positivism was an emphasis on the notion of confirmation and verification—indeed, "verificationism" quickly became shorthand for positivism. But there also emerged work that made clear the disparity between confirmation and disconfirmation.

Karl Popper's work is associated in popular terms with the work of the Vienna Circle because of Popper's origins and the influence of World War II on the travels and destinations of European scientists.[16] The problem of induction dates back, of course, to Hume and is an obvious concomitant of any development of science-related theory. Nevertheless, most of the classic work of the members of the circle focused on "verification," so that the notion of confirmation as an incomplete process (and a process the logic of which more clearly mirrors the structure of such invalidities as affirming the consequent) was seldom broached. Popper's reliance on disconfirmation, because of its avoidance of the problem of induction, pushed the positivist-influenced theory in new directions and became the benchmark for much later theorizing. Frederick Suppe glosses Popper's position in this manner:

> From the very beginning Popper rejected the verification criterion of cognitive significance, arguing that Hume's arguments against the possibility of logically justifying induction showed that scientific theories cannot be verified by any possible accumulation of observational evidence; however, scientific theories can be observationally falsified, and that empirical falsifiability is the criterion of the empirical and scientific character of theories. Popper also differs with the Received View on the issue of whether theories should be analyzed in

terms of artificial logical calculi. For he holds that the central problem of philosophy of science is the growth of scientific knowledge; and he does not think that the study of the growth of scientific knowledge can be reduced to a study of artificial languages or logical calculi formulated in terms of them.[17]

The emphasis on falsification or disconfirmation might seem to be clear-cut, but as the passage from Suppe makes clear, the other emphasis in Popper's work is equally important. The theoretical side of the correspondence rules biconditional was, as indicated in the previous chapter, a series of deductively tight theoretical statements, some of which might be deemed to hold axiomatically. Depending upon the degree of epistemological support—epistemological foundationalism—attached to the statements couched in the observation language, the statements in the artificial theoretical language might be more or less rigidly supportive of the entire theoretical structure.

In emphasizing the artificiality of the theoretical side, Popper might be thought to be pointing the way to some of the weltanschauungen views that came later, since part of his critique here is the lack of emphasis in the Received View on nonformalizable languages. Indeed, Suppe notes that Popper held that "the solutions to problems in philosophy of science offered by the Received View and other analyses which proceed in terms of artificial language systems work only because of the limitations in expressive power."[18] This concern with language and the actual operation of science mirrors the concerns of many who will come later.

The Turn Toward Weltanschauungen

A number of factors precipitated the move toward more open, more descriptively accurate, and less rigid views in philosophy of science, some of which we have seen in the preceding sections. Criticisms of the Received View along the lines examined in the immediately preceding passages, including criticisms of rampant operationalism, overuse of the notion of confirmation, and general reliance on a highly idealized logical structure of theories in logical positivism, had all come to fruition by the 1960s. But perhaps two moves were of overwhelming importance, and each is worthy of examination because they at least in some way anticipate the feminist and radical critiques of science later to come.

One such move is the at least implicit recognition of the place of value and notions related to value in science, even though the original articulations of the discussants of the Vienna Circle on this score in general denigrated such a concept. Moritz Schlick himself had written a work titled *The Place of Value in a World of Fact*, and other authors influenced by the

circle and its doctrines at least attempted to address the issue.[19] In addition, Hempel devoted an important essay to the topic in his collection *Aspects of Scientific Explanation*. The essay, "Science and Human Values," is
noteworthy for its recognition, however flatly formulated, of the place of
value in science and the question of whether much of what is constitutive
of scientific practice can ever, in any realistic sense, be value-free. What is
remarkable about these pieces is their existence, rather than any specific
formulations found in them, because the simplistic but by no means misplaced reading of the circle's pronouncements on value that emphasized
emotivism left precious little room for substantive discussions of the axiological. Although Hempel was not discussing the practice of science itself
in the following passage, the fact that the passage occurs in the piece in
question gives the reader hope that some of the thoughtfulness exhibited
by the author in these sentences will eventually be guided toward an examination of science and scientific practices:

> Without entering into details, we may say here that a person's values—both
> those he professes to espouse and those he actually conforms to—are largely
> absorbed from the society in which he lives, and especially from certain in-
> fluential subgroups. . . . Conformity to the standards of certain groups plays
> a very important role here, and only rarely are basic values seriously ques-
> tioned. Indeed, in many situations, we decide and act unreflectively in an
> even stronger sense.[20]

Most of the article is devoted to a discussion, unproblematic for its
time, of the distinction between the empirically confirmable and the value
laden, but it is noteworthy that Hempel closes the piece with an admoni-
tion to keep "undogmatic, critical and open minds."[21]

The second move during this period that led directly to a major change
in the status of the Received View and in the influence of positivism in
general on philosophy of science is the deliberate attempt to criticize specific strands of positivist doctrine in such a way as to show that it is, at
bottom, incoherent and noninstantiable. Although we have already seen
the beginnings of such a move with Popper's critical formulations of the
place of confirmability and the notion of verification, the work of Paul
Feyerabend was also crucial during this period. (We are here concerned
with some of Feyerabend's earlier writings, before the publication of
Against Method.)

In his publications of the early 1960s, Feyerabend made a number of
sharp and specific attacks against positivist doctrine, particularly against
the privileged role of observation sentences and against the notion, examined here earlier, that observation sentences could be demarcated from
other sentences by their content.[22] But more importantly for future activity in philosophy of science, Feyerabend began to speculate about the role

of large, underlying worldviews and ways of placing theories and phenomena together that might underlie the acceptance or rejection of any given theory. Observation reports and other descriptions with allegedly factual content depend on these views. As he remarked, "Scientific theories are ways of looking at the world. . . . We may even say [that what is labeled 'nature' has features] . . . first . . . invented by us and then used for bringing order into our surroundings."[23]

This emphasis by Feyerabend on underlying views, themselves perhaps subject to empirical confirmation—at least in principle—but seldom examined, will turn out to be crucially important, because it begins to damage major distinctions, generally heretofore accepted, that undergirded the Received View and the writings of those who adhered to it, such as those between observer independence and the socially constructed, fact and value, and so forth. In general, writings in the late 1950s and early 1960s still reflected the predominance of positivistic influence and to a surprising extent the acceptance of distinctions that had already been undermined by W. V. O. Quine, such as the analytic/synthetic distinction. All that, however, was to change, and the major breakthrough in this area, provided by Thomas Kuhn, paved the way for all the work that was yet to come.

The Kuhnian and the Pre-Kuhnian

If Feyerabend's comment that "[s]cientific theories are ways of looking at the world" is taken together with a budding awareness of the central place of value and with Popper's critique of the lack of allusion to nonformalizable languages, then the stage is set for a formidable criticism of the Received View. Historically speaking, this is of course what transpired; with the publication of Thomas Kuhn's *The Structure of Scientific Revolutions* in the early 1960s, philosophy of science irrevocably changed.

Because the next chapter will deal with Kuhn and the commentary on his work in an extended fashion, only a brief introduction will be given here. It is important to be precise about the relationships of the various postpositivist views to each other; without doing what we are sometimes warned against—that is, without looking for what these views have in common—it is difficult to make sense of the period after the late 1950s. More importantly, perhaps, what the views *do* have in common, aside from their criticism of the Received View, is an awareness of the larger place of the scientific enterprise that will grow to include the feminist and radical critiques. Indeed, it is probably no exaggeration to say that those critiques could not have developed without the emergence of what are loosely known as the weltanschauungen views.

Paul Hoyningen-Huene's recent work on Kuhn[24] presents a precise account of the use of certain key Kuhnian concepts, such as "paradigm," in
such a way that the reader is allowed to move chronologically over
Kuhn's development of that term. But however problematic a key term
such as "paradigm" might be, and however extensive the commentary on
it is,[25] the more crucial point here is how the concept came to be developed and what relationship it bears to the preceding theorizing.

We can see from strands of commentary by both Popper and Feyerabend that a sense had developed not only that the Received View made
too little use of the "context of discovery," or was too normative and completely lacking in the descriptive, but also that it did not refer to the critical place of background beliefs in the development of theories. Suppe remarks on this when he characterizes the weltanschauungen views
(loosely, the views of Popper, Kuhn, Feyerabend, and to some extent
Stephen Toulmin and others) as views that seem to require the recognition of the fact that scientific theorizing occurs in a context with a worldview; that is, "a particular language with meanings attached to its terms
in such a way that some theoretical principles contribute to the meanings
of terms; one's conceptual apparatus, prior knowledge and belief, canons
of experimental design and control, and standards for assessing the ade-
quacy of the theory and the relevance of information to the theory; and a
determination of which questions the theory is committed to answer."[26]

Suppe argues, as do most of those who have closely examined the various worldview stances, that none of these stances is genuinely adequate
and that moreover the notion of weltanschauung presupposed by many
of the views is too vague to do any theoretical work. But in general our
concern will be with what motivated the construction of such views
rather than with the creation of a critique of them. And it is obvious that
the chief motivators here were the various lacunae found in the established version of the tenets of positivism. Hoyningen-Huene implicitly
agrees with this interpretation when, in the middle of his discussion of
the various terms that Kuhn sometimes exchanges for the notion of "paradigm" or for other notions central to the development of this concept, he
writes:

> According to Kuhn, the discovery that many historical and contemporary
> fields, especially fields of modern science, operate in research traditions rest-
> ing on a relatively firm consensus among the participating specialists serves
> as the point of departure for the introduction of the paradigm concept. Re-
> gardless of whether or to what degree this consensus will prove truly mono-
> lithic on closer scrutiny, phases of scientific development characterized by
> such consensual traditions can easily be distinguished from those phases in
> which there is no universal consensus at all among the specialists in a given
> field.[27]

In other words, the notion of a consensus—of shared background be-liefs—that serves as the basis for theorizing is a valuable one and should not be overlooked.

In addition to the overall notion of a worldview, another impetus to views like Kuhn's was the failure of the observation/theoretical distinc-tion in its most basic formulation. What the critics take to be the failure of this distinction is not unrelated to other problems that I have discussed here; it is related, at least, to the difficulties surrounding the construction of a rigorously foundationalist epistemology. But Dudley Shapere, for ex-ample, has also presented another take on this problem—the difficulty may adhere to the very attempt to formulate observation statements that allegedly can be divorced entirely from any theoretical view.[28] Shapere's take on this particular problem, which underscores points already made here, is that any formulation of an observation statement, including those that would most closely connect to what Otto Neurath and others had termed "protocol" statements, is already rife with theory. Some of that the-ory might, of course, be articulated as parts of the very sort of weltan-schauung that Feyerabend and others had remarked upon. While denying that "red patch-here-now" is a strong candidate for this type of sentence despite what some may have claimed,[29] Shapere also wants to clarify the notion of what is actually constitutive of an observation statement. It is this part of his argument that is most important for our purposes:

> What the scientist considers to be appropriate for the presentation of empiri-cal evidence seems not to be anything like the neutral "observational vocab-ulary" of the philosophers. . . . Far from it: according to this criticism, not only is the *relevance* of observations at least partly dependent on theory; even *what counts* as an observation, and the *interpretation* or *meaning* of observa-tion terms, is at least partly so dependent. All "observation terms" in science are, in this view, at least to some extent "theory dependent" or "theory laden" in a sense which is passed over by the usual ways of making the dis-tinction. Data are not "raw"; there are no "brute facts."[30]

Part of what is being argued here is certainly the rather obvious thought that, in scientific practice, it would be extremely rare to advert or allude to data that would actually mimic the structure of the protocol sen-tences. More importantly, however, what Shapere is claiming goes much further than that—he is claiming that what does serve in the capacity of, or take the place of, a protocol statement in actual practice is a statement that already has theory built into it.

These two lines of argument (the broader line that everyone holds some background views that might be thought of as worldviews and the narrower line that there is little to count as an observation statement that is not already in some way reliant upon theory) then go a long way toward showing us how, in combination with Popperian and other criticisms of the Received View, a substantial body of critical alternatives to the Received View was built up. As noted earlier, most of the views fall under the rubric "weltanschauungen views" because the one element of commonality seems to be the notion that a great deal of inarticulate theory underlies the practice of science.

Feyerabendian Twists

In a previous section I tried to specify some of Feyerabend's criticism of positivism in general before he began his later work, such as *Against Method*. It is important to understand these criticisms because, taken in toto, they mesh with a great deal of the rest of the work that was leveled against the Received View, and again they tend to underscore the kind of bias in previous theorizing that led to later critiques.

In a piece called "Problems of Empiricism," anthologized in a volume published in the 1960s by the Center for the Philosophy of Science at the University of Pittsburgh, Feyerabend honed a long attack on some of the more cherished distinctions used by positivism, some of which I have already examined. He is worth quoting at some length, because the complexity of his argument with respect to, for example, what later came to be called "theoretical monism" is difficult to recapitulate. In general, his arguments, along with those of Popper and the lines of thought examined in the immediately preceding section, push philosophy of science strongly along a path toward views that acknowledge the difficulty of making any clear-cut observation/theory distinction.

Here is Feyerabend on the role that a confirmed theory plays:

> Assume that we possess a theory in a certain domain which has been highly confirmed. Then this theory must be retained until it has been refuted, or at least until some new facts indicate its limitations. The construction and development of alternative theories in the same domain must be postponed until such refutation or such limitation has taken place. Any doctrine containing the thesis just outlined will be called a *radical empiricism*.
>
> Radical empiricism is a *monistic* doctrine. It demands that at any time only a single set of mutually consistent theories be used. The *simultaneous* use of mutually inconsistent theories or, as we might call it, a theoretical pluralism, is forbidden.
>
> It will be argued that the demand for a theoretical monism is liable to lead to the elimination of evidence that might be critical for the defended theory; it lowers the empirical content of this theory and may even turn it into a dogmatic metaphysical system.
>
> This result has important tactical consequences. It forces us to admit that the fight for tolerance in scientific matters and the fight for scientific progress

that was so important a part of the lives of the early scientists must still be carried on.[31]

This lengthy quotation is of great assistance in understanding the developments in philosophy of science that will follow, because the "theoretical monism" referred to here is clearly very much akin to Kuhn's notion of "paradigm," however critically abused the latter term became. Feyerabend is making the valuable point that, far from serving as icons of empirical confirmation/disconfirmation, most well-confirmed theories go on, albeit only tacitly, to serve as standards or focal points around which other theories swirl, and so become themselves something more than mere theories or, as he has it, "dogmatic metaphysic[s]." The latter part of the quotation is perhaps even more important, because in acknowledging that there is a fight that must "still be carried on," Feyerabend is acknowledging that science as practiced is a flawed procedure, the flaws of which have yet to be thoroughly examined.

The foregoing discussion helps to further the notion, already abroad in the early 1960s, that more attention must be paid to some sort of descriptive account of the practice of science. Although Feyerabend is making this point in a somewhat roundabout way, it is implicit in his assertions and also in his comment about battles that still need to be fought.

In this particular essay, Feyerabend also affirms that previous philosophical systems were perhaps more open about the connection between metaphysics and various forms of empiricism.[32] His point here is that the Received View form of positivism, purporting to have escaped tendencies toward metaphysical thought, contains within it its own metaphysics, perhaps unacknowledged. Part of Feyerabend's larger goal is to acknowledge that the need for theoretical pluralism will cut short the attempt to find "one true theory," an attempt that Feyerabend regards as dangerous and misguided.[33] It was, of course, in many ways one of the original aims of at least some positivist doctrine.

The Pure View and Its Concomitants

If we pause now to recapitulate briefly some of what is entailed by the Received View, it would better enable us to understand the force of the weltanschauungen views at the time of their arrival. This work so far has emphasized the notion that positivism is associated with—and interested in—the logic of science, or what came to be known as the "logic of justification." I have shown in this examination of the correspondence rules and the place of axiomatized theory on the theoretical side of the rules that deduction is paramount and that, in a sense, everything in the structure of a theory will hang upon it.

This emphasis on the logic of science not only led to the theoretical puzzles that we have seen in this chapter but to a popularization of science insofar as the public was concerned that painted a pristine and naive view of scientific research. This would not be so important had it not had such far-reaching ramifications; much of what passed for science education in the years after the war consisted of warmed-over neopositivist accounts, with an idealized and superficial gloss on scientific activity and research. Appearing earlier than much of the work discussed in this chapter and closer in time to the appearance of articulations of positivism itself, the work of Ernest Nagel and Morris Cohen, for example, in *An Introduction to Logic and Scientific Method,* provides us with a summarization of the Received View and its reception. It is interesting to note that this work, published during the 1930s, presents a view that is taken from the whole cloth and includes little or no critical reaction. The lack of problematization of the view merely leads us to note that problems will later come up.

In the work's concluding chapter, "What Is Scientific Method?" Nagel and Cohen present the Received View version watered down for popular consumption, so to speak, without critical rebuttal or questioning. The following quotation provides the flavor of the work:

> [S]cientific method aims to discover what the facts truly are, and the use of the method must be guided by the discovered facts. But, as we have repeatedly pointed out, what the facts are cannot be discovered without reflection. . . . Sensory experience sets the problem for knowledge, and just because such experience is immediate and final it must become informed by reflective analysis before knowledge can be said to take place.
>
> "Common sense" is content with a miscellaneous collection of information. As a consequence, the propositions it asserts are frequently vague, the range of their application is unknown, and their mutual compatibility is generally very questionable. The advantages of discovering a system among facts are therefore obvious. A condition for achieving a system is the introduction of accuracy in the assertions made. The limit within which propositions are true is then clearly defined.[34]

As can readily be seen, such key concepts as "method," "facts," and "system" are presented here as if they were entirely unproblematic and as if their use were immediately available to all. It is imperative to understand the consequences of the propagation of such a view, because it is the ubiquitousness of the view and the extent to which it influenced training in both the hard and social sciences that to a large extent account for the reaction against it. No doubt the strength of physics as a discipline during this period is responsible for a great deal of the popularity of positivism, but it is important to note that part of the strength of that popularity also lay in positivism's relatively unexamined reception.

I discussed earlier the beginnings of a move toward the realization of the role of the normative and axiological in science, but even as late as the period immediately preceding the publication of Kuhn's *The Structure of Scientific Revolutions*, there was still comparatively little questioning in some quarters of what that role was to be. Although, as we have seen, Feyerabend noted the extent to which earlier large-scale views influence the development of a particular scientific theory either among a body of scientists or within the framework of a given thinker's speculation, a somewhat uncritical approach to the role of preceding normative theories was still prevalent at a relatively late point in time.

Working in the early 1960s, Nicholas Rescher noted that:

> It is a regrettable fact that too many persons, both scientists and students of scientific method, have had their attention focused so sharply upon the abstracted "logic" of an idealized "scientific method" that this ethical dimension of science has completely escaped their notice. This circumstance seems to me to be particularly regrettable because it has tended to foster a harmful myth that finds strong support in both the scientific and the humanistic camps—namely, the view that science is antiseptically devoid of any involvement with human values. Science, on this way of looking at the matter, is so purely objective and narrowly factual in its concerns that it can, and indeed should, be wholly insensitive to the emotional, artistic and ethical values of human life.[35]

Rescher gives us a clear picture of the stance, informed by positivism and postpositivistic developments, that was still predominant at that point. The question then became to what extent—and with what speed—theoreticians could begin to make headway against this view.

Introducing the Feminist Criticisms

Because of the force of the pure logicist view, what we would now regard as the feminist critique of science did not begin to develop explicitly in academic circles until the late 1970s or even the early 1980s. But although this view is preceded chronologically by Kuhn's work and other work similar to it, which will be the subject of the next chapter, an interesting juxtaposition can be set up by introducing the feminist critique in the context of a strict delineation of positivism and its outgrowth.

The pattern of scientific thinking referred to in the quotation from Nagel and Cohen above refers to a "system among propositions" and "the limit within which propositions are true." The stringency of the articulation of these points underscores, as I have maintained, the lack of problematization of certain areas of scientific research and leaves the interested reader or inquirer with the notion that, once axiomatization has proceeded on the theoretical side and observation terms are kicked into place, the development of scientific theory proceeds apace without difficulty.

But the work of Evelyn Fox Keller, for example, may be juxtaposed against this sort of view precisely because Keller, in her study of Barbara McClintock, was examining the work of someone who had been trained in the positivist tradition but knew enough to be able to leave portions of it aside when need be. In "A World of Difference," the chapter in her *Reflections on Gender and Science* that deals specifically with McClintock's work,[36] Keller is careful to note that McClintock's first reaction to the "jumping chromosome" effect noticed in corn plants was that it "couldn't" be happening. In other words, this type of chromosomal alteration went against all of the training that McClintock had received, and the first reaction of most scientists when confronted with such apparently aberrant data would probably have been to think that mistaken inferences had been made or that the data were in error. It is precisely because McClintock was able to put aside her previous training to some extent—precisely because she may not have been so concerned about a "system among propositions"—that she was able to come to conclusions that disconfirmed a great deal of previous genetic theory.

One could make a counterargument here, of course; one could claim that it was McClintock's training that enabled her to reach the correct conclusion, and so, of course, in the broad sense it was. But such an argument is only applicable in a naive and uninteresting way—her training would have encouraged her to believe that anomalous data should be discarded. It is this attentive "listening to" the data that McClintock feels best characterizes her work, and it was this focused attention that made all the difference, or as Keller has it, "a world of difference."

Speaking more broadly, one might wonder specifically what it is that feminist theory, when conjoined with both experiences like McClintock's and the encapsulated description of the Received View that I have just given, has to say to the type of logic of science that the Received View exemplifies. One of the points that the feminist critique can make is that desires for "autonomy" and "objectivity," not only insofar as rhetoric is concerned but insofar as there is a Complete Account at which theory aims (the so-called god's-eye view), are deeply rooted not only in the enterprise of science but in the male personality structure as a whole. It is this, then, that is meant when science is referred to as "androcentric"; the androcentrism of science is a matter of intellectual style and cognitive goals. And this particular style and this precise set of goals can scarcely be better depicted than in the Received View, with the rigidity of its underpinnings, conceptually and from the standpoint of theory structure.

The axiomatized nature of theory, its incorrigibly foundationalist empiricism, its logical structure—all of these elements of the original positivist doctrine speak to a desire to find that single, unifying scientific view that will provide us with a key to nature, a key that, as Keller notes in her essays on both Plato and Bacon, is a goal of the male-driven and male-identified point of view.[37] When this goal is abandoned, or even watered down, science is seen differently, more descriptive elements of scientific theorizing come into play, and a set of problematic areas come to the fore. Thus the feminist critique of science, although it chronologically succeeds rather than precedes the weltanschauungen views, aids us in seeing precisely where a system such as the Received View has gone awry and why it was so difficult for such a long time to articulate these problems. The understandable desire of male theorists, functioning at a point in time in our culture when European and male dominance was more or less unquestioned, to construct a worldview that would be airtight and not ultimately subject to disconfirmation was the dominant theme of philosophy of science for an extremely long period of time. Criticisms of this stance began to emerge only in a context in which some criticism was inevitable—in circumstances in which, as Rescher notes, science was sufficiently reliant upon government funding to call into question its own purity.[38] By comparing the Received View in its original format with sharp feminist commentary, we can see the flaws of that view in a new light.

The New Epistemological Views

In this characterization of key components of positivism, epistemic foundationalism has played a crucial role, and responses to epistemic foundationalism deserve at least some mention. As developed earlier, criticisms by J. L. Austin and others of purported or alleged incorrigibility proved to be the undoing of much of what passed for a rigid foundationalist epistemology at an earlier point in time.[39] Austinian criticisms tended to focus on word usage, but this was no small point when the phrasing of many of the protocol statements was taken into account.[40] Austin noted in *Sense and Sensibilia* that there are a variety of reasons why someone might later want to claim corrigibility for even the most severely hedged statement, including misuse of words.

Although epistemologists later tried to develop less rigidly foundationalist views—some even went so far as to develop what has been referred to as a "modest foundationalism"[41]—the attacks on foundationalism in general meant that important components of the Received View fell by the wayside.

Contemporary epistemology has been heavily influenced by views that are now known as "naturalized epistemology," and it is interesting and informative to throw these up against the type of epistemology associated with the Received View. Work by Hilary Kornblith, Alvin Goldman, and others has shown that contemporary cognitive science has much to give epistemology, including the notion that theorizing as if it did not matter whether epistemic theory was or was not instantiable in an epistemic agent is an unrealistic and ludicrously a priori way of constructing theory now that so much more is known about cognitive functioning.[42] Perhaps more important for the work here has been the intersection of feminist theory and naturalized epistemology, a way of theorizing epistemically that shows signs of great promise and that simultaneously undoes the androcentrism of much contemporary epistemology while focusing on data about how epistemic agents actually function.

Ann Garry writes of the work of several feminist theorists whose attempts to use naturalized epistemology to help develop feminist theory have drawn attention.[43] Lynn Hankinson Nelson and Louise Antony, among others, have tried to develop the notion that the "naturalization" originally called for by Quine is related to strongly developed trends in feminist theory, such as the notion of a community of knowers, the undercutting of the observation/theory distinction, and so forth. The point here is not only that a great deal of the earlier work in epistemology was noninstantiable but that much of it took as its model (and this seems to be obvious in the case of the protocol sentences) an epistemic agent working alone and with the data of only his senses.

Naturalized epistemology does a great deal of damage to any contention that strong foundationalism can be sustained because, for example, the more that we know about visual functioning, the less clear it is that anything approaching the visual "sense data" posited by theorists earlier in this century even exists.[44] Thus, with respect to the concept of a pure observation sentence, there is little that is currently available in the way of information about visual functioning that would suggest that it is even possible to think of a "percept" as something that endures for Russell's classical "two or three minutes."[45]

The upshot of combining the new epistemology with a classical feminist view as a line of criticism against positivism and positivist-inspired endeavors, as outlined in the preceding section, is that we can see clearly how arguments that would eventually develop in the demolition of the Received View were already ensconced in the proper articulation of it, so to speak. All of the stances generated against the Received View were related to problems inherent in its development in the early stages and more clearly formulated by theorists working, as I have noted, in the late 1950s and early 1960s. Although feminist critiques and naturalized critiques come much later, they too are related to material that had been presented by the positivist theorists as cornerstones of the view, hence as beyond criticism in the original framework.

Philosophy of science took its sharpest turn in the work of Thomas Kuhn, the subject of the next chapter. But the way had already been paved for significant criticism from other sources, and the strict formulation of the positivist outlook more than invited such criticism.

Part Two

The New Moves
in Science Studies

4

Kuhnian Revolutions

It is difficult to overestimate the importance of Kuhn's *The Structure of Scientific Revolutions,* originally published in 1962.[1] Perhaps few academic works in the last thirty to forty years have made as great an impression, which is all the more overwhelming when we remember that much of the work's influence finally came to bear upon disciplines not allied with the sciences—a great deal of the work's import has spread throughout the humanities, and it has had particular influence on literature and literary studies.[2]

In addition to these positive influences, Kuhn's work also spawned a plethora of critical articles and a virtual cottage industry of responses aimed at clarifying the use of terms such as "paradigm" and "puzzle." The fundamental points at which Kuhn was aiming are foreshadowed, so to speak, by a great deal of the literature in philosophy of science of the immediately preceding period, work which I have discussed in the last section. But it is either a virtue or a defect of Kuhn's project that the combination of his use of terminology and the relatively brief and concise arguments made in *The Structure of Scientific Revolutions*—the entire work in its original edition is only slightly over two hundred pages long—lends itself to something akin to a sort of spiritual plagiarism and to an excess, if such a thing is possible, of commentary.

Although much of the critical commentary on the work has focused on the notion of "paradigm," a salient concept for our purposes comes from an early chapter on puzzle solving.[3] After introducing the notion of a paradigm, Kuhn makes it clear that, within the framework of normal science, what constitutes a puzzle to be solved is, in fact, a research problem the parameters of which are so firmly set by preceding patterns of research that it is virtually indisputable that the problem will, in fact, come to be resolved. Indeed, the point here is that if the problem is not seen as solvable, then it does not count as a "puzzle." When we remind ourselves of the beginnings of the move away from the pure or uncontaminated version of the Received View delineated in the foregoing chapters, we can see how the combination of more descriptive material, and the overwhelming sense that the discovery side of the split between the "logic of discovery" and the "logic of justification" had not been sufficiently examined, paved the way for the type of material Kuhn produced.

What, according to Kuhn, is a "puzzle"? A puzzle, cast in his terms, turns out to be a relatively small problem that can be solved with contemporary methods in a comparatively short period of time. The solution to such puzzles comprises for Kuhn a good deal of the work of "normal science."[4] Kuhn gives a brief description of the concept of a puzzle within the framework of such scientific practice in the following:

> A paradigm can, for that matter, even insulate the community from those socially important problems that are not reducible to the puzzle form, because they cannot be stated in terms of the conceptual and instrumental terms the paradigm supplies. . . . One of the reasons why normal science seems to progress so rapidly is that its practitioners concentrate on problems that only their own lack of ingenuity should keep them from solving.[5]

A paradigm shift, then, results at least partly from the solution of a puzzle that has unexpected results or that does not cohere with preceding data. A difficulty both for Kuhn's work and for the notion of a paradigm shift in general, however, is trying to get a handle on what it is, precisely, that produces the shift or that precipitates the conceptual change.

It would, of course, be difficult enough to give a general account of such a procedure, since what is involved here is clearly the articulation of a model. Nevertheless, Kuhn's more sharply articulated statements about the "shift" indicate that, aside from the most broadly construed type of description, very little is offered in the way of an account of how the paradigm is altered. This feature of Kuhn's work has indeed been one of the most problematic and has given rise to some of the most extensive commentary.

The Notion of Shift

Consider the following passage, taken from the chapter titled "Anomaly and the Emergence of Scientific Discoveries":

> To a greater or lesser extent (corresponding to the continuum from the shocking to the anticipated result), the characteristics common to the three examples above are characteristic of all discoveries from which new sorts of phenomena emerge. Those characteristics include the previous awareness of

anomaly, the gradual and simultaneous emergence of both observational and conceptual recognition, and the consequent change of paradigm categories and procedures often accompanied by resistance.[6]

The conceptual difficulty here is obviously the rather extraordinary juxtaposition of the last two components of the three-step process: "observational and conceptual recognition" is described as "gradual," but then all of a sudden, so to speak, one obtains a paradigm shift, or as Kuhn has it in this passage, a "change of paradigm categories."

Perhaps the most helpful material in the chapter is the passage near the end where Kuhn attempts to build on data from a psychology experiment by J. S. Bruner and Leo Postman in the late 1940s involving the recognition of "anomalous" playing cards (cards such as, for example, a black six of hearts).[7] This material is metaphorically powerful in trying to come to grips with the notion of a paradigm shift, but it cannot rise above metaphor, since clearly there is an enormous difference between conceptual change and the recognition of salient theoretical patterns on the one hand, and minimal category change and the recognition of actual visual patterns (and minor visual patterns at that) on the other. Nevertheless, as Kuhn indicates, the one instance of recategorization can at least aid us in the understanding of the other:

> Either as a metaphor or because it reflects the nature of the mind, that psychological experiment provides a wonderfully simple and cogent schema for the process of scientific discovery. In science, as in the playing card experiment, novelty emerges only with difficulty, manifested by resistance, against a background provided by expectation. Initially, only the anticipated and usual are experienced even under circumstances where anomaly is later to be observed. Further acquaintance, however, does result in the awareness of something wrong or does relate the effect to something that has gone wrong before. That awareness of anomaly opens a period in which conceptual categories are adjusted until the initially anomalous has become the anticipated. At this point the process has been completed.[8]

This example is helpful in providing a model for the notion of paradigm shift, but it is still lacking in specificity. Since the anomalous data faced by the scientist are not, as I have articulated, anomalous in the same way that the card pattern is anomalous, the notion of change or "completion" is much more difficult to assimilate. Approximately how much anomalous data is needed to force the shift? Over what period of time does this occur? How many instances, roughly speaking, of anomalous data must be brought to bear before the shift occurs? These answers are not easily obtainable, whereas the card experiment can be delineated crudely in number of trials. (Interestingly enough, Kuhn notes in citing the Bruner and Postman material that "[a] few subjects, however, were never able to make the requisite adjustment of their categories."[9])

Theory Change

Kuhn attempts some clarification of the notion of theory change as concomitant to paradigm shift. Again, there is some fuzziness in the categorization, but this particular chapter of the book is aided by a perhaps somewhat clearer and more familiar set of examples.

As Kuhn explores the notion of theory change, the lacuna that we have seen previously is at least somewhat ameliorated by advertence to such factors as length of time involved in the intellectual crisis and the notion of "penetration." In other words, a paradigm shift (or theory change) can occur at least partly because the anomalies are evident for such a long period of time and with respect to so many, or such important, phenomena that real intellectual movement is generated. Kuhn writes:

> Shifts of this sort [paradigm shifts] are, I have argued, associated with all discoveries achieved through normal science, excepting only the unsurprising ones that had been achieved in all but their details. Discoveries are not, however, the only sources of these destructive-constructive paradigm changes. In this section I shall begin to consider the similar, but usually far larger shifts, that result from the invention of new theories. . . . If awareness of anomaly plays a role in the emergence of new sorts of phenomena, it should surprise no one that a similar but more profound awareness is prerequisite to all acceptable changes of theory. . . . Furthermore, in all these cases except that of Newton [changes of theory] the awareness of anomaly had lasted so long and penetrated so deep that one can appropriately describe the fields affected by it as in a state of growing crisis.[10]

Although it would not be fair here to say that Kuhn is running together the two notions of paradigm shift and theory change, one can see, as Kuhn himself admits, that there is a great deal of overlap between the two. The dual phenomena of length of time and depth of crisis are relevant to many of the situations preceding paradigm shift, so that it would not be accurate to say that these descriptive factors play a role in theory change only. In fact, in attempting to articulate the major difference between these two concepts, Kuhn speaks in terms of size.[11]

The Copernican revolution turns out to be, unsurprisingly, an example of both paradigm shift and theory change—Kuhn writes of Copernicus's preface as "one of the classic descriptions of a crisis state."[12] What is remarkable about Kuhn's work, even with the apparent conceptual muddiness affecting parts of it, is its descriptive flavor. Such a growth in the emergence of the validity and relevance of historical data to scientific conceptualization and to accounts of scientific theory making could scarcely have occurred at a much earlier point in time, since, as we have seen, the preceding work in philosophy of science was still driven largely by concerns with the logic of justification.

A Feminist Overview

I pause here briefly at the beginning of a more specific adumbration of the feminist critique, largely because we do indeed possess developed feminist commentary on Kuhn and because the nature of Kuhn's work pushes us in this direction. Sandra Harding, among others, noted that Kuhn brings to bear a number of "naturalized" lines of argument, each of which is helpful in pursuing the development of a new historiography of science without reference to gender issues. Harding writes:

> The post-Kuhnian studies have moved past these dogmas [of empiricism] to provide naturalistic and critical interpretive accounts of the history and practice of science. To the extent that they avoid examining the effects of gender identity and behavior . . . however, their explanations and interpretations are both incompletely naturalized and distorted.
>
> [N]atural science is a social phenomenon, created and developed at particular moments in history by particular cultures. Gender . . . is a variable not only in the beliefs about gender differences but also in the most formal structure of beliefs about nature and culture.[13]

This quotation from Harding accomplishes two things simultaneously: It provides us with a quick reason as to why Kuhn's work was so immensely appealing—it did, as I have indicated, address as central issues other than the ubiquitous logic of justification—but it also provides us with a brief take on what is lacking in Kuhn's view. Although I will examine further aspects of *The Structure of Scientific Revolutions* later in this chapter, nowhere in Kuhn's work, social though it may be in its emphasis on the reception of paradigms and the notion that what is constitutive of a "puzzle" has to do with how a paradigm is defined, is there any awareness of issues such as gender, social class, or, of course, race. In other words, Kuhn takes it for granted that the practitioners of the tradition about which he is writing (the practitioners of, in fact, normal science) are white males, and there is no hint within the text of the social pressures that caused this division of intellectual labor. Then again, as is indicated in the last portion of the Harding quotation, there is also such a thing as "androcentric style" insofar as the demarcated structure of thought is concerned, and although it hardly would have been realistic to ask Kuhn

to inquire into this phenomenon, it is nevertheless not a source of speculation for him.

Thus Harding reminds us of the fact that reference to the "social" can
come in many forms and guises and that a bare-bones introductory account
of what provides the sociological form of the logic of discovery can hardly
do justice to a broader view of its structure. That feminists were later to take
the formulation of such questions somewhat for granted is indicative of a
great deal of movement in this area, for as we have seen, when Kuhn's
work was first published these questions were nowhere in evidence.

A further twist on the relationship between what will come to be the
feminist critique and all of the weltanschauungen moves, Kuhn's taken as
exemplary, comes from the disparity and tension between what Harding
refers to as "internal" and "external" stories about science.[14] Since this
distinction is similar to the distinction between various sorts of histori-
ographies of science that Kuhn himself made at the beginning of *The
Structure of Scientific Revolutions*, it is important to try to clarify the relationship of this cleavage to feminist and other views.

The "internal" story is, of course, cast not only in terms of the logic of
justification and the epistemological rigor that those who, for example,
were associated with the Received View of positivism would often espouse, but also in terms of lack of relationship between science and society as a whole. Thus, with regard to the "internal" story, there is virtually
no importance to be attached to the social strands that weave the back-
drop against which science occurs. This view attributes an undue emphasis—even, one might assert, in comparison to many strictly empiricist
views—to the purity of standards and the notion that these standards can
be adhered to without allusion to social functioning. Interestingly
enough, Harding insightfully casts part of the motivation for the blind acceptance of this view to those who had so carefully articulated the justificatory logic. She implies that part of the psychological motivation here
was the effort involved in having constructed the logic in the first place:

> The internalist program assumed that a rational reconstruction of the devel-
> opment of science would simultaneously provide the entire *relevant* history
> of science. This is the assumption that motivated the heirs of logical posi-
> tivism . . . to try to construct ever more nearly perfect logics of justification.
> . . . The internalist program tried to produce a rational reconstruction of the
> development of science for which the history of science would provide no re-
> futing evidence. After all, what point would there be to a logic of justification
> from which one could draw the conclusion that the historical development
> of science . . . was irrational and *not* logically justified?[15]

As Harding notes, much of the work since then (and certainly since
Kuhn) has been "external" in the sense that it usually is categorized as "so-

ciology of science," "history of science," or some other "——— of science" with sociological factors filtered in, but this work, too, is often androcentric in the sense that it relies on disciplines that have not themselves been suffi- ciently informed by feminist critique. Because so many of these "external" studies were, until recently, heavily reliant on Marxist criticism, they suf- fered from the defects, not always subject to scrutiny, already implicit in such lines of argument. Thus any neologistic discourse that purported or alleged to examine science was, until the 1970s, usually itself a victim of the masculinist bias that informs the disciplines generally. (As Harding notes of these sorts of critiques, "If we have no grounds for judging the reliability of beliefs apart from their coherence with cultural arrangements of which we do or do not approve, why should anyone who is not moved by the Marx- ist vision of social progress find the externalist accounts plausible?"[16])

It is now clear, given the relevance of the general notion that the weltanschauungen views were themselves informed by what Harding is labeling as "external" accounts, how sociology of science in its more con- temporary manifestations came to assume its current role. What is needed here is clearly a meshing of the various theoretical varietals, and no one "-ology" of science can bring more to bear than another, given that conceptual clarification is the ultimate goal. Kuhn's work, then, is central not only in the overwhelming critical response it received but because it opened the door to many other sorts of "external" critiques. Harding em- ploys the phrase "post-Kuhnian" in her work to signal to the reader that *The Structure of Scientific Revolutions* is indeed a watershed insofar as fem- inist and radical critiques of science are concerned.[17] Kuhn's book is not the only such work published during this period, but it is the work against which all others must be measured.

Hesse and Metaphor

The intersection of the arrival of the weltanschauungen views and the de- velopment of the feminist critique points us in the direction of other orig- inal views promulgated during this period. In the remainder of this chap- ter I will examine the work of more than one such theorist, but an underexamined area that deserves special mention, especially in this con- text, is the work of Mary Hesse.

Writing as a woman philosopher of science in a time well before the ar- rival of the feminist overview, Hesse nevertheless developed a strikingly formulated theory with respect to the importance of metaphor in sci- ence—one that, in its own way, was prescient.[18]

Hesse forwards the argument that "the deductive model of scientific ex- planation should be modified and supplemented by a view of theoretical explanation as metaphoric redescription of the domain of the explanandum."[19] This in and of itself might not be so striking were it not for the fact that, in her book-length work on the topic, Hesse devotes entire chapters to the role of metaphor, the function of models, and so forth. Taken in conjunction with the theoretical descendants of positivism (such as Carl Hempel, whose work I examined in Chapter 3), it is clear that part of the power of Hesse's work derives from her assumption that it is possible to use nonreferential or quasi-referential language in science and, indeed, that such language may be beneficial for our understanding. If we think of the insistence on correspondence rules characteristic of positivism, the importance of the notion of reference, and so forth—what we might describe as the general rigidity of the view—then we can see that Hesse's work represents not only a variation of what might be called a weltanschauungen outlook but specifically a variation that is precognizant with respect to some of the feminist critique of science that will emerge. Hesse's work seems intuitively to understand that there is an amount of stylistic aggression involved in, for example, the Received View.

Hesse writes:

> We start with two systems, situations, or referents, which will be called, respectively, the "primary" and the "secondary" systems. Each is describable in literal language. A metaphoric use of language in describing the literal system consists of transferring to it a word or words normally used in connection with the secondary system: for example, "Man is a wolf," "Hell is a lake of ice." In a scientific theory, the primary system is the domain of the explanandum, describable in observation language; the secondary is the system . . . from which the model is taken.[20]

Hesse's work here shows an attention to the power of metaphor that moves the language of science in a new direction. Hesse actually takes pains to contrast poetic and scientific metaphor—she notes that "it is characteristic of good poetic metaphor that the images introduced are initially striking and unexpected."[21] She also discusses the power of the metaphor to "cause us to 'see' the primary system differently."[22]

Although Hesse's work is brief, it represents a valuable alteration and one that was in keeping with the spirit of the time, if we think of that spirit as a decided move away from positivism. Any move that would allow for the exploration of literary and metaphorical uses in the language of science or in the construction of scientific models was a powerful breakthrough in the period immediately after the predominance of positivism.

Lakatosian Research Programs

Among the responses to the collapse of positivism were several views that, although sharing with Kuhn a new approach to the difficulty of moving from one research view to another or from one paradigm to another, differed from Kuhn by trying to articulate the process as possessing a fundamentally greater degree of rationality.

Imre Lakatos's concept of a research program that involves both "positive" and "negative heuristics" provides us with a stance that exemplifies responses to positivism predicated on the underlying rationality of science.[23] He is especially sensitive to the notion, stressed by Kuhn, that the anomalies that may ultimately give rise to paradigm shifts are not somehow foreseen or anticipated by researchers. Thus what Kuhn labeled a "puzzle"—something that, as we have seen, is demarcated and solvable within a given research tradition—is for Lakatos only one sort of problem. Many other problems and instances of theoretical difficulty that are not solvable within a given tradition are for Lakatos possible counterexamples that, in many cases, have already been noted by researchers. Lakatos himself can perhaps best articulate what separates him from Kuhn:

> Kuhn is wrong in thinking that by discarding naive falsificationism he has discarded thereby all brands of falsificationism. Kuhn objects to the entire Popperian research programme, and he excludes *any* possibility of the rational reconstruction of the growth of science. . . . *In Kuhn's view there can be no logic, but only psychology of discovery.* For instance, in Kuhn's conception, anomalies, inconsistencies, *always* abound in science, but in 'normal' periods the dominant paradigm secures a pattern of growth which is eventually overthrown by 'crisis'. There is no particular rational cause for the appearance of a Kuhnian 'crisis'. 'Crisis' is a psychological concept; it is a contagious panic.[24]

Lakatos may exaggerate, to some extent, the lack of attribution of rationality to the scientific process that he finds in the Kuhnian view, but he is correct insofar as Kuhn's original text assimilates the notion of paradigm shift into the perceptual gestalt change that one obtains when faced with anomalous playing cards. In any case, what Lakatos develops and delineates particularly clearly in his long article "Falsification and the Methodology of Scientific Research Programmes" is a view that allows for a gradual alteration of the research program by a series of maneuvers involving falsification in a steplike sequence. This overview of more gradual change allows for a greater attribution of rationality to the process while at the same time moving away from the classically grounded notions of confirmation and the tie-in to rigorous epistemology that characterized the Received View.

Lakatos indicates that one of the hallmarks of the worth of a research program is its "heuristic power": "[H]ow many new facts did they produce, how great was 'their capacity to explain their refutations in the course of their growth'?"[25] Again, Lakatos is the best proponent of his own view:

Even the most rapidly and consistently progressive research programmes can digest their 'counter-evidence' only piecemeal: anomalies are never completely exhausted. But it should not be thought that yet unexplained anomalies—'puzzles' as Kuhn might call them—are taken in random order, and the protective belt built up in an eclectic fashion, without any preconceived order. The order is usually decided in the theoretician's cabinet, independently of any *known* anomalies. Few theoretical scientists engaged in a research programme pay undue attention to 'refutations'. They have a long-term research policy which anticipates these refutations. This research policy . . . is the positive heuristic of the research programme.[26]

Here Lakatos informs us of the notion that what can be anticipated can also be rationally accounted for; that is, it is anomalous only in the sense of a given set of hypotheses that may have been previously articulated, and not in the sense of a larger, expanded view. This argument certainly resuscitates the concept of an overall rational order to the progress of research, but it is not absolutely clear that, historically, such a program can be ascribed to the proponents of the views that preceded what Kuhn would call "paradigm shifts."[27]

On the whole, we may think of both Lakatos's and Kuhn's views as responses to the Received View that provide for a much greater degree of fluidity both in the construction and in the emergence of theories than was originally provided for in the theorizing of members of the Vienna Circle. Other key proponents of such views enjoyed a certain popularity during the 1960s and 1970s, before the advent of views more decidedly associated with the sociology of science.

Toulmin and Change

Stephen Toulmin makes similar challenges to Kuhn's overall view, and his essay "Does the Distinction Between Normal and Revolutionary Science Hold Water?" has the virtue of stating these challenges succinctly.

Like Lakatos, Toulmin sees science as an enterprise that already has at its disposal, at least to some extent, devices for the conceptualization of category change that do not have to encompass "revolutionary" activity. Thus Toulmin is able to acknowledge, as have most theorists, the enormous categorical changes and shifts without, as he phrases it, buying into a view that assumes that there are "discontinuities in scientific theory far more profound and far less explicable than any which ever in fact occur."[28] Toulmin reminds us that there is very little evidence, anecdotal or otherwise, that the shifts in theory that occurred in the past (the sorts of shifts that Kuhn has labeled "revolutions") were viewed in that way by the participants themselves. In other words, part of Toulmin's point is that sea changes of that sort should yield at least some minimal evidence about what transpired; in general, no such evidence is to be found. Toulmin writes:

> If the complete breakdown in scientific communication which Kuhn treats as the essential characteristic of a scientific revolution had in fact been manifested during this period, one should be able to document it from the experience of the men in question. What do we find? If the conceptual change involved in the transition was as deep as Kuhn claims, these physicists at least appeared curiously unaware of the fact. On the contrary, many of them were able to say, after the event, why they had changed their own personal position from a classical to a relativistic one. . . . Taking Kuhn at his word, however, such a change could have come about only as a result of a 'conversion'.[29]

What Toulmin means, of course, is that the provision of reasons indicates that there was no such conversion. More tellingly, perhaps, Toulmin likens the battle between those who would accept Kuhn's account, with its large-scale, monumental, and sudden changes to the dispute between the uniformitarians and the catastrophe theorists in nineteenth-century geology, and those who would not. As Toulmin notes, the debate was at least partially resolved simply because each side modified its position and moved somewhat closer to the other. With respect to the catastrophe theorists, he claims: "In a word, the original 'catastrophes' became uniform and law-governed just like any other geological and palaeontological phenomena." He also notes that the acceptance of this notion by the theorists in question did, of course, destroy the original point that they had been making about catastrophic occurrences and undercut their ability to claim that enormous nonexplicable changes had occurred.[30]

In this brief article, Toulmin's task is similar to that of Lakatos: Both thinkers want to be able to account for the nature of scientific change without resorting to Kuhn's terminology or his conceptual apparatus. What the thinkers have in common, however, as I have already remarked, is an inability to move back to the sort of theorizing characteristic of the Received View. In this respect, the two thinkers have a great deal in common.

Watkins's Critique

One of the most valuable pieces of critical commentary on Kuhn's work published in the 1960s is by J. W. N. Watkins of the London School of Economics. This particular piece has the virtues of maintaining sharp clarity and of focusing the attacks on Kuhn to a manageable bundle, most of which can be articulated with brevity. Watkins treats extensively an area which I have already examined here: the disparity between Kuhn's account

of puzzle solving and the kind of activity that would, at least under suppo-
sition, be necessary in order for the revolutions to which Kuhn makes reference to occur.[31] As Watkins points out, the solving of the puzzles under the
puzzle-solving rubric has little to do with confirmation or disconfirmation
of theories, in the Kuhnian view, and everything to do with a closed system
of scientific activity that may, in fact, be overtly hostile to change.[32]

But, as Watkins is also careful to note, without a more fully adumbrated
view of what it is, specifically, that leads to paradigm shift and of the time
lapse necessary for paradigm shift to occur, the concepts become somewhat vacuous. The difficulty, as Toulmin also asserts, is that the shift itself
becomes more like a religious experience (or at least an extrarational experience) and less like a shift involving the growth of scientific knowledge, unless these concepts can be properly set out. What later becomes a
problem for a number of disciplines, not just the sciences, is the purported "incommensurability" of the paradigms. Holding that the paradigms are indeed incommensurable does nothing, of course, to help delineate the specifics of paradigm shift. Watkins develops his critique
along these lines:

> By contrast with the relatively sharp idea of testability, the notion of ceasing
> 'adequately to support a puzzle-solving tradition' is essentially vague; for
> since Kuhn insists that there are *always* anomalies and unsolved puzzles, the
> difference between supporting, and failing to support, a puzzle-solving tra-
> dition is merely one of *degree:* there must be a critical level at which a tolera-
> ble turns into an intolerable amount of anomaly. Since we do not know what
> the critical level is, this is the sort of criterion that can be used only retrospec-
> tively: it entitles us to declare, *after* a paradigm switch has occurred, that em-
> pirical pressure on the old paradigm *must* have become pretty intolerable.
> This fits in well with Kuhn's idea that a reigning paradigm has such a sway
> over men's minds that only strong empirical pressure can dislodge it.[33]

In other words, as has been said by a number of commentators (but
said clearly by Watkins), it is by no means obvious how the paradigm
shift occurs, since it only looks feasible, so to speak, with hindsight. What
happens here is that the conceptual analysis that is necessary to sustain
the notion that the paradigm shift was inevitable is a sophisticated case of
post hoc ergo propter hoc; after such a shift has taken place, all of the key
components of the theoretical moves leading up to it look as if they, by
their lack of fit, caused the breakdown of the old paradigm and the emergence of the new. At various points in his text, and with some qualifica-
tion, Watkins accuses Kuhn of formulating "Gestalt-Switch" and "Instant
Paradigm" theses—these labels seem apt precisely because of the fact that
there is little explication, as we have already seen, of how it is that the
paradigm shifts actually take place.

All of the foregoing helps us understand two very important considerations: first, that the arrival of the weltanschauungen views—Kuhn's, any of the others, or all of them together—marks a decided break with the preceding logic-of-justification period, and that this move itself pushes us, as we have already seen, toward the feminist and radical critiques; and second, that the barrage of criticism addressed specifically to Kuhn helped develop these alternative theses, even if it did little to clarify Kuhn's text. The Kuhnian debate tended to dissolve into extended commentary on the use of the term "paradigm," as I have noted, and this part of the debate may not contain any material that is, in and of itself, particularly forward looking. But insofar as these views advert extensively to history of science, sociology of science, or a philosophy of science that is more focused on the logic of discovery than on the logic of justification, they pave the way toward another round of theory development and they open the door to critiques that are descriptive rather than prescriptive.

The lack of reference to gender, gender-related issues, and issues of race and social class is still apparent in the work of the theorists at this point, but the amount of descriptive material inherent in the debate—the assertion, for example, that there must be further elucidation of *how* shifts occur, because it does not make sense to think that they appear suddenly in the middle of the night—indicates an environment in which it will soon be possible to ask rather more difficult and penetrating questions about the sociological structure of science and science activity. This material will begin to move to the fore in the 1970s.

Hanson's Patterns

Still one other theoretician whose work is associated with the rise of weltanschauungen views is Norwood Hanson. In the opening chapter of *Patterns of Discovery*, Hanson manages to make the point that the observation/theory distinction is undercut—a point that, as we have seen, is related to the prominence of the weltanschauungen views in the first place—in a discussion that focuses wonderfully on the notions of "seeing" and "seeing as."[34]

Hanson uses some of the same examples employed by Wittgenstein in the *Investigations* (the duck-rabbit, for instance) to discuss the nature of the different kinds of seeing involved in scientific discovery and scientific theorizing. Like Hesse's work on metaphor, Hanson's work here already has one overriding virtue: It pushes the debate in new directions and alleviates the flat-footedness of some of the previous claims. Like Kuhn's work itself, it provides a new frame for seeing changes in science and awakens our sense that much is going on that had not been addressed by previous theorizing.

Hanson begins his work with a simple biological example, but it is a telling example because it will influence all that follows. With respect to biological "seeing," Hanson notes:

> Imagine . . . [two observers looking at] a Protozoan—*Amoeba*. One sees a one-celled animal, the other a non-celled animal. The first sees *Amoeba* in all its analogies with different types of single cells: liver cells, nerve cells, epithelium cells. These have a wall, nucleus, cytoplasm, etc. Within this class *Amoeba* is distinguished only by its independence. The other, however, sees *Amoeba*'s homology not with single cells, but with whole animals. Like with all animals, *Amoeba* ingests its food, digests and assimilates it. It excretes, reproduces and is mobile—more like a complete animal than an individual tissue cell.
>
> This is not an experimental issue, yet it can affect experiment. What either . . . man regards as significant questions or relevant data can be determined by whether he stresses the first or the last term in 'unicellular animal.'[35]

Hanson is careful to insist that this is more than mere "interpretation," but it is also more than mere biological "seeing." (This has little to do, for example, with images produced on the retina.) Instead, as Hanson is indicating, this involves, at least, minimal conceptions of theoretical frameworks that are already in place, so to speak, before the data are encountered. Another example encapsulates the same issue in a single sentence. Kepler and Tycho stand on a hill at dawn, each with differing beliefs about the earth and the sun. As Hanson puts it: "Do Kepler and Tycho see the same thing in the east at dawn?"[36]

As Hanson later goes on to argue, "seeing as" and "seeing that" are significantly related to the points he is making, even if neither of these conceptualizations completely captures the relevant distinction. As he also says, "'Seeing that' threads knowledge into our seeing; it saves us from re-identifying everything that meets our eye; it allows physicists to observe new data as physicists, and not as cameras."[37]

In articulating these points, Hanson, like Hesse, Lakatos, Toulmin, and Watkins, cleared the path for the development of other views related to lines of development that ran contrary to the Received View and that pushed philosophy of science in new directions. The feminist critique and the radical critique emerged from these new ways of seeing.

The New Criticism

The emergence of the new criticism involved not only the disparity of the views that manifested themselves as responses to the Received View but also public jadedness about the perceived dominance and barrenness of science. The cold war, the space race, the nuclear threat, the continuing problems with environmental pollution—all of these obvious areas of public debate rose to prominence in the 1960s, at the same time that massive social changes forced Americans to become more aware of points of view that might be thought of as radical or counterculture.

A gradual sense emerged among academics that part of the hegemony of science, as it were, was related to the dominance of scientific discourse and to the notion that science had somehow replaced other belief systems as the leading exemplar of rational thought in the postwar developed world. Now that a plethora of views has emerged, not one of which takes obvious precedence, it is somewhat difficult to reconstruct a public-policy atmosphere in which science and the alleged or purported progress of science are dominant, but such was the case until at least the early 1970s.[38]

Both the feminist and radical critiques of science began in the general atmosphere of public criticism brought on by the war in Vietnam, the Watergate scandal, and the decline in importance of the space race, especially after the much-publicized and somewhat anticlimactic series of moon shots. As Geoffrey Gorham writes in a journal article that provides an overview of feminist epistemology and the feminist critique of science:

> The challenge is to find a conception of knowledge that captures the objective (epistemic) superiority of the feminist sciences without resorting to the objectivist 'god-trick' of traditional epistemology. . . . The knowledge obtained in masculinist sciences can only be weakly objective, according to Harding, because its causal history is confined to the interests and perspectives of the dominant social class.[39]

This paragraph skillfully summarizes two of the outstanding motives behind the attempt to ameliorate the practice of science. Feminist epistemology and the overall critique of science generated by feminist concerns are first of all motivated by a desire to find an epistemic stance that does not involve the kind of "ground-all" foundationalism inherent in positivism and its offshoots. But, perhaps more importantly, because this kind of epistemology is itself masculinist and androcentric—because it so overwhelmingly exhibits the stylistic aggression of a personality run through the alembic of male developmental distortion—it fails to be responsive to the concerns of others, both in its epistemology and in its practice and effects. Thus Gorham encapsulates what drives both the radical and the feminist critiques in just a few lines; the force behind both is the goal of bringing to bear on the sciences as we know them the voices of the disenfranchised.

The Kuhnian and post-Kuhnian concerns that I have followed in this chapter also have in common an important element not categorizable solely under the rubric of either of the main critiques, and that is the aim of providing at least some minimal account of how science is practiced. This was not only Kuhn's target, as we can readily see from his work, but was to some extent the goal of the other thinkers whose arguments I have examined here. Thus, as I have noted before, the turn toward the logic of discovery rather than the logic of justification was more or less simultaneous with the emergence of other concerns, and all lines converged in the establishment of science studies, a domain that refused to settle for logic-of-justification questions and in which, indeed, justification has played a comparatively small role.

The rise of French theory at a still later point has given us the kind of postmodern criticism of science that we currently find in the work of Bruno Latour and others, but this take on science could come to the fore only after the preparatory work of the other critiques had been laid. Chief among the tiles in this mosaic of preparation was the sociology of science.

Related to the sociology of science but still distinct from it is the radical stance on science; one of the most important works published in this vein in the 1970s was *The Political Economy of Science* by Hilary and Steven Rose.[40] As the turn toward the weltanschauungen views had signaled, and as even some of the most standard work in philosophy of science had presaged, the pretensions toward a complete divorce of science from the world of the mundane had always been grandiose at best. A more sophisticated view would have taken the complex ties of science to industry and production into account, and the work of the Roses furthered analysis along that path.

Much of the initial work in the radical critique had a Marxist flavor, since part of the argument was that industry's need for science was overwhelming and spoke to greater concerns about productive forces in general. But some of the critique merely pointed out the inevitable consequences of the complexity of scientific research—its ties to other areas, its inherent entanglements, and so forth. In a chapter titled "The Incorporation of Science," the Roses wrote as follows:

> The capitalist mode of production requires continuous innovation in all spheres of life, the creation of new commodities, new technologies, new ideas and new social forms. It is the business of natural science to aid in this process of innovation. Thus under capitalism natural science acts as a direct productive force, continuously invading and transforming all areas of human existence. Marx himself saw that nineteenth century science acted both as a direct force of capitalistic production and also as a means for social control—for the maintenance of the capitalist order. . . . The point is, that despite the paradigm within which bourgeois historians, philosophers and sociologists of science have operated, modern science and technology are indivisible.[41]

Capitalism needs science, because science provides for expanded forces of production and hence expanded markets. And, unfortunately, science needs capitalism, because high-level scientific research cannot be done without the multiple sorts of apparatuses that capitalism supplies.

The radical critique of science was also extremely sensitive to the brutal exploitation of the Third World by science, and the merging of the feminist and radical lines meant that there was a developing awareness of, for example, such phenomena as the utilization in the Third World of improperly tested or even overtly flawed birth control devices and other products of technology.

In sum, the emergence of the new critiques, along with the burgeoning growth of sociology of science, spelled an end to a good deal of the logic-of-justification emphasis in science studies in general and even to some extent in philosophy of science itself. More importantly, the entire direction of work in and on science began to subtly change as a result of these efforts. Since the 1970s, an explosion in science studies has attempted to focus our attention on how it is that science actually functions in our lives.

5

Philosophy/ Sociology of Science

We may think of sociology of science as an offshoot of sociology of knowledge, an endeavor that goes back at least to the classic work of Karl Mannheim, if not before.[1] Although it could be argued that enough material descriptive of the procedures and processes of science was already contained in the weltanschauungen views, sociology of science further disabused those interested in the science community of the notion that science contained any purity qua intellectual endeavor. Sociology of science also helped merge the lines of radical critique and nascent feminist critique, to which I have already alluded, and the upshot has been that, more recently, science has begun to look less and less like a formalizable endeavor and more and more like an accidental process with elitist and hierarchical overtones, the results of which are occasionally written down, promulgated, and codified.

Sociology of science has also drawn from the type of work in epistemology that now goes under the rubric "socialized epistemology" or even "naturalized epistemology." Although I will draw on the latter work later in the text, it is interesting to note that any alembicated account of sociology of science must at least minimally make reference to social features of cognitive processes and their relationship to scientific theorizing.[2]

Writing on "the elusiveness of consensus," Steve Fuller has noted that what passes for consensus is a seldom articulated process that may be comprised of a number of strands, some of which may bear very little comparison with the ordinary use of the word "consensus." This type of work has been typical of some of the more recent endeavors in science studies and is indicative of the trend toward demystification that is provided by allusion to material more purely descriptive. Here all of the original concerns about the context of justification have virtually dropped out. Fuller writes:

> [T]he last thing [a theoretician] would want to learn is that consensus formation is largely an *accidental* phenomenon, the result of a statistical drift in allegiances, in which the reasons invoked by the individual scientists may have little to do with each other. A discovery of this kind, which would amount to an 'invisible hand explanation' . . . of science's cognitive success, would obviously be difficult to implement *deliberately* as a piece of rational science policy.[3] (Emphasis in original)

Fuller goes on to differentiate between several types of situations, some of which result in what has ordinarily fallen under the rubric "consensus" and some of which do not.[4] More instructive for our purposes, however, is the variety of comments that Fuller makes about the sociology of actual historical situations known to have transpired that, at the time, passed for scientific consensus. The lack of rationality inherent in some of the situations (indeed, in some cases, the lack of contact sufficient for anything like consensus building to have occurred) is indicative, Fuller argues, of the kind of post hoc tinkering that frequently occurs in theoretical accounts of science, many of which are designed to heighten the notion that science is a more rational, or in some sense purer, endeavor than it actually is. Fuller sets this out in the following passage:

> Admittedly, historians of science often mention the names of such theories as 'Newtonian mechanics,' 'Darwinian biology,' and 'phlogiston chemistry.' However, they tend to use the names as a convenient way of individuating camps of scientists, often simply on the basis of the fact that these scientists either have appropriated the labels for themselves or—and more likely—have had the labels foisted upon them by their rivals. And perhaps every scientist would assume that the other scientists in his camp adhered to the same core tenets. The commonality of labels normally has been enough to dissuade the scientists from delving into the matter, united as they seemed to be against a common foe. Consequently, it is not unusual for a historian to examine the microstructure of a scientific camp only to find that the scientists must have been presuming of each other quite different core tenets—a fact that may surface only much later in internal disagreements.[5]

Here Fuller takes what might be thought of as paradigmatic cases of consensus and demonstrates that that apparent agreement may be just that—more apparent than real. Particularly important in the above paragraph is Fuller's phrase "united as they seemed to be against a common foe," because in many cases this, in fact, is the basis for what has been taken by others as consensus.

I have spent some time on these selections from Fuller's brief article because I believe it to be indicative of the new directions in which sociology of science has pushed science studies. As I have noted in the preceding sections, although these directions might appear somewhat obvious simply from the arrival of, say, Thomas Kuhn's material and responses to it at a given time, it is not tendentious to suggest that the overall direction of science studies as we approach the contemporary period tends to attribute less rationality to science rather than more. In this chapter I shall examine the effect that sociology of science has had on science studies and show its intersections with the various feminist theories that come to the fore during this period.

The Class Structure of Science

Sociology of science and the radical critique of science converge in some of the work that addresses issues of the class-based origins of scientific research, the reproduction of the notion of social class in such research, and related matters.

In a piece called "On the Class Character of Science and Scientists," Andre Gorz presents an analysis of the special structure of science, qua activity, within society that leaves observers of the phenomenon with the impression that the true nature of scientific activity is frequently concealed under bourgeois trappings.[6] Gorz's primary argument is that work that would ordinarily be deemed "scientific"—because it contributes to a body of knowledge, because it aids in the betterment of human life, and so forth—is often held to be less than scientific because it is produced under conditions that do not replicate the bourgeois structure of science that is so paramount to overall social reproduction.

In other words, contemporary capitalist society requires a division of labor such that skilled knowers and workers receive special status labels that tend to cut them off from other workers, regardless of the inappropriateness of such labels when considered in terms of actual labor or of actual contribution to human functioning. Gorz indicates that the structure of scientific activity is thus concealed—and this concealment is similar to the concealment of other phenomena. Although neither author tries to make the intersection, Fuller's argument with respect to consensus is similar to Gorz's argument with respect to class; both stances traditionally attributed to science (that consensus does not happen accidentally and that scientific workers are not "proletarians") mask the accidental day-to-day workmanlike quality of much scientific research.

Gorz addresses the untruths told about the scientific enterprise in the following way:

Our whole education has been devoted to telling us that science cannot be within the reach of all, and that those who are able to learn are superior to others. Our reluctance to consider ourselves as just another type of worker rests upon this basic postulate: science is a superior kind of expertise, accessible only to a few.

This is precisely the postulate which we must try and challenge. Indeed we must ask: why has a science—or systematised knowledge generally—been so far the preserve of a minority? I suggest the following answer: because science has been shaped and developed by the ruling class and for its benefit in such a way as to be compatible with its domination—that is, in a way that permits the reproduction and the strengthening of its domination.[7]

Gorz's concern is that this specialization of knowledge, insofar as it is related to class structure, is concealed from society at large by the same series of mechanisms that creates much of the bourgeois false consciousness. More importantly, however, and not plainly addressed by Gorz's piece, is the notion that the systematized knowledge that is constitutive of science is produced by some mysterious process not accessible to mere mortals and relatively uncontaminated by the usual sorts of human needs and concerns.

It is here that the radical critique and standard sociology of science merge, because the pretension of science to a special epistemic status, bolstered by the Received View and other theories that were essentially offshoots of it, is undermined by contemporary science studies.

The rise of the sociology of knowledge was also crucial in leading to the sort of critical stance with respect to science associated with contemporary sociology of science, and most of the work done in this area makes at least tacit acknowledgment of such a debt, as I indicated in the beginning of this chapter. If the class structure of science, as indicated by Gorz's piece, recapitulates claims of transcendental purity, it is partly because (as we know from the investigations here) the original epistemology tied to the Received View actually articulated an incorrigibility. But Mannheimian concerns pushed anyone with even a remote interest in sociology toward recognition of the situatedness of knowledge claims, the interests of knowledge producers, and the relevance of this material to science.

Seen in this light, then, the aims of the Vienna Circle were formulated almost entirely in response to the demands of the new physics, and the explanatory power of alluding to the push of those demands becomes much stronger than any argument that could be made on the logic-of-justification side. Fuller ably expresses some of what goes on when sociologists of knowledge become sociologists of science in the following passage from his book *Social Epistemology:*

However, one can be more or less naive about the relation of words to deeds in knowledge production. More naive is the classical epistemologist, who takes the expressed justifications literally as referring to a common method with a track record of getting at an extrasocial reality. A little more astute were the original sociologists of knowledge, who nevertheless continued to think that behind similar forms of expression must lie similar forms of constraint, even if they turn out to be nothing more than the ideological force exerted by a discipline's dominant interest group.[8]

In other words, purity of relationship between word and object is on a collision course with an analysis that sees such putative relationships as driven by bias and social positioning. To put it bluntly, the latter analysis won. The overwhelming appeal of this kind of analysis drives much of science-related inquiry today, so that even approaches that might be thought of as more purely philosophical frequently find themselves subjected to lines of criticism that are essentially sociological or that represent a merging of historical and sociological arguments. Because so much has been done on these fronts, and because originally important claims and distinctions such as those between theory and observation, the analytic and the synthetic, and the claims that underlay attempts to develop sense data theories were largely discredited on their own terms, it is no exaggeration to say that sociology of science is currently the driving force behind science studies.

The Social Structure of Knowledge

A number of lines of argument and evidence may be cited in support of the contention that the social structure of knowledge has existed all along, and was perhaps better recognized by at least some philosophers before our time. The split between accounts of knowledge acquisition and accounts of other philosophical activities dates back only approximately to Kant, at least according to some.[9]

More importantly, perhaps, even a cursory examination of the works of philosophers whose interest in "knowledge" was thought to be completely normative shows at least some awareness of a social element. Oddly enough, or maybe not so oddly, Plato's *Theaetetus*, often described to undergraduates as the first major work in Western epistemology, itself exhibits some of this minimal awareness, since it is clear that many of the examples and counters that Plato has Socrates provide as stepping-stones for the definitional account employ social and/or perceptual situations involving other persons.[10]

If it can be claimed that there are trends in epistemology and Western philosophy in general that support the notion that knowledge is social, then the opposite can of course be maintained, and it may very well be the case that the opposing side has had the most publicity. We cannot easily find social elements in, for example, Descartes's *Meditations,* and this work is often cited for its paramount importance in the creation of the theory of knowledge as a subsidiary discipline. But the point here is to try to show how the tendency in science studies to bring sociology of science to bear heavily on the material is but one stance that can be taken with respect to knowledge acquisition in general.

As Fuller notes in *Social Epistemology:*

> And so, my short answer to the alleged self-contradictoriness of "social epistemology" is that epistemology has been a well-motivated autonomous field of inquiry only insofar as it has been concerned with the social organization of knowledge. Such had clearly been the case with the first epistemologists, Auguste Comte and John Stuart Mill, and it had continued to be the case in the twentieth century with the logical positivists. The continuity of this concern is nowadays lost, however, mainly because logical positivism's legacy has been greater in the techniques it introduced for doing epistemology than in the actual project for which those techniques were introduced.[11]

Fuller is simply making the point that there is a way to interpret the history of epistemology that makes a project like that of the Vienna Circle appear somewhat anomalous, and thus sociology of knowledge and sociology of science move more smoothly into place.

Bloor and Social Imagery

If there is a point of departure for much of what currently passes for breakthrough work in sociology of science, it is probably David Bloor's important book, *Knowledge and Social Imagery.*[12] Published in the mid-1970s, the work is crucial for a variety of reasons: It offers an argument against those who would try to maintain (as the positivists and others had done) that some "knowledge" had a special epistemic status and hence was invulnerable to relativistic concerns; it offers an articulated version of what a sociology of science would encompass (Bloor's "strong programme"); and it offers counterarguments to classic rebuttals, such as the line that sociology of science undermines itself through its own critique.

Bloor's work is focused and cognizant of scholarship in both philosophy and history of science, and Bloor is aware of much of the research, particularly in logic and mathematics, that would tend to dismiss sociological concerns as trivial and not worthy of serious investigation. More importantly, perhaps, Bloor recognizes that the work of philosophers of science before him, particularly Karl Popper and Kuhn, indicates a profound turn that requires further guidance and development, rather than elision of the lines of argument that might be thought to flow from it quite naturally.

Bloor's "strong programme" became a staple of discussions in the sociology of science, and although he is indebted to a number of other theoreticians from the Edinburgh school, his work is worthy of examination on its own. In the first chapter, Bloor gives us a taste of what is to come when he condenses an argument extolling the relevance of sociology of science into the following paragraph:

> It is quite possible to sweep . . . empirical observation aside and declare it to be irrelevant to the true nature of science. Science as such, it may be said, develops according to the inner logic of scientific enquiry and these [priority] disputes are mere lapses, mere psychological intrusions into rational procedures. However a more naturalistic approach would simply take the facts as they are and invent a theory to explain them. One theory which has been proposed to explain priority disputes sees science as working by an exchange system. . . . Because recognition is important and scarce, there will be struggles for it.[13]

In clear and concise language, Bloor reminds us that the notion that priority disputes about who came to scientific knowledge first, so to speak, can only be seen as "lapses," holds for someone who is wedded to a certain way of thinking. Taking an empirical approach to science itself—or as Bloor has it, "taking the facts as they are"—yields the conclusion that such disputes are central to science and may even in some sense define scientific activity. Although a devotee of a more normalized view might find such an interpretation inherently offensive, it is Bloor's point that it is this very interpretation that, in this case, is a priori and nonempirical. The prevalence and frequency of such disputes demand some sort of theory to explain them, and sociology of science provides such a venue.

Bloor's work is rich in such arguments, as sociology, itself professedly one of the sciences, examines the enterprise of science. If, as I have claimed, Bloor is up against a formidable set of obstacles in attempting to forward such a view, he is able to marshal counters with surprising ease. A typical assault can be found in his chapter contrasting the styles of Popper and Kuhn; Bloor indicates that their styles represent little more than the appropriation of a certain kind of thinking by philosophers of science (Bloor labels the one "Enlightenment," the other "Romantic"). Far from demonstrating that science or the philosophy of science is sacrosanct, Bloor indicates that they are, of course, a part of the larger circulating intellectual endeavors of the time, and that anyone involved in these academic circles is bound to be infected by the variety of styles and types of thinking available.

Hence the difficulty would be in arguing that someone engaged in philosophy of science would be invulnerable to the prevalence of these various intellectual styles; that these philosophers would be above the fray in the sense of shielding themselves from information presented in these forms. Bloor notes:

> It is the mechanics of the transfer of the ideas from the one realm [epistemological] to the other [ideological] which remains to be examined.
>
> It is not difficult to make plausible conjectures. The ideological opposition is widely diffused through our culture. It is a prominent and repeated pattern, so any reflective person is going to encounter it—whether through reading history books, novels or newspapers, or in responding to the rhetoric of politicians. The pattern may not be encountered as a stark, fully articulated opposition. It may come first through experience of one side of the polarity, then through the other.[14]

In other words, Bloor is saying, we have to go a much greater distance to maintain that scientific thinking is protected—an argument that we would in any event have difficulty sustaining—than to simply admit that scientific thinking, too, is part of our culture, and hence subject to the vagaries and whims of intellectual currents.

Among Bloor's contentions here is that thinkers who theorize in ways that our culture finds intellectually acceptable are so deeply embedded in practices and conventions about our culture that they may find it impossible to distance themselves. In a sense, Bloor's analysis is similar to much of the analysis that is constitutive of Freudian theory. We accept, when dealing with psychoanalytic explanations, that a great deal of what is under discussion is difficult to formulate at the conscious level, and the fact that analysands frequently deny the motivations that they have been charged with does nothing to forward evidence for what is being denied and in fact may undercut it, since we understand that denial is a classic defense mechanism. So, too, Bloor is reminding us that the fact that theoreticians may not be aware of broad tendencies in the range of intellectual styles available to them does nothing to bolster the contention that these theoreticians are still not operating under the influence of a given style, or are not susceptible to it.

Rather, the ubiquity of these styles indicates that it would be virtually impossible for someone to theorize without resorting to one or more of them, and so their very presence in the culture indicates that they are being picked up and employed even though we may not be aware of it. The power of Bloor's argument resides simply in the fact that an analysis of the styles available to us reveals that empirically he is on the right track, and that his claim that it is virtually impossible to divorce oneself from one or more of the available styles is also significant.

Perhaps more controversially, Bloor also attempts to similarly characterize mathematics and logic; that is, he attempts to show how work that might be considered beyond sociological analysis—Gottlob Frege's attack on Mill, for example—may actually require just such an analysis. However successful one thinks Bloor's attempt is, it is noteworthy that he makes the effort; it is also noteworthy that part of Bloor's analysis uses material that is relatively uncontroversial (Mary Douglas on purity, for example) and applies it to areas where it might not normally be applied. Bloor would no doubt add that the fact that such an analysis is not often applied to these areas tells us something about the sociology of mathematics.[15]

Only a small portion of Bloor's work in this section can be recapitulated here, but the argument is an intriguing one and turns on what Bloor takes to be the aim of Frege and others in distancing themselves from Mill's psychologizing. In other words, it is part and parcel of Bloor's argument that style of presentation is an overwhelming factor, and that sociologists are just as entitled to investigate the motivation behind the style in this rather arcane area as they would be in other, more empirically driven areas. The comparative strength of Bloor's claims is underscored by the obvious motivations of Frege in attempting to distance himself from Mill's work—motivations that might themselves be linked to prestige, status, and similar qualities. Bloor writes:

> The importance of the common sense experience of mathematics . . . is that it represents a body of facts for which any theory of the nature of mathematics must account. . . . The unique, compelling character of mathematics is part of the phenomenology of that subject. An account of the nature of mathematics is not duty-bound to affirm these appearances as truths, but it is bound to explain them as appearances. It is a notable characteristic of some philosophies of mathematics that they uncritically take over the phenomenological data and turn them into a metaphysics.[16]

Bloor notes that "there is a sense of urgency and a sharp awareness of professional esteem" in Frege's *The Foundations of Arithmetic.* Employing a consistent line of analysis, Bloor notes that the main difference between the methods with which Mill and Frege attack the notions of mathematical foundations and the status of mathematics has to do with their differing styles and their differing concerns for their professional reputations. Although Bloor's analysis leaves relatively untouched the core of Frege's work, it does provide a biting commentary on why certain works deemed to have groundbreaking intellectual value occur at certain times. In that sense, Bloor's work is like Kuhn's—Bloor recognizes that there are social considerations behind the "revolutions" that affect intellectual history and thought in general.

Knowledge and Social Imagery is but one of a number of works published during a decade-long period that signal the strong emergence of the sociology of science. The continued turn in any field purporting to examine science toward an account of what underlies work in science could only bode well, of course, for the concerns of feminists and others, such as the radical critics of science, who were seeking allies in their endeavors to construct a strong body of criticism.

Winch, Philosophy, and the Social Sciences

Some time before the work of Bloor and other members of the Edinburgh school, Peter Winch had published a small book frequently cited in the same context, *The Idea of a Social Science*.[17] Winch's work drew heavily on Wittgenstein, but it was surprisingly forward looking in the extent to which it anticipated some of the other work cited in this chapter.

Winch argued that epistemology and sociology were much closer, disciplinarily, than some had believed. Taking into consideration Winch's background as a philosopher rather than a social scientist, this rather extraordinary thesis required a great deal of argumentative support. Winch found this support in Wittgenstein to some extent, but much of his argument simply turned on the notion that knowledge arises from social conditions and is hence a social production—rather a strong move for its time. Winch noted that it was possible to clarify the somewhat hoary notion that epistemology provided the general framework under which other philosophical considerations could be examined. Ameliorating this cliché of philosophy, Winch claimed:

> [T]he relation between epistemology and the peripheral branches of philosophy [had been considered to be] that the former concerned the general conditions under which it is possible to speak of understanding while the latter concerned the peculiar forms which understanding takes. . . .
> But to understand the nature of social phenomena in general, to elucidate, that is, the concept of a 'form of life', has been shown to be precisely the aim of epistemology. It is true that the epistemologist's starting point is rather different from that of the sociologist but, if Wittgenstein's arguments are sound, that is what he must sooner or later concern himself with.[18]

Drawing on work on the relationship between language, conceptualization, social phenomena, and knowledge, Winch pushes the line that epistemology is much closer to becoming a social endeavor than had previously been thought. Concepts, Winch argues, depend on group or social life, and one puts the cart before the horse to speak of any kind of categorical generalization without allusion or advertence to the circumstances under which the conceptual apparatus that makes such generalizations possible springs into place. Winch also draws on Ernst Weber's notion of sense or *sinn* to make this point, which also ties into other Weberian concepts, such as ideal types.

If, as Winch claims, epistemology has a much greater social component than has generally been recognized, then without further ado the pure science whose epistemic foundations are tied to the singularized theory of knowledge is done for, and it not only makes sense to look at the sociology of science but sociology, science, and some sort of epistemology are more closely related than had previously been believed. It is interesting that Wittgenstein is cited in this context, because so much of the work that is associated with the *Investigations,* for example, seems to examine only linguistic phenomena or phenomena that might more properly be thought to fall under the rubric of philosophy of language. But it is a virtue of Winch's work that it takes another direction.

Winch examines Weber's concept of *Verstehen* (or interpretative understanding), a notion that has been absolutely crucial to the social sciences, and he does so in the light of Wittgenstein's comments about rule following. Rules, of course, are never followed explicitly; rather, practice and rules go together in ways that are difficult to untangle. This insight, combined with Winch's further appropriation of *Verstehen,* allows Winch to point out that the distinction so often made in the social sciences between strictly quantitative and purely qualitative work is more or less a bogus distinction. Even work that is demarcated as quantitative cries out for further interpretation (i.e., further understanding). Although Winch does not use the expression "hermeneutic circle," it is clearly something like this that he means, since the interpretations themselves, like the rule following, lead us in further interpretative directions.

With respect to the common moves made against Weber and *Verstehen,* Winch writes:

> [Weber] is very insistent that mere 'intuition' is not enough and must be tested by careful observation. However, what I think can be said against Weber is that he gives a wrong account of the process of checking the validity of sociological interpretations. . . . Weber is clearly right in pointing out that the obvious interpretation may not be the right one. But I want to question Weber's implied suggestion [and the suggestions of his critics] that *Verstehen* is something which is logically incomplete and needs supplementing by a different method altogether, namely the collection of statistics. . . . I want to insist that . . . [w]hat is then needed is a better interpretation, not something different in kind.[19]

Thus Winch sees the social sciences as a network of interpretations, many of which themselves become part of or demarcate activities that we would ordinarily call "epistemological" and so forth. As indicated earlier, it is part of the strength of Winch's analysis that it lets us see a relationship between philosophy and the social sciences that has not previously been articulated, so that Winch's work falls not so much under the categorization of sociology of science as under its own categorization—the relationship between sociology and philosophy or, as Winch would have it, the relationship between sociology and epistemology.

Although John Rawls's work on two concepts of rules comes chronologically later, it is clear that Winch's insight about rule following does indeed bear some relationship to Rawls. The concept of rule that is most useful to the social sciences is the "practice concept"—a great deal of what we call rule following is embedded in the practice of an activity, and the activity does not make sense qua activity without this notion. What passes then, for an epistemology is something not distinct from the practices that it would purport or allege to guide; it is a part of those practices, and the attempt to separate the epistemological from praxis can only result in a fundamental sort of misguidedness. Indeed, here Winch reminds us somewhat of John Dewey, and his remarks on the irrelevance of the a priori and the necessity for merging theory and practice.

Winch sees the importance of ideas as wedded to a conception of life; hence these ideas should not be subject, in any important way, to an analysis that purports to "separate them out," as concomitant to a general understanding of those ideas. This view leads to Winch's remarks on the relationship between epistemology and sociology. Winch pushes us in the direction of social understanding in general, although there is no question that what he says is au courant with respect to the more contemporary takes on sociology of science that would attempt to strip science of most of its remaining pretensions.

Toward the end of his work, Winch remarks:

> These [social science theories about data] can then be applied to history itself in order to enhance our understanding of the ways in which its episodes are mutually connected. I have tried to show . . . how this involves minimizing the importance of ideas in human history, since ideas and theories are constantly developing and changing, and since each system of ideas, its component elements being interrelated internally, has to be understood in and for itself; the combined result of which is to make systems of ideas a very unsuitable subject for broad generalizations. I have also tried to show that social relations really exist only in and through the ideas which are current in society.[20]

What Winch is getting at here is, of course, the notion that "social relations [are] an equally unsuitable subject for generalizations and theories of the scientific sort."[21] But if this is true, as Winch is at pains to claim, it is because the relationship between the social and the epistemological has never been adequately explored. Here Winch is on sure ground, at least with respect to his own claims, since these, of course, have been the focus of his work.

In the preceding two sections I have focused extensively on the work of David Bloor and Peter Winch, since this work is of paramount importance (Bloor's, especially) in paving the way for contemporary sociology of science. Each of these theorists insists that science adopts the pretense of standing outside of systems of which it is really a part; Winch focuses on the extent to which lived lives reflect epistemological practice that is itself social, and Bloor makes the more flat-footed claim that it does not make sense to attempt to separate portions of science from sociological analysis.

Still missing from these critiques is any attempt to deal with gender issues and (except for work briefly examined earlier, such as Gorz's) any attempt to specify what will later become the more radical critique and its variants. That this is the case reveals, I believe, particularly with respect to feminist theory, the overwhelming androcentricity of what has passed for theory in the past and the difficulty that we all experience, as theoreticians, in attempting to divorce ourselves from it.

More so perhaps than any other forms of critique that are in current exchange, the feminist critique demands that we step outside the viewing apparatus that we have used up to this point and employ some other lens or filter for the examination of the intellectual enterprise as a whole and science in particular. That this is no easy task is underscored, again, by the fact that this type of broadside criticism has only recently come to the fore.

The Importance of Elster

Among recent theoreticians whose work has become extremely influential is Jon Elster, although in a sense his work defies categorization. In a lengthy series of works that might be thought of as a combination of philosophy of the social sciences, sociology, and even sociology of science, Elster examines a broad range of problems from contemporary theory, but does so in a way that signals the shifts and movements that have been the topic of discussion throughout this chapter.

In general, much of Elster's work does not fall under the rubric "sociology of science," so in that sense his work is not similar to Bloor's, for example. But the range of the work undertaken by Elster is significant because it signals the merger of many lines of argument concerning the sciences, their place in the general culture, their relationship to one another, and so forth. In this sense Elster is still another harbinger of a profound change in the attitude toward the sciences and scientific theorizing, because his crosscutting work moves away from the easily categorizable, rigid work of the preceding theorists.

Although it is virtually impossible to give an account of the complexity and depth of Elster's work, just one book that has become important, *Ex-*

plaining Technical Change, may suffice to illustrate the broad nature of his theorizing.[22] In this rather condensed work, Elster takes on all of what is normally regarded as the sciences and even occasionally portions of the humanities to try to account for how the various sciences explain change and how these explanations relate to each other. Elster works first with the physical sciences, comparing causal accounts to, for example, functional accounts, and then moves on to the social sciences, comparing evolutionary, Marxist, and other accounts.

At an earlier point in time, work like Elster's would have been unthinkable because the static division in thinking about the sciences, caused in part by the residual influence of the Received View and its adherents, would most likely have prevented the synthesis of such an enormous amount of material. It is a strength of Elster's work that this synthesis does not seem forced. For example, in his introduction to the second part of the book on work in the social sciences, he writes:

> Let me set out informally what these [Marxist] theories are trying to explain. More formal and precise statements are given in the following chapters, but there is a common background to the theories that can be stated here. Basically, they are concerned with explaining the rate and direction of the change in technical knowledge. Assuming that technical knowledge can be measured cardinally, the term 'rate of change' should not pose any technical difficulty. . . . These are not the only aspects of technical change one might want to explain. One might also, for instance, try to account for the location of technical change.[23]

It is not the substance of what Elster says here that is so surprising—it is the scope of the overview he provides that astonishes. The importance of the work is related to the growth in science studies in that the work required an overview of what the various sciences were about before such theorizing could become possible.

One more example of Elster's scope may be instructive, because this further example will also provide an interpretation of contemporary work bridging the gap between philosophy, sociology, and science studies. In an unusual intersection with literature, Elster contributed a piece, "Deception and Self-Deception in Stendhal," to an anthology titled *The Multiple Self.*[24] Again, the piece is remarkable for the extent to which it bridges gaps that, however artificial they may have been, were nevertheless predominant until only recently.

Employing some analysis that is straightforwardly philosophical and some that is more sociological or driven by the social sciences, Elster develops the notions of the contradictions and tensions in Stendhal's work that result from Stendhal's goals, as stated in his diaries and autobiographical work, of striving to be natural and free from hypocrisy. Elster notes that such strivings are similar to those of the person with insomnia; the more one strives to be "natural," the less natural one becomes. More importantly, not only are there tensions between action and goal but there are also tensions, in the major novels, between the Stendhalian narrator and the protagonists themselves, these two voices representing, as Elster sees it, the two developed halves of Stendhal's own split identity. In analyzing these layers of the Stendhalian oeuvre, Elster uses a combination of literary criticism and, as mentioned, work in the social sciences and philosophy. The result is a startlingly original essay on a major literary figure. Here is a sample of Elster's analysis in this vein:

> Similarly, it might be possible to bring about spontaneity by acting deliberately, to use the will to phase out the will. This indeed is a central idea in Buddhist thought. One then has to take care, of course, that one never requires more will for the next step than what is left after the preceding step. Also, one might try to overcome timidity by using what little courage one has got to build up a bit more, which can then be employed to further development. . . .
>
> Stendhal's presence in his novels takes several forms. There is the voice of the narrator, who intrudes with ironic and affectionate comments on the behaviour of his heroes and heroines, mock protestations when they behave too outrageously and so on. There are the young protagonists who enact, by proxy, Stendhal's desire for requited love. And there are older, wise, often cynical, always gay father figures, such as Count Mosca and Leuwen père.[25]

Here Elster takes up the problem that Stendhal set out for himself on an individual level—that is, of achieving spontaneity, as if spontaneity were something that could be achieved—and shows how it informs the structure of his novels. That this particular essay can be constructed concurrently with a work such as *Explaining Technical Change* is indicative not only of changes in academic disciplines as a whole but of a certain integration in analysis that is concomitant to those changes. An analysis of self-deception has in the past tended to be a purely philosophical endeavor, with perhaps some reference to the work of the ancients or of such major philosophers as Hume. But an integrated theory of self-deception, using literary criticism, philosophy, and other disciplines as springboards for further analysis, is a move that could probably have been made only after the conscious advent of science studies, studies informed by the history, philosophy, and sociology of science.

Bruno Latour

If there is one thinker whose work has been of paramount importance in the broadly construed area of sociology of science, it is probably Bruno

Latour. Works such as *Science in Action* and the more recent *We Have Never Been Modern* have garnered enough attention that, like Kuhn's work, they may be said to have altered the direction of the field.[26]

Latour places new and profound emphasis on what might be called the "social construction of science," except that to phrase it that coarsely does not do justice to the originality of his theorizing. The opening chapter of *Science in Action*, for example, is revelatory: Not only does Latour provide the reader with an analysis of three exemplary cases of scientific work, but he also provides drawings, charts, and cartoonish images that, when taken in toto, underscore his points.

Latour's constructed image of the social progress of the revelation that "The DNA molecule has the shape of a double helix" is a paradigmatic piece of work. The reader sees a page with several cartoonish boxes; each box, some depicting human figures and some simply with statements about DNA, purports to represent a stage in the development of the social recognition of the alleged "fact" that DNA has this structure. The move from the third to the fourth boxes—difficult to describe in words—is particularly illustrative. In the third box, two figures say simultaneously, "If it had the shape of a double helix . . ."; and then in the fourth box, one figure says to the second, "This would explain Chargaff" while the second figure replies, "and it would be pretty."

The reader does not need prognosticatory equipment to understand that Latour is making the major point that the "hypothesis" that DNA has the shape of a double helix is an attractive hypothesis for a number of reasons, some of which have more to do with the personalities of the thinkers involved than anything else, and thus becomes "confirmed." Many have found Latour's demystification of science offensive, since presumably the process of confirmation is somewhat more reliable than Latour implies. (Two of the last three boxes on the page indicate that the core of this process is repetition among scientists—that is, verbal repetition at conferences and in hallways—and that, after a sufficient amount of time, the repetition becomes received wisdom.)

Latour, however, is apparently unswayed by much of the criticism directed against him, because it is obvious from a number of his statements that he believes that his interpretations authentically capture what is going on. The following quotation, on the page facing the boxes I have just described, is illustrative:

> This is the general movement [the boxes] of what we will study over and over again in the course of this book, penetrating science from the outside, following controversies and accompanying scientists up to the end, being slowly led out of science in the making.
>
> In spite of the rich, confusing, ambiguous and fascinating picture that is thus revealed, surprisingly few people have penetrated from the outside the

inner workings of science and technology, and then got out of it to explain to the outsider how it all works.[27]

From his use of the term "outside," we can see that Latour takes his enterprise to be one that has indeed successfully "penetrated" science. Whatever the merits or demerits of his approach, there is no question that the demiurge of science has suffered a blow at Latour's hand and that science studies on the whole has gained fame, if not notoriety, from his work. In addition, the general critiques alluded to here many times, in particular the feminist critique, benefit from any approach that attempts to break down the process of science, and Latour's work of course does just that. Thus the androcentric style of the logic of justification—that very endeavor on which much of my first two chapters was focused—turns out to be, according to *Science in Action,* little more than knots of scientists (almost all of them male) talking to each other, passing information along, and coming to believe that this information has some epistemic status that, according to Latour, it cannot possess. Science is not only masculinist in its construction of the various logics, then, and not only androcentric in terms of numbers and style, but masculinist in a rather crude sort of way in that its core process consists of groups of men talking and discussing among each other, if seen from this rampantly sociological point of view.

Much of what we have looked at in this chapter is underscored by Latour's work. The Gorzian radical critique is of course bucked up by it, and the work of Bloor and Winch (Bloor especially) is certainly deeply connected. Bloor's take on the sociology of the process of Frege's response to Mill's original work is, in its own way, very similar to Latour's boxes. Putatively epistemic motivations give way to gossip, manipulation, repetition, and the search for fame and one-upmanship. Thus a turn that I had originally labeled "Kuhnian" becomes something quite a bit more than that.

Gleaning from Sociology of Science

Our progress through sociology of science in this chapter has given us increasingly relativistic, or even antiscience, takes on the enterprise as a whole. In other words, the radical critiques and the Edinburgh school's "strong programme," with which I opened, do not do as much damage to the traditional enterprise of science as does, for example, Latour's work.

Part of the reason for the switch is not only the notion of demystification, to which I have already alluded, but the general cultural strains that tend toward the abandonment of the "Enlightenment project."[28] For a variety of reasons, some of which seem to have precious little to do with academic life in general or even intellectual life at all, a number of currents in society indicate an increasing breakdown of categories and an increasing sense that old categories, formerly revered and employed with ease, are now irrelevant and should be abandoned.

Some of these currents do indeed derive from intellectual experiments, and I have already referred to them by allusions, for example, to French theory. But other currents may have more to do with demographic shifts, or with the growing importance of technology as an equalizer and a destroyer of formerly cherished conceptualizations.

In any case, it is certainly clear that since the 1970s science and anything having to do with the scientific enterprise have come to be seen as increasingly meretricious and subject to alembicated public criticism and doubt. Thus the tendency has been even for organizations that themselves might be thought to represent conservative, science-bound interests to take on the aura of the new science studies and, at least to some extent, to promote a view of science that they might not have tolerated twenty years ago.[29]

When Latour gives us little boxes purporting to represent the socializing process in which scientists engage—a process that, Latour would claim, has everything to do with what scientists will later claim to be "confirmed" data—he is merely voicing what a great many feel, including those without any special training in this arena. Here a number of different approaches run together; Gorz's pronouncements on the bourgeois aims that science is bound to serve, despite its claiming to be apolitical, mesh well with the general feminist critique that science possesses a stunningly androcentric bias. Both of these lines of criticism are obviously concomitant to arguments that we have seen from Bloor and Latour.

There are, of course, notions of a successor science, and there is sufficient feminist work in this area to be able to set out large portions of it, work that I will engage at a later point. But some are understandably troubled by the antiscience view (as they see it) and want to set out a response to it now. A number of works have appeared in the last few years that do just that, even if there is some doubt about their prospects for turning the tide.

The Attack on the Critiques

Chief among the works that have drawn attention to the sociological and science studies–based approach to science, but in a negative vein, has been Paul Gross and Norman Levitt's *Higher Superstition*.[30] The book is a vitriolic condemnation of science studies in general, of the work of some of the particular thinkers examined here, and especially of the radical and feminist critiques of science (particularly of the latter).

The authors are constrained to point out from time to time that they do see a place in science studies and the sociology of science for at least some acknowledgment of the ways in which the procedures and processes of science are influenced by greater social forces, but they appear to believe that little has been done in the way of this sort of research that actually meets rigorous intellectual standards. (There are very few positive citations in the book.)[31]

Gross and Levitt make one point rather well, and that is that, unfortunately, most of those who have engaged in the various critiques of science do not possess a level of scientific training such that they are actually qualified to engage in scientific research themselves. This, of course, comes as no surprise. Although such a scenario is certainly possible—and the authors admit its possibility—very few who have the training of professional scientists are willing to distance themselves from the scientific enterprise fully enough to engage in the critique.

So it is clear from the outset that one cannot have one's cake here and eat it, too. Nevertheless, it can be conceded to the authors that, especially insofar as the more technical areas are concerned (particularly mathematics, the status of Kurt Gödel's work, and so forth), it would be wonderful if the critics did indeed more fully comprehend what they were criticizing. But this relatively modest thesis does not, of course, form the core of Gross and Levitt's book. Rather, the core is an attack on the critiques, and it may rightly be said that this attack on the various strands of science studies is no more well informed than some of the studies themselves. The authors want to maintain the classical notions discussed here, such as confirmation/disconfirmation, theory construction, place-of-observation statements, and so forth, as relatively untouched core parts of the work of science; and they disagree vehemently with critics who claim that confirmation, for example, can be a highly politicized process.

Here is part of their attack on Latour:

> [An example taken from Latour's work] illustrates an important aspect of current intellectual life, especially among the trendier doctoral movements to which the academic left has proved susceptible. Self-consistency is no longer considered to be much of a virtue; and logical coherence, in the version that working scientists are obliged by their peers to honor, is viewed as a chimera. One must understand that a large part of the reason for Latour's success and celebrity is rhetorical. He provokes and challenges with his insistence on paradox and contrarian whimsy.[32]

Note that the authors assume that "logical coherence" is something that "working scientists are obliged . . . to honor." Whether or not this is true, its assumption in the text appears to be an instance of question begging.

Higher Superstition is probably at its most provocative with respect to its attack on the feminist critique. The authors heap ridicule on feminist philosophy of science, but are themselves guilty of a great deal of what they impute to others. In general, the feminist critique of science has not focused merely on numbers or exclusion, and instead has been informed, to a great extent, by the object-relations portion of psychoanalytic developmental theory, which purports or alleges to explain to us how gender differences occur during the period of rapid growth from infancy to approximately five years of age.[33] But despite the fact that the notion of theoretical confirmation is, presumably, one of the notions up for grabs in such a discussion, the overwhelming weight of lived evidence that tends to support the contention that much gender construction is already in place by the time a child starts kindergarten is ignored by the authors, as is any argument that might be made with this apparatus serving as a platform.

Gross and Levitt seem to believe that the feminist critique of science, if it were to be "properly" done, would require evidence of "palpable defects, due to the inadequacies of a male perspective, in heretofore solid-looking science"[34] In other words, feminist theory would have to, in some sense, tell us how some of our "solid-looking" theories were wrong. But the feminist critique does not, of course, engage on that level—rather, like the radical critique, it is aimed at the practices, assumptions, and processes that appear to be the guiding constructs of science. Because the authors take as implicit a view of science that is informed by, roughly, a sort of 1950s post-Hempelian outlook, they fail to understand a great deal of what the feminist critique is about.

One of the milder passages (and it would seem, perhaps, unfair to quote extensively from some of the less mild passages), a continuation of the sequence cited above, runs as follows:

> Keller's position rests upon unsupported speculations about psychosexual developmental differences between men and women; and its examples of consequences of such differences, in science, are questionable at best. Yet on such a basis, an already large body of writing has come to be taken with utmost seriousness, indeed to be celebrated, especially among cultural critics. What is most curious, though, is the acceptance of a form of essentialist doctrinaire by these anti-essentialist feminists. Keller presumably does not believe that the proposed cognitive differences between men and women are inborn. But so pervasive and fundamental a pattern, if it exists, fails of essentialism only in the feminist denial that *genes* are in any way involved.[35] (Emphasis in original)

It is by no means clear what the authors mean here, since Keller is at some pains in her work to indicate that the gendered styles are just that—simply styles—and that they can be appropriated by persons of either sex. But this is not mentioned by the authors, regardless of the fact that the relevance of style to gender development theory is one of the key points made by Keller repeatedly throughout her work.

Other portions of the Gross and Levitt work are not so palatable. The authors seem to be under the mistaken impression that part of the feminist-derived critical overview is to show that a great deal of what has already been done in science (actual theories, constructs, paradigms, and so on) is flatly wrong or can be disconfirmed. But even a cursory reading of much of what the authors themselves view as core work in feminist theory shows that this is not the case—the evidentiary basis for the claims that they attempt to make with respect to this set of contentions simply is not there. That does, of course, undercut the force of their work.

Taking some of the weaker attempts at feminist critique as exemplary in the opening part of their book, and mixing this with their own somewhat tendentious reading of feminist theory on the whole, the authors manage a remarkable tour de force of erroneous and wrongheaded accounts of feminist theory. The glibness of their attack does not seem to prevent its repetition. They claim that "The reigning posture is that the weight of men's historical misdeeds is so great that it is bad form, in fact indecent, for male academics to object, even to the most aggressive and speculative announcements of their feminist colleagues."[36] Shortly after this pronouncement, pages of analysis are expended on a piece of work that Gross and Levitt find exemplary of feminist theorizing; this work is titled "Toward a Feminist Algebra," and is obviously intended as a pedagogical piece, a point that Gross and Levitt, with their tightly constructed rationale, seem to have missed. That American universities frequently harbor graduate schools of education on their premises is a fact of which Gross and Levitt seem to be unaware. In any case, some of the analysis of this particular piece is as follows:

> It may seem to innocent readers, if any such remain, that we are putting words in the authors' mouths, but no: they disapprove of a particular problem in which a girl and her boyfriend run toward each other (even though the girl's slower speed is carefully explained by the fact that she is carrying luggage) because it portrays a heterosexual involvement. They object to a problem about a contractor and the contractor's workers because they assume that the student will envision the workers as male.[37]

What is particularly objectionable about the foregoing is that, other than their opening remarks in the chapter, the example in question is the first cited piece of feminist theory to undergo a sustained analysis by the authors in that particular chapter.

Gross and Levitt's work has achieved a fairly large audience, and one can assume that this is because many do indeed find the attacks on science threatening. Of course, those involved in science studies (particularly those in the enterprise of radical critique) can easily point out that science serves vested interests in American society, and that many stand to lose if the authority of science is diminished. The difficulty with a work such as *Higher Superstition* is not merely that it represents an attack on cultural studies, feminist critique, and so forth; it is the way in which it is done. Dealing with material that, in some cases, is virtually parodic does not help the authors building their case.

In summing up this overview of the recent work in sociology of science and science studies, two strands of argument or analysis are notable. Insofar as the radical analysis and more traditionally centered theorists such as Bloor and Winch are concerned, there are pressing epistemic issues that undercut any attempts by the standard lines of analysis to try to suggest that science rests on some inherently foundational basis. Bloor, in particular, has been able to show that there is no such thing as an issue in philosophy, science, or even mathematics that is immune from the effects of politics or of the sociology of day-to-day functioning. The project of the Received View—which, in fairness, we must remember was never intended to be descriptive—when viewed in retrospect was flawed not only because of its failure to allude to actual levels of functioning in scientific behavior, but also because it rested on the kind of rigid foundationalism that has since been sharply attacked by many theorists. The combination of these two defects—its lack of reference to instantiated behavior and its reliance on too rigid a foundationalism—has been overwhelming in the sense that it is no longer plausible to even attempt to defend such a project.

Secondarily, the more nonstandard (and more chronologically recent) theoreticians, such as Latour, have pushed the line of analysis with respect to science in such a direction that, although it may be possible to counter their arguments, any move that is made to that end is already located in an unusual space. The very fact that Latour has a wide readership indicates that many find his construal of the "confirmation" of the structure of DNA, for example, a coherent and believable account. This fact cannot be heartwarming to many who have been trained in the sciences, but it is an undeniable event and one that has brought a great deal of attention to Latour's rampantly social-constructionist line.

One might be tempted to reply that there is a middle ground here that has not been fully articulated. There might be a way of constructing, for example, some kind of coherence epistemology for science, and then of providing an overview of the scientific process that is simultaneously at least moderately descriptive and equipped with a firmer epistemic base than mere social construction. This will, indeed, be examined in a later chapter. But more importantly, some of the material covered in this chapter not only paves the way for a full-scale analysis of the feminist critique, but makes the feminist critique appear more standard by comparison. That is, insofar as the feminist critique adverts to a more standard take on science to begin with, it does not always involve those who would agree with it in adherence to a stance on the scientific enterprise that is as deviant as Latour's.

Sociology of science can be thought of as an antidote to the type of theorizing that I addressed earlier in this work, wherein crucial questions about the functioning of scientists and about the structure of the scientific enterprise qua social process were in general not asked. The necessity for the antidote is obvious from the lack of advertence to the realm of the social in the construction of the Received View. What can be gathered from the overall critique provided by sociology of science, however, is that science has little or no epistemic basis. Whether that particular view can be supported will be part of the debate in the coming chapters.

6

The Advent of Feminist Theory

The feminist critique and the work of feminist theorists in science studies, philosophy of science, and history of science have burgeoned in the last decade. Theorists whose work we have already briefly examined here such as Sandra Harding and Evelyn Fox Keller have gone on to produce further volumes; other theorists, whose work might not have been as important or as well known in the early 1980s, have now become extremely influential. One thinks, for example, of Donna Haraway, Helen Longino, and feminist epistemologists such as Lynn Hankinson Nelson whose work overlaps with the critique of science.

The importance of the feminist critique across disciplines is such that it cannot be ignored—indeed, in many disciplines, feminist criticism has become a staple and is no longer merely a peripheral part of the scene. Academic conferences in the humanities, for example, such as those which are part of the Modern Language Association, are now dominated by feminist theory and its offshoots. On still another note, the feminist critique and the radical critique have merged to some extent, and it is now somewhat difficult to distinguish between them, at least insofar as the productions of certain theoreticians are concerned.

Just as what was the weltanschauungen turn in philosophy of science gave way to sociology of science and finally to something more broadly construed as science studies, so a more standard feminist critique that commented on, for example, the androcentrism of the type of thinking that informed positivism finally gave way, in many quarters, to a version of feminist criticism that itself fused with cultural studies and science studies to assume a broadly based stance with respect to the general "narrative" of culture. The importance of the French theorists here is hard to minimize, of course; without French theory, such a painting-in-broad-strokes level of criticism might have been difficult to construct. But however this critique is positioned, its influence has been undeniable, and the growth of these interdisciplinary disciplines, as it were, signals a new era in social thought.

Because some of the types of criticisms leveled by feminist theorists against the work of those in the sciences is now familiar, and because we have already examined at least a small portion of such work here, I want to begin this chapter with a look at the work of Donna Haraway. In a sense, Haraway's work is not as important to traditional philosophy of science, or to the type of philosophizing and theorizing discussed in the beginning of this volume, since it is much less concerned with actual core components of the older philosophy of science. On the other hand, Haraway's work has now assumed such general stature that it would appear to be a mistake to begin without it. Her work on the importance of primatology, both as metaphor and as actual scientific endeavor, has been among the most crucial work done in feminist theory in the last decade.

The Work of Haraway

Employing the now familiar language of cultural studies, Donna Haraway writes of science's "stories" and their construction.[1] It is not merely that Haraway takes this approach to science; at this point, such an approach is familiar. Rather, Haraway sees that certain kinds of stories are told at certain key points to promote certain kinds of social interests—she finds such stories, especially in the field of primatology, exceedingly interesting. Primatology is itself a field of the biological sciences that has an unusually high percentage of women investigators, especially considering the virtual blockage of women in the sciences until about the 1960s.

In an intriguing chapter of *Simians, Cyborgs and Women* titled "Daughters of Man-the-Hunter in the Field," Haraway is able to show how an overwhelming percentage of the important work on langurs in primatology during the 1960s and 1970s was done by just a few women investigators who were all either students of, or students of students of, the University of California at Berkeley anthropologist Sherwood Washburn. Here is Haraway on the importance of these relationships:

> Washburn students were not members of a particularly authoritarian laboratory; they chose their own topics. They also opposed Washburn in several ways and worked independently of his ideas and support. But several report the sense in retrospect that the intellectual excitement of a new synthesis in physical anthropology and Washburn's nurturance of students' choices and opportunities (as well as indifference to other choices) suggest the existence of a more explicit plan. For example, since functional anatomy appropriate to a hunting way of life was an essential part of the story, it should not be surprising to find students in the 1960's working out new anatomical adaptational complexes made visible by the man-the-hunter hypothesis.[2]

In this passage, Haraway reminds us that social needs often determine exactly which topics are pursued and, more importantly, what conclusions are reached about them. The most salient phrase above is probably "since functional anatomy appropriate to a hunting way of life was an essential part of the story." The hunting-way-of-life tale was already in full swing, and evidence to support it needed to be found, and needed to be found in a hurry. It would be very convenient if langurs (or any other primates under investigation) somehow began to look as if they could, by dint of anatomical examination, be made to support this story. In this vein, Haraway's work borders on Latour's—what drives the process of science here is the need created for certain kinds of evidence. When there is need, then evidence begins to appear.

Haraway describes the relationship of the four women primatologists whose work she tracks in this chapter as a "patriline"; she says that these women were "raised to speak in public, to author stories, to have authority."[3] Authoring stories is, of course, one way of depicting the scientific tradition, and Haraway does not choose these words for no reason. "Patriline" is another interesting term here, especially since the field is primatology and presumably what is under investigation is how human behavior might be said to be related to the behavior of primates.

Insofar as research on baboons and langurs is concerned, Haraway is careful to note that there is a divergence of stories among the daughters of the patriline. She does not discount the seeking of evidence, and she does not try to establish that there is anything nonstandard (or nonscientific) about what is going on in the observations of primates conducted by Washburn's students and their students.[4] Rather, her point is that what is good scientific practice is a great deal more socially determined than one might ordinarily think. Observations of langurs and of baboons can be affected by behavior instigated by the investigator, and that behavior itself can be prompted by what is perceived as a need at the time, even if the perceived need may be on a fairly inarticulate level. Prior to 1960, Haraway notes, stories about baboons and langurs were constructed around male dominance, and in some cases the activities of the investigators were designed to provoke incidents that would specify patterns of male dominance; at least some of the time, one could hypothesize that the incidents might not have occurred (or might not have occurred so readily) had they not been provoked by the investigators.[5] Later investigations highlighted the activities of females, although these activities, too, could be interpreted in a multiplicity of different fashions, depending on who was doing the reporting. Haraway is at her most incisive when she is able to position her protagonist in such a way that the protagonist has some obstacle to overcome or some obvious narrative to tell; it is instructive to cite the text in this regard. She has the following to say about the widely cited work of Sarah Blaffer Hrdy:

[Hrdy] did . . . write her dedication and acknowledgements, both marvel-
lous icons, or stories in miniature, suggesting public meanings that open a
book replete with the language of heroic struggle and Odyssean voyages to
preserve the products of genetic investment in dangerous times. . . . Hrdy's
book is a sustained polemic against what she sees as group selection arguments and structural-functional social selection theory. Dolhinow and her
students are Hrdy's principal antagonists in a 'heroic' struggle for correct vision. The purpose, like the purpose of the stories in the orthodox Washburn
lineage, is to illuminate the logic of the human way of life by telling scientific
stories, thereby producing public meanings.[6]

Haraway places Hrdy in a context that allows us to see how the
rhetoric of Hrdy's work replicates Hrdy's own struggle to try to forward
a sociobiological account of primate behavior against other competing accounts. Thus the primates under discussion are not the only agonists
here—another level of struggle is that between the authors (investigators)
whose stories contest in the mapping of the terrain.

The work of Donna Haraway has attained the importance that it has at
least partly because of the rise of "science studies" as opposed to traditional philosophy, history, or sociology of science. This rise has been a
comparatively recent phenomenon, as was seen in Chapter 5. The very
phrase "science studies" indicates that the realm of endeavor here is now
more or less on a par with, say, cultural studies; and this new situation, of
course, tells us a great deal about the status in which the scientific enterprise as a whole is now held (a status that might be presumed to be a
great deal lower than during the heyday of the Received View). In any
case, Haraway's writing and similar work have greatly affected feminist
theorizing in the sciences. Sandra Harding's most recent work is, in some
ways, in a similar vein.

Harding's *Whose Science? Whose Knowledge?*

The original impact of Harding's work in the mid-1980s had been to set
out at least three types of feminist epistemologies that, in their various
ways, might be used to combat androcentric styles of scientific knowledge acquisition. But Harding's most recent book-length treatment is, like
the thinking of those involved in the radical critique or in science studies,
more concerned about a wholistic account of science that shows how the
standard story of scientific progress has left much out.

In *Whose Science? Whose Knowledge?* Harding spends some time elabo-
rating the notion that there are alternative histories, not only of science itself but of the relation between the rise of Western science and Third
World cultures in general. In other words, the growth of science in the Eu-

ropean cultures was accomplished not only because of the colonization and exploration of other cultures, movements that provided the impetus for the kind of economic growth needed to provide a leisure class, but also at least partly because those other cultures were, so to speak, robbed of their own sciences. This particular take on the moves that led toward scientific development in Europe during the seventeenth to the nineteenth centuries owes a great deal to African and other Third World theorists who have conceptualized alternate frameworks for an understanding of the rise of science. Noting that the growth of European science was far from inevitable, Harding writes:

> Three recent books by Third World scholars challenge the idea that Western science can be adequately understood within the constraints of conventional Western history. . . . They make a persuasive case for considering Western obliviousness to these constraints not as an innocent oversight on the part of Westerners but as an important piece of racist and imperialist ideology that has helped to justify to Westerners the inevitability of the scientific and technological gap between the First and Third Worlds.[7]

Citing the work of specialists in African traditions, Harding argues that the situation could have been the other way around—Europe could have been exploited and millions of Europeans captured and taken into slavery. Had such a sequence of events indeed occurred, one would not have expected the European rise of science.[8]

Harding's point here is an important one: Too often, internalist or externalist histories of science seem to take it for granted that the geographical and cultural factors that gave rise to science made its peculiar current form inevitable. This, of course, is not so. To take but one example, the depredations visited upon Africa as a result of the slave trade and extensive colonization prevent us from seeing how the continent was the victim of cultural thievery, and prevent us from coming to grips with what other cultures, particularly African cultures, might have known at a much earlier point in time.

The same emphasis on the "inevitability" of the intellectual and social structure of science and on the lack of necessity for attention to its explicit construction informs at least some of what has passed as the general feminist critique of science, a point that Harding was at pains to make in her previous book. In *Whose Science?* Harding presents a chapter with the title "How the Women's Movement Benefits Science: Two Views."[9] As might be expected, the contrast that she wishes to draw here is between feminist empiricism, which is willing to make some accommodation to rearrange what it regards as "bad science," and the more rigorous feminist critique, especially that shaped by standpoint theory or overt Marxism, which makes the claim that "science as usual" is what should go. Painting in broad strokes, one of the chief criticisms that Harding has of feminist empiricism here (a point that was also made sharply in *The Science Question in Feminism*) is that a critique so weak and mild-mannered can, in the long run, benefit only white women. Feminist empiricism does little to alter the social structure of science insofar as Third World cultures or persons of color are concerned, and it does little to request a more probing examination of the kinds of topics dealt with in scientific research.

It is here that the feminist critique meets the radical critique, and it does so in a charged way. Just as Haraway's comments on the "patriline" give us a clear indication of how it is that "top" work in primatology gets done (and who does it: i.e., largely students of former "top" workers), Harding's assessment of the comparative lack of strength of a critical position such as feminist empiricism provides us with a clearer view of the structure of science. Both critics would converge, apparently, on such points as Haraway's assumption that the models employed or questions asked in baboon research are closely related to the social needs of the investigators and the larger society in which they find themselves. Harding writes of the conflicts between the two sorts of feminist agendas she has delineated in the following passage:

> However, feminists who must struggle together against these conventionalists disagree among themselves about other important issues. One such disagreement separates those who believe that the task of feminist analysis is to object to "bad science" from those who think that "science-as-usual"—the whole scientific enterprise, its purposes, practices and functions—should be the target of feminist criticism. Indeed, feminists from one group are often surprised to find just how different their agendas are from those of people in the other group who also see themselves as feminists. The critics of bad science sometimes see the critics of science-as-usual as undermining the former's attempts to end sexist hiring practices and sexist and androcentric biases in the sciences, and as raising issues about race, class, and imperialism that seem to them to have only marginal relevance to the advancement of (white, Western) women in (white, Western) science.[10]

Harding's critique here could scarcely be more focused—the main problem with feminist empiricism is that the results it achieves (were it to be instantiated) will benefit primarily white women from the same social class and background that already dominate science and the construction of scientific problems deemed worthy of investigation. It does little, if anything, to ask the more probing sorts of questions that are brought to the surface by a set of criticisms like Haraway's, or like those of Andre Gorz or Hilary and Steven Rose. Harding does not believe that this critique is "good enough"—a more sustainable critique that speaks to the core of the issues is needed.

Putting together what we have grasped from both Haraway and Harding might at first blush appear to be difficult, but it is not so recondite a task. Haraway's general take meshes well with what Harding refers to as criticism of "science-as-usual"—although it probably does not intersect so well with what Harding describes as the more conservative, feminist empiricist approach that focuses on "bad science." What the first two views have in common is the acknowledgment, subsumed under perhaps a larger heading having to do with cultural narratives, that science constructs a number of stories, replete with evidence to support them, that tend to sustain whatever view needs support at the time, in most cases the views of a dominant, privileged group. (Although Haraway's writing frequently seems to divulge that she is more concerned with the perhaps smaller notion of privilege within a discipline, nothing that she says is inconsistent with a critique of the larger notion.) Harding's feminist position criticizing the practice of "science-as-usual" is very largely consistent with what, in her earlier work, she had dubbed "standpoint theory," since both of these views derive heavily from Marxist theorizing about class and social power and its impact on science.[11] Haraway's critical focus is somewhat more driven by the powerful lens of cultural studies—its target is an amalgam of issues that sometimes do not neatly separate into class, gender, and race categories—but, as I have pointed out earlier, "patrilines" do not come into being for no reason, and although one might indeed make sense of the concept of a matriline, there are few matrilines in the academic sciences, or indeed in the academic disciplines as a whole.

Harding is not hostile to the critics of "bad science," although it might be argued that she finds the efforts of the less conservative group somewhat more laudatory. Instead, she pointedly notes that both sorts of critical stances are necessary for movement within the sciences to occur; it is neither necessary nor desirable to make do with just one critique. She clearly articulates the need for both approaches when she writes:

> I have explored two views of what resources the women's movement can provide for science. It seems clear that feminists who hold these views have different audiences for their feminisms. Each of us may well find one set of beliefs more congenial than the other to our own projects and the institutional worlds in which we carry them out. Historically, we have too often tended to express these affinities in terms that devalued the projects of the "other feminism." I think it would be a great loss for the women's movement to abandon either approach.[12]

Harding goes on to a judgment that might be analogous to a political point made during the 1960s: It is possible to effect at least minimal change by working "within." (As it is, Harding notes that "[w]e need women within the existing sciences for many reasons."[13]) More importantly, she might well agree with the coarse-grained interpretation of this position, that working within and working without are themselves two stances that are not completely identical to the previous divisions, so that they constitute still another way of "seeing." In any case, the work encompassed in *Whose Science? Whose Knowledge?* clearly pushes feminist theory in new and refreshing directions.

Nelson and Quinean Criticism

Lynn Hankinson Nelson's *Who Knows: From Quine to a Feminist Empiricism* is an extremely important book because it bridges something like traditional epistemology and philosophy of science in ways that are both crucially feminist and, inter alia, theoretically astute.

Unlike either Haraway or Harding in her later work, Nelson's vantage point is less that of social construction than of the original philosophically pressing questions that underlay much of the work that I examined in Chapters 2 and 3. One might consider it urgent for feminist theory to have a go at such technique, because it is comparatively easy to effect a marriage of components of feminist theory with science studies or with the sociology of science, but more difficult when it comes to the original core questions. One might also think that this task parallels, to some extent, the program that Bloor, for one, set for himself when he attempted to move from the straightforward task of showing how sociological factors affect empirically derived theory to the more arcane task of attempting to show how they affect theory that is largely mathematical.

Still another virtue to work such as Nelson's is that it helps bring together some of the postpositivist theorizing with W. V. O. Quine's criticisms of it in ways that may actually be clearer and, ultimately, more comprehensible. If Quine is critical of views that might be thought of as "Hempel-Nagel" views (a label taken to some extent from Nelson herself),[14] then it is just possible that postulating feminist takes on these views may actually make Quine's criticisms more easily understandable.

It is a virtue of Nelson's work that she does not see empiricism, qua scientific method, as at all incompatible with feminist goals and themes. Rather, what Nelson tries to do is to show how Quinean criticisms of some of the constructs used to buttress the Received View—constructs that I have set out earlier, such as the observation/theory distinction, the notion of the given insofar as sense-data are concerned, and the importance of biconditional correspondence rules—can also be used to help develop a feminist epistemology and a feminist overview of science.

Nelson argues that most of us are, most of the time, functioning as empiricists, and that it does not make sense to attempt to deny this.[15] If empiricism is the idiom of everyday life, then what we need to do as feminist theoreticians is to come to grips with how we can make some version of empiricism plausible as a feminist theory, without sacrificing the insights (or, in some cases, the critiques) that have been built up against it over the history of feminist theory. Nelson reminds us of the importance of Quine's concept of communities of knowers and takes this as a point of departure for further theorizing.

Not only would the use of Quinean theory obviate the need for such formulas as a foundationalist epistemology, according to Nelson; it would also undergird many other aspects of contemporary feminist projects that have not been examined in sufficient detail to date, or the examination of which would seem to have precluded (according to some) the development of adequate theory. As Nelson notes:

> The ensuing discussion will be reactionary neither in rationale nor in conclusions. Though I believe that empiricism warrants deeper consideration than it is now accorded in feminist science criticism, I do not take the views underlying the feminist move away from empiricism as obstacles to be overcome in the development of a feminist empiricism. Rather, they are indications of what an adequate empiricism must be like. . . .
>
> At its most serious, contemporary empiricism represents a far more radical departure from traditional and positivist empiricism than has been taken into account in feminist criticisms of empiricism.[16]

Nelson's point is that both feminist critique of science and contemporary empiricism (without advertence to feminism) have something to offer each other, but too frequently this has not been acknowledged. Her overall project has the virtue of sustaining science in something like a recognizable form—problems of evidence, construction of theories, and so forth, do not receive the dismissal that they do at the hands of some of those in science studies, for example, because it is assumed that there are criteria for evidence gathering and that we can set those criteria out. By the same token, Nelson, relying on Quine, articulates a view that not only divorces itself from the aspects of the postpositivist tradition that are still foundational, but also insists on the criterion of communities of knowers and on the insufficiency of the once ideal standard of the single investigator whose sense-data were supposed to serve as the springboard from which further theorizing could begin. Unlike either Haraway or Harding, then, Nelson is more concerned with questions that we might originally deem to be classical questions for philosophy of science. Like the two preceding thinkers, however, Nelson recognizes the importance of the feminist critique of science and the stinging appropriateness of the lines of

Quinean criticism that have now become classic. It is surely a virtue of Nelson's work that we can see the enterprise of science in it without seeing science as necessarily cast in an antifeminist mode.

Hubbard, Biology, and Women

The work of Ruth Hubbard has inspired an exciting transformation in our understanding of biology and how biological issues come to shape women's lives. In a series of essays, some of which are commentaries on the work of other women engaged in the critique of science, she has tried to untangle the various strands of argument that constitute feminist criticism and also that work in science itself.

Like Nelson, Hubbard is perhaps more sympathetic to a great deal of what is ordinarily taken for granted as the structure of science, no doubt because of her training and her actual functioning in a scientific role. But like Haraway, Harding, and others, she is sensitive to and aware of the nuances of contemporary theorizing that drive both the debate over science and the larger epistemological debates as well.

Hubbard's ability to see from both perspectives is evident in her recent essays published in a collection titled *Profitable Promises*.[17] In a piece reviewing Donna Haraway's *Primate Visions*, Hubbard steers a coherent middle course between an all-out assault on science and the old-fashioned view, derived from positivism and postpositivistic practices, that sees science as inviolable. With respect to the intermingling between various metonymic takes on science and actual scientific terminology itself to be found in the writing of Haraway and some of the other science studies critics, Hubbard notes:

> Haraway's interweaving of the iconography of "high science," science fiction and popular science as presented in films and magazines, makes fascinating reading.... As the reader is led back and forth among scientific expeditions, field notes, popular films, laboratory experiments, histories of individual researchers, museum exhibits, all contextualized in political and historical time and space, it is sometimes hard to hold onto the story. But the common threads are there and always worth seeking out.... [But] not all her readers will be familiar with the ways of modern literary criticism. She erects unnecessary barriers by requiring them, again and again, to translate "semiotics," "inscription devices," "tropes," "discursive fields" and the like into plain speech.[18]

Hubbard's wonderfully commonsensical style does much to alleviate the reader's premonition that science and its results are incomprehensible, or that the intermeshing of the feminist critique with contemporary results is simply too hard to understand. Writing about the human genome project and contemporary work on genetics, Hubbard warns that the fascination with such work is to be found partly because it distances us, without our knowing it, from actual human beings. The fetus seen in ultrasound somehow takes on a life of its own (as if no biological mother were necessary), and the reduction of human conditions to genetics keeps us from looking at the hard social problems that still need solutions in real time regardless of what progress is or is not being made with respect to genes. It is easier, Hubbard notes, for geneticists and others to attempt to define phenomena in genetic terms, for it simplifies the phenomena and makes them seem more manageable. But that simplification, Hubbard argues, is largely a falsehood: Very few phenomena can actually be captured in this way, and the "waste" of focusing our efforts in this direction prevents us from seeing what actually *does* need work, regardless of how difficult these "real" issues may be.[19]

Although some of current feminist critique may suffer from the liability that it is perhaps insufficiently formulated with respect to scientific rigor and insufficiently aware of the overall track of science, Hubbard's work cannot be said to suffer from the same deficiencies. Combining a take on the capitalist exploitation of the Third World that shows a sensitivity to the construction of science in that regard with her own formal training, Hubbard is easily able to show the deficiencies of contemporary research in clear, readable prose.

Ruth Hubbard is at her best when discussing the poverty of the sociobiology stance. Here she is able to use her accomplishments as a biologist to good advantage, because her knowledge of biology enables her to undercut the classic sociobiological position as articulated by E. O. Wilson. That feminist theory needs such direction should hardly have to be stated; it is one thing to find sociobiology politically offensive and another to be able to engage in the relevant level of precise and specified criticism. Hubbard is easily able to do this, and her promulgation of an opposing point of view should fill feminists with gratitude.

In an essay titled "Sexism and Sociobiology: For Our Own Good and the Good of the Species," Hubbard undertakes to demonstrate how Wilson's popular works in the 1970s distorted and, in some cases, simply falsified a great deal of biological evidence. Part of Hubbard's point here is that Wilson's use of language did nothing to assist his case. Noting that she considers Wilson's work to be similar in spirit to the work of Edward Clarke (also of Harvard), who in the late nineteenth century had argued that lack of care in designing formal education for girls could interfere with their menstrual cycles,[20] Hubbard tries to show how a parallel structure in Wilson's arguments could drive a reader to analogous conclusions about reproduction and the role of women.

Hubbard writes:

> What is all this [Wilson's Pulitzer Prize and similar honors] about and how does it relate to the way scientists have used their purportedly objective expertise to support the status quo against women's striving for equality? Before examining Wilson's sociobiological arguments in greater detail, I want to make clear that sexism lies at the center of sociobiology because of the way that sociobiologists deal with the concept of "reproductive success." Following Darwin, reproductive success is measured by the number of offspring an individual produces who themselves grow up and reproduce. . . . Many things are wrong with this line of argument [the section that refers to sperm and eggs as "investments"]. First of all, it is a metaphor, and a questionable one at that, to speak of eggs and sperm as investments. . . . Yet Wilson and other sociobiologists use this purported asymmetry in the reproductive investments of women and men to account for the division of labor.[21]

Wilson's books—and other material similar to and derivative of them—have become staples in many popular and even academic arenas. A critique such as Ruth Hubbard's is sorely needed if we are to be able to tackle some of the most salient points of these arguments on their own terms. It is not even so much that sociobiology requires undermining as it is that specific strategies used by sociobiologists to lure the reader need critiquing, and the critique should come from someone who has the relevant training. Here one can say that the sort of criticism that Hubbard employs, coming straight from science rather than aiming at the rhetoric of science, is part of the reason that her work is so successful.

Other feminist theorists have come to the fore since the publication of Harding's original work, and many of them, if not actually practicing scientists, have a great deal of technical training. The trick has been to combine these approaches with the more interdisciplinary, cultural-studies strategy of much of feminist theory.

The New Approaches

An interesting anthology of pieces in feminist ethics, feminist epistemology, and feminist critique in general is *Knowing the Difference: Feminist Perspectives in Epistemology,* edited by Kathleen Lennon and Margaret Whitford.[22] This English-language compendium is noteworthy because most of its authors are not American; thus, a slightly different twist is given to controversies with which we are already familiar.

Janna Thompson contributes a piece on moral theory that accomplishes the near impossible, and does so in a way that sheds light on some of the controversies insofar as they relate to science studies and the critique of science. As we have seen, a large part of the feminist critique has always been that the normative and detached view of the androcentric theorists purports to have a universality that it does not; this universality is undermined by any reasonable attempt to situate it in time and place. The object-relations theory that has been employed by Evelyn Fox Keller and others to help establish a critique of science that relies on gynocentric (or at least not androcentric) concepts is also related to a great deal of the work in feminist ethics, and is cited in the work of Carol Gilligan and others. In this particular article, Thompson does for ethics what some of the other theorists have attempted to do for straightforward epistemology and philosophy of science: She attempts to show how at least some of the classical male-constructed theory may be interpreted in ways that are friendly to feminist ethics, and in so doing she illuminates both areas.

One of Thompson's main concerns with respect to ethics is the notion that "caring" is somehow incompatible with the usage of moral rules or with the general set of presumptions about moral theory. Part of what she does is to take portions of a now classic piece from the early John Rawls and show that at least one reading of it is not incompatible with concerns driven by feminist critique.[23] In other words, the conundrum here is whether it makes any sense to think that there are readings of, say, standard ethics that allow for the notion that the feminist concern for particularity can be meshed with some kind of subsumption of standard rules and principles. Using the notion of a discourse-based decision procedure, Thompson notes:

> What, then, is the meta-ethical justification for the assumption that ethical knowledge should be determined by a discourse in which everyone is an equal participant? If ethical belief were simply a matter of individual conviction, then there would be no point in the discourse about ethical matters. . . .
> It is notable that the approach to ethical reasoning of the women Gilligan studied resembles the approach of the collectivist. These women were not inclined to think of themselves as judges or moral arbiters. They were more inclined to regard their view as a contribution to a discussion, as one opinion among many, and were anxious to maintain the relationships in which a reasonable solution could be found. I am not saying that these women actually held a collectivist view of ethical reasoning; but it does mean (if this position is indeed correct) that the women had a rational approach to solving ethical problems.[24]

Here Thompson attempts to mediate between standard ethical theory and the so-called feminist approaches, with the upshot that the feminist takes are not seen as necessarily playing an antithetical role to at least some portions of standard theory. Rather, Thompson claims, it is possible to find common ground, and in so doing to shed light on both approaches.

Diana Sartori makes a similar attempt in an article in the same anthology titled "Women's Authority in Science."[25] Again, the point is that feminist theory is closer, perhaps, to some lines of theorizing that might be deemed "classical" than has previously been thought. Ironically, it is probably the influence, at least to some extent, of cultural studies that allows us to see this: By viewing almost all endeavors as on all fours with each other, the relationship between competing areas is smoothed over.

Sartori's point is that much feminist critique has been written as if the main target of science was its impersonality, its putative universality, and so forth, when a closer examination reveals that much of what makes science so androcentric is the male-based communities from which it springs.[26] The point, then, is to look for female-defined communities in science and to see what influence this has on our overall estimate of what science appears to be. Sartori writes:

> The aim of the 'practice of relations between women,' privileging female mediation in its various forms, is to re-establish the greatness of the mother-figure and 'female genealogy' through the mother and daughter line. Perhaps the most important mediation, surely the most discussed in the Italian debate, is *affidamento* or entrustment, a relation between two women which functions as a means of mediation with the world, in which disparity and the authority of the other are recognized. . . . I have reached the conviction that there is a need for women to have scientific authority, and this must be the aim of the political work that needs to be done.[27]

In other words, relationships look different when they are based on female-female rather than male-male models, and science could benefit from the former.

Sartori's argument reminds us, once again, of the importance of the object-relations theory as set forth by Nancy Chodorow and Dorothy Dinnerstein; this importance lies not so much in what it tells us about male-female relations, perhaps, as in what it tells us about the notion of male competition and distancing as a hallmark of male-male relations. These are the relations, professional and otherwise, that dominate science. The *affidamento* relation described by Sartori reminds the reader of the "dynamic objectivity" referred to by Keller in *Reflections on Gender and Science* and exemplified in the work of Barbara McClintock. This dynamic objectivity, in a sense a kind of empathetic relationship between the observer and the observed, allows the observer to develop a sense of union with the observed; as McClintock is quoted as having said in *Reflections on Gender and Science*, she felt as if she could write the "autobiography" of a corn plant.[28]

Maura Fricker's piece, "Knowledge as Construct: Theorizing the Role of Gender in Knowledge,"[29] is perhaps the most important of those to be examined here because it goes a long way toward achieving closure in the

debate that I have implicitly alluded to in this chapter—the contest between those who, while still employing feminist theory as a way to critique science, would like to construct at least a minimal empiricism (if for
no other reason than that the world does not make a great deal of sense
without it), and those who, postmodernly, want to abandon most pretensions to empiricist reasoning and to any kind of a strong claim for science.
Interestingly enough, Fricker sees the proponents of these two positions
as being largely Haraway and Harding, and the extent to which she is
able to navigate between these two theorists and come up with something resembling a synthesis of their work is in itself remarkable.

Fricker is herself somewhat closer to feminist empiricism. It is a virtue
of her essay that she gives a long, complex argument to try to sustain the
notion that the kinds of political changes that feminist and radical critiques envision do not emerge as genuine possibilities without at least
minimal empiricism; otherwise, claims are seen as being on all fours with
each other, and claims to political victimization cannot really be documented. As Fricker clearly and concisely notes:

> The view that empirical claims underwrite political ones . . . is borne out if
> we think of the form that political arguments usually take. Arguments for a
> given political action, say, writing off Third World debt, or increasing fund-
> ing for women's refuges, invariably turn on empirical claims respectively
> about the economies of developing countries, or the numbers of women who
> are battered. (This, of course, does not entail that empirical propositions are
> sufficient to determine political ones—empirical agreement is clearly no
> guarantee of political agreement.) Yet without a realist account of these em-
> pirical claims, we cannot invoke them as reasons for or against different po-
> litical views or actions. Without an account of empirical belief which says
> that, if true, they pick out real states of affairs in the world, why should any-
> one's political opinions be influenced by them?[30]

This gets at the heart and core of the valuable point that Fricker makes,
and also lets the reader see why it is that many who have more technical
training find, for example, that Haraway's work has a metaphorical import but does not really answer the relevant epistemological questions. If
virtually everything that is said about, for instance, primates and their behavior can be reduced to political motivation, without privileging one
story about the orangutans of Borneo over another, then anything that
could potentially be learned by observing these orangutans goes out the
window and all potential observations of them are on an equal footing—
equally worthless. This is why a form of feminist empiricism looks attractive, and why arguments that try to forward such a stance keep recurring.

It may very well be the case that, attempting to summarize the views
examined in this section, particularly Fricker's, there is some inherent

tension in feminist theory that makes feminist empiricism a very difficult position. It is not merely that postmodernism is attractive—postmodernism appears necessary, at least to some, both because of the difficulty of attaching epistemic privilege to any position and because of the difficulty that feminists have with a general notion of privilege or foundation, regardless of whether the notion is used epistemically or not.

In other words, the feminist emphasis on community and connection (an emphasis that we have seen here with Thompson, Sartori, and Fricker) means that notions of consensus occur throughout levels of theory with respect to discourse, emotions, knowledge, and many other levels and components of theorizing. Feminist empiricism seems to be a contradiction in terms, at least to the theorists who refuse to acknowledge that any "stories" are better or more accurate than others, or that there could be anything "feminist" about admitting this. On the one hand, one is tempted to say, with respect to the debate about primatology, that there are versions of what the orangutans are doing that are somehow more careful, less politicized, and so forth. On the other hand, it is difficult to know how one could reach this judgment. This particular example, then, crystallizes much of the debate and leaves us with little room to maneuver.

In the final essay in the Lennon and Whitford collection, Anna Yeatman connects the notions of epistemic privilege and political power in an explicit way. "Subalterns" do not have this privilege precisely because they do not have this power. To fail to see this, Yeatman argues, is to err.

> These oppositional intellectuals agree with what is arguably the core feature of postmodernism: the critique of epistemological foundationalism. Put simply, this critique is based in a rejection of mirror theories of knowledge, where knowledge, if it is to be true or accurate knowledge, mirrors an order of being outside itself. In such accounts of knowledge, all that matters is that the knower is trained correctly to use the techniques and methods which permit him direct, 'objective' access to reality. . . . A rationalist metaphysics of this kind turns out to be a rationalist version of the divine right of kings. . . . We can see here how the authority of a foundationalist science ensures that the voice of the scientists not only prevails over but silences all those who are not scientists.[31]

Those who have political authority, then, are in a position to decide who the knowledge producers are, and they are also in a position to decide who becomes objectified and who lacks the status that is required to enter into knowledge seeking.

This position might be thought of as the most popular among those that would currently merit the label "feminist." Whatever its other advantages or disadvantages, Yeatman's position does have one particular virtue: It demonstrates an awareness of the fact that, if a culture or a people lack the status of being seen as knowledge producers, they then become the objects of knowledge producers. It is this—the awareness of the importance of objectification—that is at the heart of much of the work being done in what can be labeled contemporary feminist postmodernism.

Feminist empiricism is attractive because it allows us to make distinctions. But feminist postmodernism is attractive to many precisely because it undercuts that ability, since that ability is seen as predicated on oppression. There does not appear to be, at the moment, any way out of this contretemps.

Longino and the Social

The importance of Helen Longino's *Science as Social Knowledge* can scarcely be overestimated, because it ties together so many of the threads that I have addressed in this chapter. If there does not seem to be any way out of the postmodernist dilemma, then it might be helpful to articulate, with some precision, at least some of the ways in which science appears to be social, so that a conceptual handle can be gotten on this material.

Longino is philosophically sophisticated, precise about the nature of the social insofar as it relates to science, and conceptually au courant with respect to the material to be found at this intersection. Thus, for example, one could query the assertions that are made about the social nature of science at a number of different foci—one could ask whether the social shows up mainly in practice, to some extent in theory, at the level of what used to be called the observation/theory distinction, and so forth. *Science as Social Knowledge* attempts to cover all this ground and more; it is not merely that the social appears in the practice of science but that the practice cannot be divorced from theory, since the theoretical is shot through with the ramifications of practice from the outset.

In her chapter titled "Values and Objectivity," Longino notes:

> The social character of scientific knowledge is made especially apparent by the organization of late twentieth-century science, in which the production of knowledge is crucially determined by the gatekeeping of peer review. Peer review determines what research gets funded and what research gets published in the journals, that is, what gets to count as knowledge. Recent concern over the breakdown of peer review and over fraudulent research simply supports the point. The most startling study of peer review suggested that scientific papers in at least one discipline were accepted on the basis of the institutional affiliation of the authors rather than the intrinsic worth of the paper.[32]

The social not only determines what counts as knowledge but also determines the conditions under which knowledge production occurs, which in turn has still a greater ramifying effect on what does count, since place of origin is of paramount importance here. Not specifically mentioned in this passage, but still relevant, is the notion of style—as Haraway had indicated, "patrilines" influence the theorizing of those who are trained in a certain way and by certain parties. The influence of the "pater" not only affects the positions that his academic offspring obtain, but the prestige of those positions influences the reception of their work, and so forth. The social comes into play at every point in the process.

Longino also has a particularly apt analysis for why it is that earlier versions of the scientific story may have been able to escape recognition of the social—or may have been able to engage in self-deception, as it were. As she notes, the positivist distinction between the context of discovery and the context of justification allowed for a certain leeway in coping with the social—if social elements were thrust under certain rubrics, they could more easily be dispensed with. As Longino notes, "They [the social or nonempirical elements] are treated as randomizing factors that promote novelty rather than beliefs or attitudes that are systematically related to the culture, social structure or socioeconomic interests of the context within which an individual scientist works."[33]

Longino's distinction between constitutive and contextual values in science allows her to show how some of what might be deemed contextual undermines the constitutive or reveals itself in ways that cause core aspects of the practice of science to be reexamined. Part of the story here is that the practice of science is also affected by such variables as publicity and the media—factors that once may have been in relatively short supply as potential influences on scientific research but that are now rather too abundant. Citing the case of the development of interferon and of the first waves of publicity surrounding its emergence, Longino notes:

> In January 1980 interferon was being tested for effectiveness against cancer and as an antiviral agent generally. In that month the microbiological firm Biogen announced in a press conference featuring its director and one of its active researchers that it was the first laboratory to achieve the bacterial production of human interferon. . . .
>   [There] is a rule about communication of results—that research should first be presented in professional journals or at papers read at conferences. . . . When results are communicated by means of a press conference, there is no opportunity to study them for their soundness before they are absorbed into and begin affecting the public mind.[34]

How do we characterize the specific violation of scientific "rules" that is exemplified by the interferon debacle? Clearly, one wants to say that it is merely a contextual rule of science that the mode of presentation of research be in a scholarly forum. But the difficulty that immediately presents itself is the obviousness that the violation of this tradition carries with it other freight—in an effort to get to media outlets, so to speak, the quality and character of scientific research can be undermined, and there is a risk of compromise (above and beyond the usual compromises) at each step of the way. Another obvious example is that of the alleged cold fusion research.

Clearly, the media have been around for a long time, but just as patently they did not always have the power that they have enjoyed since the 1970s. It is this rather mundane fact (that a researcher can present research results before television cameras) that alters the fact of scientific research and that also alters what counts as science.

As Longino herself says:

> Once contextual considerations of any sort are admitted as relevant to scientific argumentation, however, values and interests can no longer be excluded a priori as irrelevant or as signs of bad science. The argument, therefore, does establish the legitimacy of examining research and research projects that are perfectly "good science" for the influence of value-laden considerations.[35]

The contextual affects science at every step of the way, and attempting to ferret out the ways in which these effects are achieved helps illuminate the structure of science itself, once again dismantling its pretensions of purity and uncontaminatedness.

Finally, there is that which is scientific that affects society and social functioning. Here we turn around, so to speak, the levels of impact, attempting to analyze what it is in contemporary work in the sciences that makes them so important to developed societies and that has helped them displace religion and achieve an unparalleled secular prominence.[36] One of the chief factors is undoubtedly the importance of anything that is perceived, rightly or wrongly, as sociobiological or vaguely Darwinian—a variety of material that appears to have this provenance can be used to buttress certain social programs and to dismantle others, a point not lost on those doing the research. Since the research is done by "scientists," and since laudatory commentary on the sciences and scientists is published regularly in the popular press, it is almost impossible to try to redress wrongs that might have their origins in this type of research. Longino succinctly encapsulates the salience of such programs and their offspring when she writes:

> [These] programs [compensatory government schemes] assume that innate differences in ability are uniformly spread throughout social classes and that compensatory education will eventually mean a distribution of significant social groups—the sexes and racial groups—in proportion to their distribution throughout the population.

Research supporting the biological basis of observed group differences has a contrary implication, one not lost on the champions of current research. . . . Their [Anke Ehrhardt and collaborators'] behavioral neuroendocrinology attributes, at a minimum, higher levels of "energy expenditure" to the male hormonal profile than to the female one. . . . The suggestion that racial differences in I.Q. scores are biologically based was used explicitly to support claims that efforts at compensatory education for Black children were futile.[37]

The point is that the legitimacy of science can be used to bolster almost any cause, and, of course, given the social construction of American life, it should come as no surprise that one of the causes it can legitimize is an inequitable social structure. No matter how wrong it may seem to create such areas of justification, some workers in the sciences are easily able to perform these tasks, not only to protect their prestige as scientific investigators (remember Haraway's "patrilines") but also because the social situation virtually demands it. The combination of these two effects—the strength of science and the rocklike structure of the inequalities that its research results might be used to support—creates a formidable obstacle indeed, one that is not easily overturned or surmounted.

The importance of Longino's work lies in her careful detail, her overall grasp of philosophy of science (which makes her feminist critique of it all that much more powerful), and her sensitivity to social nuance. One might almost say that the relationship between science and the social itself constitutes a hermeneutic circle of understanding; the influences run both ways, and it is virtually impossible to separate out the various channels of influence or to determine with precision what influenced whom or who influenced what. But this, surely, is part of Longino's overall point—that uncontaminated science has never existed, and never will exist.

The Postmodernist Dilemma

Throughout this chapter, the feminist theory that we have encountered can be broken down broadly into two camps. Haraway and the body of critics whose work comprises the Lennon and Whitford anthology are of the postmodernist stripe—eschewing attempts to develop "an epistemology," they tend to insist that all claims are politicized, that there are no independent standards for judging claims, and so forth. Their work is provocative; in a sense they are like the *agents provocateurs* of the 1960s who engaged in radical activity largely with the goal of breaking up whatever the relevant power structure was. As with those agents, it is never really clear whose side the theorists are on. Harding is to some extent in the same camp with her latest work, although this is debatable.

Nelson, Longino, and Hubbard, however, do have some interest in the enterprise of science, and one can see in each of their critiques that it is the uses to which science has been put that are, if anything, under greater attack. Although it might be the case that none of these writers would be comfortable wearing the "feminist empiricist" hat (with the possible exception of Nelson, whose work is the most epistemological and who is avowedly empiricist), it does not seem likely that any of them would assent to the proposition that one set of observations is as good as another, or that all sets of observations are so hopelessly enmeshed in and contaminated by political commitments as to be inseparable and indistinguishable.

The postmodernist crisis has, then, infected the intersection of philosophies of science and feminist theories, and will undoubtedly continue to do so. If the use of the term "crisis" seems to elide some important set of claims, it is probably because we want a term that is more precise and that will enable us to do more theoretical work. But there does not seem to be any other suitable term immediately at hand—those who would espouse something close to feminist empiricism have to face the contentions of others like Haraway who are unable to distinguish between sets of "stories" because each story is putatively the result of its own causes or agendas. On the other hand, those who would identify with postmodernism must acknowledge (as some have) that any sort of radical critique of an intellectual enterprise is seriously undermined by the failure to make distinctions and by the placing on all fours of disputed sets of claims.

Can feminist theory, in its barest form and shorn of most of its contentiousness, be of any help here? A staple of feminist theory—and one that has been alluded to in this text from the outset—is the notion, articulated by Chodorow, Dinnerstein, and others, that male and female development differ in crucial ways and that these differences eventually give way to gender-related styles. If there is anything to this particular take on things (and most feminists have used this material, in one form or another and in one place or another), then communities and community-oriented thinking would be crucial in developing a feminist epistemology. If this interpretation can be accepted, then it does indeed do something to bolster the case for feminist epistemology on the whole, because it would enable some claims to be distinguished from others.

If there were a way to try to develop a feminist epistemology, the notion of community might be a key. But the important point to grasp here is that this notion, presumably, carries its own empiricism. In other words, when we speak of a "community" of knowers or of a knowledge-based community, we are able to refer to such an entity because we know that, within a given group of persons, a combination of the empirical and the social usually presides. It could, indeed, be the case that within a given community, standards that are nonempirical will prevail, for some idiosyncratic set of reasons (one thinks, sadly, of the Jim Jones commune in Guyana in the late 1970s). But such an example is, of course, an exception. In the villages of India and Bangladesh, group decisions about planting and crops are made on the basis of empirical evidence about the monsoon, about the locations of wells, and so forth. And insofar as the behavior of women is concerned, women in such societies cannot, in general, afford the sometimes exercised male prerogative of ignoring the empirical in favor of an a priori religious teaching or a speculative conceptualization—women have generally been excluded from the segments of such societies that engage in this type of thought. (In Varanasi, India, for example, there are no female scholars to be found among the groups of men who pass their days in the study of the Upanishads and other sacred documents.)

Thus much of what we know about the world encourages us to believe that women are natural empiricists and that a feminist epistemology would not be based on speculation or pure ratiocination; rather, it would be a theory of knowledge based on everyday life.

This is the key toward the partial resolution of the postmodernist dilemma, if such key exists. The preeminence of empiricism in a feminist worldview helps to resolve the tendency to assert that claims are indistinguishable or that the highly politicized nature of claim making prevents one from being able to choose. A commitment to the world of experience and the world of the senses forces one to try to look for that which would confirm, and here the confirmation is a posteriori—a given set of claims.

None of this, of course, completely destroys the force of the arguments that undergird postmodernism, and it does not give us much advice on what way to go. But the fact that postmodern malaise or ennui can at least be countered should give some hope to those who would like to rectify a number of wrongs. These wrongs cannot be rectified—claims cannot be addressed and/or adjudicated—until acceptable levels of evidence are encountered and labeled as acceptable. The taking of such evidence and the marking of it is at variance with the claim that any assertion is, epistemically, as good as any other assertion.

It may be worthwhile at this point to recapitulate the three traditional stances that have been taken with respect to feminist epistemology, and then to see if it is at least possible to adjudicate any of the claims that seem to leap out at us from the contemporary material in science studies and philosophy and sociology of science. Taking a leaf from the set of positions originally adumbrated in Harding's *The Science Question in Feminism*, the three stances traditionally associated with feminist epistemology are feminist empiricism, feminist standpoint epistemology, and feminist postmodernism.[38]

I have already given a cursory overview of feminist empiricism, but it could be argued that some resolution of the debate might come about through advertence to feminist standpoint epistemology. This stance, developed by Nancy Hartsock, Jane Flax, and other theorists and derived at least partially from the Marxist notion of material grounding and division of labor, postulates that women are immersed in the world of the sensuous, the concrete, and the material and that this adds to or filters what would count as women's modes of knowing. Notice that this account is not necessarily at variance with what we have termed object-relations theory; rather, the two tend to reinforce each other. The connectedness and the attachment that Chodorowian object-relations theory teaches us is characteristic of the female modes of functioning that manifests itself in women's ties to the division of labor into which they have historically been forced, and it also manifests itself in the tendency not to detach or to engage in the kind of speculative ratiocination that is the hallmark of male thinking.

Feminist standpoint epistemology is important here—one might be tempted to say crucially important—because it may help decide, in Solomon-like fashion, between the tensions inherent in the other two positions. In other words, standpoint epistemology relieves us from having to conclude that we are left with one horn or the other of an unsatisfactory epistemic dilemma. The lack of structure and of criteria provided by postmodernism, and the comparative lack of political sophistication inherent in empiricism, need not be the only alternatives for the feminist philosopher of science and the feminist epistemologist.

Standpoint epistemology not only helps to clarify women's standpoint, but the very nature of the view reminds us that there are other standpoints as well. It is because of this, for example, that the theorist Patricia Hill Collins has felt free to develop in her work *Black Feminist Thought* a chapter titled "Toward an Afrocentric Feminist Epistemology."[39] One standpoint reminds us of another, and thus no standpoint is, in principle, inarticulable. Feminist standpoint epistemology has the further merit that it provides us with a lens through which certain data may be captured; thus, to work with Haraway's material, if the daughters of the patriline have implicitly politicized their take on the behavior of the primates by reading into it what the pater or the patriline demands, one antidote to the situation is for other daughters (hopefully of matrilines, not patrilines) to read into their necessarily politicized takes on the behavior of gorillas, orangutans, or chimpanzees something that is required by a feminist view of the circumstances—something that might, in fact, result from the feminist standpoint epistemology.

There are, of course, no clear answers to the debates surrounding philosophies of science and feminist theories. But there are questions, and how we frame those questions is an inevitable result of other decisions made at earlier points. Feminist standpoint epistemology has the still further advantage that it may to some extent be naturalized, a topic that I will take up at a later point. In any case, awareness of it as an epistemic construct ensures that the notion that a daughter is beholden to a patriline will not be the only notion of obligation informing our take on the world.

Part Three

Extensions of Philosophy of Science

7

The Radical Critique of Science

The radical critique of science is an enterprise that might be said to have its origins in Marx.[1] The notion that there is a material reality underlying our endeavors, our acquaintance with which should inform our intellectual projects, is also a Marxist notion and was a point that Marx and Engels were at some pains to articulate throughout their work. But the radical critique has been able to gather steam, and do so in a dramatic way, partly because of the trajectory of science itself, particularly since World War II; partly because of the relationship between this critique and feminist theory; and partly, no doubt, because of an emerging awareness of conditions in the Third World and their political origins.

The radical line of attack on science is not only an epistemological critique—as indeed it is, since part of Marxist theory here would ask us not to divorce our thinking from our practice—but also a critique of uses. Radical thinking about science reminds us of the failure of science to investigate reality in a manner consonant with our material grounding in the world as human beings, and also that the fruits of science have been employed in ways that all too frequently continue to marginalize those who are already outcast and fail to help or give succor to those who require such succor.

Steven and Hilary Rose were among the first social scientists having any acquaintance with the way in which science is normally practiced to attempt to explicate what might be "wrong" with science. In this series of explicit claims, the Roses identify why a Marxist critique of science is completely consistent with the rest of Marxist theory:

What distinguishes human history from the history of the rest of nature, including that of other animals, is that man has learnt to produce the means of his own existence. And hence men produce their own material life. This production occurs by acting upon nature, and it is through this practice that the

social and natural worlds are changed. The very fact that human beings
learn to be more productive, to objectify themselves, to create more material
objects, makes possible, and actual, new ways of living.

The first practice springs from man's conflict with nature, including other
men as part of nature in order to survive. (Not for nothing did Marx want to
dedicate *Capital* to Darwin.) Knowledge comes from this conflict with, and
action upon, nature. Natural science is the form of knowledge of the actual
world which developed in the specific historical context of capitalism.[2]

In other words, in nonindustrial modes of production (particularly, one
assumes, in the ancient mode of production), humans lived in greater
contact and harmony with the earth and its products, and this kept human beings somewhat more intellectually honest about their endeavors.
The rise of science is consonant with the rise of industrialization, and
both of these realms of activity have in common the distancing from a
more organic wholeness with human life that Marx finds characteristic of
"alienation."

How can one salvage science? This concern, found in both the feminist
and radical critiques, preserves the notion that scientific activity mani-
festly has something to offer us while divorcing us from the too easy categorization of science as all-valuable enterprise. Part of what might be at
stake here is the merging of the type of critique that originally formed
part of the philosophy of the social sciences (here, for example, we might
think of the Frankfurt school) with other forms of criticism originally directed against the natural sciences. Marxist theory would ask us to recognize areas of commonality here, and if the organicity alluded to above is
married to a concept of the sciences that, oddly enough, mirrors to some
extent the positivist concern for the continuity thesis, then perhaps some
work ameliorative of the sciences can be performed.

Giovanni Ciccotti, Marcello Cini, and Michelangelo de Maria, also writing in the Roses' anthology, note the relevance of this line of argument:

> The problem therefore is real and cannot be ignored; it is to investigate the
> links that exist between science as a particular form of social human activity,
> and the social relations of production that in general regulate the activity of
> human work in *this* society. This is the significance of moving from a general
> recognition, now largely accepted, of the 'non-neutrality' of science, to a
> more precise identification of the various levels and mechanisms of recipro-
> cal interaction of these activities, and of the possible interventions available
> to transform the social role of science through the explicit recognition of al-
> ternative social goals.[3]

Because of the relationship between industrialized post-Enlightenment
science and the modes of production available to European and other developed societies, unraveling these links is no small task, but an aware-

ness of the conceptual networks helps us to understand why it is that, again according to the postmodernist critique, all claims are politicized and no claim can have any special epistemic privilege.

When Ciccotti, Cini, and de Maria also remind us that the original subject-object distinction in Marxist theory, if applied properly, reduces rather than entrenches that distinction insofar as the sciences are concerned, they are simply telling us that the world of practice and the world of theory merge in ways that are unpredictable, crucially important, and in need of explication. Much of what has now passed under the banner of radical critique is concerned not only with science as institutionalized endeavor but with the technological consequences of even "pure" research and how these have come to have social effects. An investigation of what is now being done in science and technology studies helps us come to a clearer comprehension of the relationship between these fields.

If technology is to some extent the unintended offspring of science, it is only because researchers have failed to even attempt to foresee any of the consequences of their research. This blind spot with regard to the possible social utilization of research is long-standing—it affected work done in the eighteenth century just as much as it has affected work done more recently.

Radical Critique and Reproductive Technology

An exemplary debate for the setting out of radical critique is that surrounding reproductive technology. Although a great deal has been done recently to advance criticisms of the reproductive technology market and reproductively related science in general, it is interesting to note that this dialogue got off the ground in the mid-1970s, and has been connected to issues surrounding the position of women in medicine and in medically related research in general. Thus many of those who were foresighted enough to see, for example, the advent of phenomena as disparate as in vitro fertilization and surrogate mothering also noticed that the dominance of gynecology and gynecological research done by men was not unrelated to the kinds of ethical dilemmas posed by the research.

Writing on the general topic of women in medicine and the history of women physicians, Regina Markell Morantz-Sanchez notes:

What have been the implications of these changes [in numbers] for women? Has capitalism really achieved what feminism could not? Certainly an important contribution of the recent influx of women into the labor corps has been the maturation of what Harry Braverman called "the universal market"—the transformation of society into a giant exchange for labor and goods.

Ironically, women's new and unprecedented freedom to make career decisions has also made the social and structural impediments to their success
more visible. For this reason those now entering the professions will have to
struggle with powerfully subtle barriers to their achievement of equality
with men. . . . [W]omen must contend with the persistent social assumption
that their, and not men's, primary obligation is to the family.[4]

In these paragraphs, Morantz-Sanchez is reminding us that women
come to the fore in professions that are science related, particularly medicine, at a time when the conceptual work necessary to provide a foundation for women's participation has not yet been made. Because of this, it
is doubly ironic that some of the greatest "advances" made in medicine
since the 1970s have been in the area of reproductive technology—precisely the area in which women's interests might be thought to be paramount, but in which women continue to have little say.

Noting that this would become a problem, Hilary Rose and Jalna Hanmer wrote in the mid-1970s that feminists such as Shulamith Firestone,
who seemed to think that the new technology would benefit women,
were probably being naive. Rose and Hanmer claimed: "Her [Firestone's]
conception of science is almost nineteenth century in its confidence in the
inherently progressive nature of science and technology. The naïveté of
this view is reinforced if we examine the social structure of science, for it
is historically a stronghold of men and it is difficult to understand why
science and technology should appear to be the allies of women."[5]

With prescience, Rose and Hanmer describe work that, only a few
years after the publication of their essay, would lead to the first recorded
and publicized in vitro fertilization.[6] Deploying Marxist arguments
against the general commodification of cultural trends, they are rightly
quite concerned that such techniques might lead to a commodification of
mothering. The conundrum is made even more severe by the knowledge
that many of the techniques that might be used to alter female fertility, or
to change the conditions under which and through which women give
birth, are not unrelated to other schemes that might be deemed to be irretrievably capitalist. Thus, as Rose and Hanmer note:

[T]here are three possible ways of looking at the role and image of women in
a situation in which women are no longer forced to produce children but are
to be actively discouraged. The first is a continuation and intensification of
the traditional view of women as the most flexible part of the industrial re-
serve army (last hired, first fired). The second relates to women not in the
paid labor force, or in the unpaid as producers of children; these need to
learn to accept themselves as 'super consumers' in the 'none is fun' image.
The third is to encourage women to take on wider social roles and hence
have fewer children.[7]

In this passage, the second stated viewpoint notes that childless women may be encouraged to see themselves as capable of having a greater degree of economic freedom and as being relatively unharried and free-choosing consumers. Needless to say, in a society that already encourages enormous expenditures of disposable income on such items as makeup, clothes, shoes, and hair care products, the catalytic power of further consumption and its tie to childlessness does indeed call for reflection.

Although a contemporary view might connect this scientific research in reproduction to consumerism and also to women's "sexual freedom" (the freedom to indulge in relatively cost-free heterosexual intercourse), it is interesting to note that, as Morantz-Sanchez reports, the original movement toward developing reproductive technology was not only tied to the eugenics movement but tied to it in such a way that it seemed to define many aspects of female sexuality as perverse. Morantz-Sanchez asserts that "[f]ears of 'race suicide' and an inordinate respect for motherhood led many of these same women physicians to reject artificial birth control and to sanction only sexual continence for the sake of a woman's health."[8] The long and the short of this analysis seems to be that the growth of reproductive technology has been largely at the expense of women's interests and certainly tied to a type of capitalist expansion that seems to benefit everyone except those who most need it.

The dumping on Third World countries of shoddy and rejected methods of birth control (including the loop) is still another example of the issues in which the feminist critique has a broad intersection with the radical critique. Other types of medications may also be given to developing nations, and there is real reason to believe that aid projects in the Third World are frequently tied to the implementation of population control programs, many of which rely on the devices just mentioned, whereas those countries whose populations are in fact stripping the planet of its resources because of their conspicuous consumption are relatively uncriticized by arguments extolling the necessity for fewer births. The radical critique of science is on relatively sure ground here, because the combination of the sexism inherent in the reproductive technology market and the general lack of sensitivity to the living conditions and cultural constructions of developing countries means that only a radical view of technological advances will be able to speak to these issues.

Still another take on this very broad topic reminds us that obstetrics and gynecology in general, without regard for reproduction in particular, achieved growth during the early years of the twentieth century by problematizing the natural processes. Thus the impact of technology on the portions of medicine concerned with reproduction and women's health as a whole is not only relevant to a standard feminist position on science but also to the radical critique, especially because of its intersection with general childbirth-related issues in Third World cultures. Writing in *Science, Technology and Human Value,* Anja Hiddinga and Stuart Blume note:

> How were obstetricians to "capture childbirth, all of it, treat it, and hold it firmly as part of their project"? The professional concerns of obstetricians in the first decades of the twentieth century were different from those of their nineteenth-century predecessors. The common project would now entail not demarcating the normal from the abnormal but problematizing the normal. The recognition of "potential abnormality," the characterization of "borderline cases," and procedures for the avoidance of "potential risk" would become priorities in the further development of obstetric practice and would lead to quite different demands being made upon technology. How these priorities were implemented, the kinds of procedures developed, differed from country to country.[9]

Here we can see clearly that rising professionalization, growing technological advances (such as the X ray), and the need to justify and unify the foregoing played a large role in the development of what became the field of gynecology. Although the authors claim at least some disagreement with Gina Corea, a radical critic of such interventions and the author of *The Mother Machine,*[10] it is clear that much of what they have to say either advertently or inadvertently sustains many of her theses.

To be fair, it is clear that humanitarian motives were at the heart of at least some of the research that transpired from a combination of the development of technology and the increasing disreputability of midwifery. But, as is so frequently the case when we analyze the social factors in the growth of the sciences, we find the self-perpetuating cycle of research and technology justifying further research and technology, of increasingly dubious value. That this was especially the case with respect to obstetrics and gynecology is, of course, not unrelated to the general lack of status accruing to all things female and the comparative stature of the medical profession as a whole, dominated as it was by men (a point made by Morantz-Sanchez).

Thus radical criticism here assumes from the outset that it is not enough simply to categorize efforts as noble minded; the complicity of other, less high-minded components of human endeavor in medical and scientific fields must be alluded to and examined. The radical critics of the obstetrics-gynecology practice have just this kind of politicization in mind. Hiddinga and Blume themselves quote Corea, who wrote: "Interventions in normal childbirth began accelerating in the 1980's and are now so extreme that any woman who, avoiding a cesarean, manages to actually go into labor and push a baby out of her body, can count it as a victory."[11]

There are very few facets of the intersection between medicine and the growth of technology not examined by the Marxist and Marxist-influenced critics of science. Even without the flavoring provided by radical critics of science, certain portions of the current critique as practiced by those conducting social studies of science achieve a kind of radicalism simply by virtue of the types of categorization employed.

In another journal article informed by this stance, social scientist Susan Hornig concludes that women, in responding to mock news stories about scientific advances, were significantly more likely than men to claim that the advances had deleterious effects or were possibly not beneficial to society. Noting her belief that this outcome has to do with "cultural differences"[12] between women and men, Hornig reports that:

> For example, a female respondent stated that the use of artificial intelligence to assist in making medical diagnoses could be plagued by breakdowns, viruses, and other types of malfunctions, resulting in major errors. Another female respondent stated that if the ELISA test for agricultural diseases described in one mock article was successful, it would become political, economic greed would enter the picture, and there would not be enough checking and verification of the results. A third female respondent stated that the development of a solar laser could result in economic downturns. . . . One of the male respondents also expressed concerns about the impacts of this development, but his concerns centered on costs and the feasibility of economic applications.[13]

In general, one might describe the female responses as more imaginative, but one might also claim that a great deal of what informs the female responses not only derives, as Hornig asserts, from "cultural differences" but stems perhaps—as indicated in the immediately preceding sections—from the very real disadvantageous experiences that women have had with technology, especially reproductively related technology, throughout the course of this century. Thus a combination of what might be taken, in Chodorowian or Gilliganesque terms, to be a greater female responsiveness to perceived problems and an experience based on the results of those problems as they actually, not hypothetically, occurred yields an intense skepticism about science, the results of science, and the efforts of scientists. It is particularly noteworthy that one respondent reported that "economic greed" might enter into the picture, since the radical critique of science is, of course, a critique to the effect that economic greed has been in the picture all along.

Graham and the History of Technology

In an important work published in the early 1980s titled *Between Science and Values*,[14] Loren Graham advances the arguments drawn up by the radical and socialist-oriented critics by presenting a history of the development of science and its conflict with values. More intriguingly, perhaps, he includes two chapters near the end of the work that provide neat and cogent summaries of much of the critique as it existed at that point in time; one of the chapters has the prescient title "Public Concerns About Science and Technology: The Question of Limits of Inquiry."[15]

Graham's work provides a chart of the types of worries that are most often expressed as being at the intersection of science and values, many of which have featured prominently in the work of the Marxist theoreticians. But again, the intersections themselves are almost more noteworthy than the bare-bones list of the actual concerns. Just as I have indicated here that part of what drives radical criticism is its awareness of the capitalist complicity between science and impure social concerns—an awareness, of course, that was virtually never manifested or even hinted at in the work of the members of the Vienna Circle and other theorists examined earlier—the capitalist exploitation of scientific and technological advances occurs most rapidly when there is a tie-in to some other social need. It is for this reason that reproductive technology, for example, is more or less at the mercy of market forces. Graham's work is strong in that it clearly delineates other portions of the inevitable intersections— the gray areas of development in the general advances in medicine (other than reproductive), the abuse of human subjects, and, again, the market-driven alterations in research.

Graham specifically labels some of these areas "slippery slope technology," and in a section devoted to these changes, he writes:

> Obviously, every act of physical damage contains an ethical dimension, and no clean separation of the two can ever be made. Nevertheless, there exists a significant difference between, on the one hand, a concern whether the physically damaging effects of a certain technology can be excused within existing ethical systems, and, on the other, whether a certain technology may be destroying the ethical system itself. The present category deals with the latter concern. Issues in this category can be described as "expansionist," since they are instances in which technology is affecting human values. . . .
>
> New possibilities for prenatal diagnosis by amniocentesis, prolongation of life through the use of dialysis and respiratory machines, psychosurgery, *in vitro* fertilization, and DNA therapy, or genetic engineering, are only a few examples of issues that have been widely discussed in the press. . . .
>
> One of the major concerns expressed by observers of technological developments in the biomedical field has been that by blurring or erasing ethical boundaries that were earlier considered absolute, we will go into a "slippery slope" of relativistic ethics on which we may lose our balance and tumble to the bottom.[16]

In other words, we are again faced with a circle: Alterations in science and technology affect the way in which we value human life, and these changes in values create or help open the way to new work in science that then creates further changes, and so forth. Although one would like to naively rejoin that these kinds of differences and alterations have been in evidence since the beginning of human history, it has only been for the past few centuries that the changes have been sweeping enough that they can truly be said to have made lasting and monumental differences in our lives and lifestyles.

Graham is also sensitive to the fact that it is not merely that contemporary work in science is often market driven, but that only those who are tied into the market, so to speak, can really afford to do scientific research. The research itself becomes an exorbitant investment, and thus having a certain kind of background can greatly prohibit one from ever being in a position to undertake the research in the first place, a point that has been made again and again. Graham writes: "Now even a member of the Rockefeller family who was a radio astronomer would probably not be eager to undertake the building of a very large array radiotelescope."[17] As Graham also indicates, this inability of a contemporary Rockefeller or someone from the same social class to fund scientific research in certain areas virtually guarantees that for many realms of research, direct and indirect government involvement will increase, not decrease, over a period of time. This, of course, may affect the notion of freedom of inquiry, and it certainly affects the notion of freedom to conduct research that is not seen as being of any immediate practical value.[18]

Graham also provides a constructive criticism of an area that, if anything, has become more prominent in the fifteen years since his work was originally published. Drawing on an area of controversy that he refers to as "ways of knowing" and pairing that with another bone of contention that he calls "subversive knowledge," Graham goes the feminist critique one better by alluding to the general problem of the distancing and objectification of scientific knowledge as opposed to, for example, the mystical experience or the experience of human intimacy; he indicates that this particular line of criticism has been around for quite a while and was broached earlier in this century by Arthur Eddington.[19] In addition, Graham reminds us that there is still a great deal that might emerge from science that humans will find offensive in other, less easily articulable ways—ways that involve, as in the Darwinian controversy, the status of human beings, speciesism, and our desire to find ourselves "special."

Graham is quite right to bring up this topic as a separate line of argument, for there is much in the current popular press, even if it has not been subjected to academic scrutiny, that reminds us of this line of argument. Graham notes:

> Some of the resistance to studies in the fields of ethology and primatology discussed [in previous chapters] can be related to concerns about the

diminution of the uniqueness of man, the narrowing of the distance between humans and the rest of the animal world. The possibility of increasingly successful explanations of human behavior in terms of animal behavior often evokes resistance among intellectuals who would usually consider themselves far from being anti-science. One does not have to accept the vulgarized interpretations of ethology of the type of Robert Ardrey or Desmond Morris to agree that at least part of the resistance here is the ancient restrictionist one of concern for man's place in nature.[20]

Graham's analysis is particularly salient, since it touches on areas that I have already examined in the course of perusing Haraway's work. Graham, of course, is by no means in obvious agreement with Haraway, and is concerned to make a different point—but what is remarkable is that Loren Graham's analysis converges with Haraway's general stance in agreeing that it is absolutely obvious that "stories" about primates, whatever their epistemic status, are of the utmost importance to human beings. It may very well be the case that one reason an analysis of the "patriline," as Haraway would have it, involved in baboon or gorilla research is so important is that anything having to do with primates still touches on us deeply and profoundly and to some extent shakes our conception of the world.

Woman the Gatherer

In a widely cited piece originally published in Rayna Reiter's *Toward an Anthropology of Women,* Sally Slocum identifies the pitfalls of a thesis that was, in fact, originally associated with Sherwood Washburn, the same anthropologist who is cited by Haraway as the father of the patriline of female primatologists. Washburn's take on early hominids had followed the now-classic lines of man-the-hunter and woman-the-gatherer, and had emphasized male development (cognitive, athletic, and so on) at almost the complete expense of female development. With hindsight, Slocum's response to this may not seem as radical as it was at the time, but Slocum preceded Haraway and several other feminists in arguing that the androcentrism of the "man-the-hunter" view concealed important facts about the structure of science and scientific power.

As Slocum says at the outset of her paper,

> We are human beings studying other human beings, and we cannot leave ourselves out of the equation. We choose to ask certain questions, *and not others.* Our choice grows out of the cultural context in which anthropology and anthropologists exist. Anthropology, as an academic discipline, has been developed primarily by white Western males, during a specific period in our history. Our questions are shaped by the particulars of our historical situation, and by unconscious cultural assumptions.[21]

Again, of course, all of the foregoing is tied to structures of power about which we already know, but it affects the development of important theses and hypotheses in ways that are not always readily visible.

Anthropologists of the period during which Washburn's work was at its peak of influence generally seemed to feel that that very important human capacity, tool making, stemmed from male hunting activities, and that somehow this capacity, and others like it, led to the growth of other features of hominid culture that might be thought to be uniquely human.[22] But as Slocum shows us, an intellectual breakthrough of sorts can be achieved by moving the debate in another direction and asking what we have in human culture that might be an outgrowth of activities not related to violence or aggression. Turning things around, as it were, achieves a twist that allows us to see that certain features of our culture were probably designed, invented, or otherwise originated by females. Slocum notes:

> We know that gathering was important long before much animal protein was added to the diet, and continued to be important. Bones, sticks and hand-axes could be used for digging up tubers or roots, or to pulverize tough vegetable matter for easier eating. If, however, instead of thinking in terms of tools and weapons, we think in terms of *cultural inventions*, a new aspect is presented. I suggest that two of the *earliest and most important* cultural inventions were containers to hold the products of gathering, and some sort of sling or net to carry babies.[23]

In other words, as so frequently happens, a hypothesis forms and then produces its own evidence—all of the evidence that allegedly or purportedly confirms the hypothesis originates from the hypothesis itself and the intellectual activities that it generates. Not only did this sort of self-fulfilling thesis generate, among the female primatologists, a desire to look for evidence of male violence (for example, as noted earlier, among the baboons) but, perhaps more importantly, it places an emphasis in human culture on the sorts of activities that stem from violence and aggression. Conversely, because no search is ever made for the cultural outcomes of such peaceful and, indeed, nurturing, activities as carrying babies or hauling vegetable growth, no evidence is ever found for their development or their influence.

Slocum also notes that the wish to perpetuate the "man-the-hunter" view led to several instances in which countervailing circumstances were irrationally ignored; it is a plain fact, for instance, that half of the human race, or half of the hominids, must have not been hunting at any given time. If they were not hunting or engaged in acts of aggression, the thoughtful investigator might have asked the simple question: What were they doing? An analysis that looks at the complete picture, as Slocum suggests, might run along the following lines:

Food sharing and the family developed from the mother-infant bond. The techniques of hunting large animals were probably much later developments, after the mother-children family pattern was established. When hunting did begin, and the adult males brought back food to share, the most likely recipients would be first their mothers, and second their siblings. In other words, a hunter would share food not with a wife or sexual partner, but with those who had shared food with him: his mother and siblings.[24]

This way of looking at the phenomena suggests that to take seriously the "man-clubs-woman, man-starts-family" stereotypes found in cartoons is to err. The first family units were headed by females, and males either fit into these units as other relations (usually sons, as suggested above), or perhaps did not fit into them at all.

As Slocum notes, cooperation, and not competition, may have been the byword of early hominid development,[25] but, as she also notes, it may not be possible for a female researcher to see the world this way unless she becomes "politically conscious of [herself] as a woman."[26] This, of course, implies that male researchers may never be able to attain the requisite degree of consciousness. On a more serious and substantial note, Slocum is clearly saying that only political movements like the feminist movement enable one to adjust the lens and look at the evidence from a completely new perspective.

The combination of Slocum's piece, Haraway's work that I discussed earlier, and the general focus of the radical critics makes it seem as if all of the research done on hominids and primatology is inevitably tainted. This may or may not be the case, but it does leave one shaken to think of the effect that the popularization of this kind of research—most effectively through the media—has on the culture at large. Here is one area where to say that more research needs to be done is to engage in gross understatement.

Bleier and the Biological Critique

In her work *Science and Gender* (and in a string of other works), the biologist Ruth Bleier does an impressive job of putting together the feminist and radical critiques. Since she is a trained biologist, her criticisms penetrate in the same way that Hubbard's do. If anything, Bleier's comments are even more pronounced, for she not only sees science as an intellectual enterprise that too often reeks of oppression (some of it specifically patriarchal), but she also sees all of our contemporary intellectual discourses through eyes informed by Foucaultian critique. Thus Bleier is unimpressed even by the formulation of many "scientific" questions, since she agrees with Foucault in the belief that the ways in which the questions are formulated involve relations of power.[27]

It is scarcely possible in contemporary science to ask a question or to frame a hypothesis that is free of this kind of taint. It has affected all of biology, and it encroaches upon every area of science. Bleier writes as follows:

> Always the "scientific" opinion is polarized, and the questions are basically and ultimately unanswerable scientifically as they are posed. But the questions persist as scientific issues because their significance and purposes are social and political. The very existence of discourse on the subject, the very fact that the question is raised, serves the issue that the discourse presumes to be seeking to understand: the asymmetrical distribution of power between women and men or blacks and whites.
>
> Thus, in Foucaultian terms one could say that truth is not a collection of insights or information floating about, parts of which are sooner or later revealed or discovered, nor does it lie deep within us waiting to be freed. Truth is produced through discourse . . . and its production is imbued with relations of power.[28]

Bleier is, like many of the critics whose work I have examined in this chapter, especially concerned to further the notion of biology as a vulnerable discipline because so much of what has passed for "knowledge" in biology has been blatantly politicized. Throughout this work I have adverted to notions having to do with intelligence and intelligence testing. Bleier not only examines this area but explicitly states the little-known fact that Alfred Binet did not originally develop his tests in questions as measures of general intelligence (or the mythical "g"); his goal at the outset had been to devise some kind of psychometric device that would allow for "identi[fication of] learning disabilities in children and measuring the children's progress after remedial treatment."[29] That this is hardly the use to which these tests were put is obvious—despite the fact that IQ testing remains controversial and that much that is both informed and critical has been written on the subject, this pertinent information about Binet's aims is rarely circulated.

If Bleier is concerned to identify relations of power and their effect on science, she sees these relations as both those of gender and race, and of social class and power. This particular constellation is not new, but Bleier is acutely sensitive to the intermingling of these focal points. Each one of them alone is strong enough, in a given situation, to exert an influence over the formulation of questions and topics for investigation; all of them put together constitute formidable obstacles indeed.

Bleier is concerned about sociobiology and its influence—it is one of the motivating factors behind the writing of her book—but she is also sensitive to the issues so frequently addressed in these pages, such as hypothesis formation, the logic of justification and its relationship to discovery, and so forth. Ruth Bleier has a knack for the terse and telling statement, and her pronouncements on the relationship of values to science are among the best and most concise to be found. With respect to the extent to which science is infused with the axiological, she writes:

> Unfortunately, there is no single correct scientific methodology; these biases, values, and beliefs—a scientist's worldview as well as mundane daily life circumstances—can and do affect scientific methodology itself. Even though scientific methodology is meant to constantly examine and challenge established scientific beliefs, including the investigator's own, it can be manipulated to support and strengthen those beliefs. The actual questions that a scientist finds interesting to ask and chooses to investigate may be biased; the questions may presume certain truths and premises that are not supportable but incorporate the informal opinions, values, or judgments of the scientist. Thus, the question both precludes asking valid and fundamental questions and also determines the nature and limits of the answers, which were predetermined; in fact, production of those answers was the reason for asking the questions in the first place.
>
> For example, the question "Why are all males aggressive?" produces very different answers from one asking "Are males of all species aggressive, and under what circumstances and how is 'aggressivity' displayed?"[30]

As this quotation from *Science and Gender* attests, Bleier is acutely sensitive to issues revolving around the formation of hypotheses and the posing of questions; these issues are, of course, central to the process of science. Bleier's larger claim here is obviously something like the following: We would like to be able to convince ourselves that the sorts of scientific "procedures" alluded to in the idealized and logicized versions of philosophy of science described in the earlier chapters of this book safeguard the construction and conduct of science and prevent bias from creeping in. But, again, we can find nothing in the actual evidence about how science takes place that would allow us to believe this—rather, if anything, the inferences we can make are the other way around. It is this emphasis on how some questions are valorized and prioritized over others that allows Bleier to make her strong criticisms of sociobiology, a phenomenon that had reached perhaps its highest level of influence around the time her work was published (the late 1970s and early 1980s).

That sociobiology is shot through with the political hardly needs to be argued here, because the issue has been examined sufficiently elsewhere. But Bleier notes that the sociobiological theories of Harvard's E. O. Wilson, for example, were immediately picked up by right-wing groups in Great Britain and were even cited in the literature of that country's semi-fascist National Front from the 1970s.[31] The sociobiologists could always try to claim innocence, but the history of the twentieth century precludes our believing that those who work in the sciences have no conception of the uses to which science can be put.

Lewontin and the Critique of the New Right

Richard Lewontin, Steven Rose, and Leon Kamin collaborated in 1984 on a work called *Not in Our Genes,* a valuable compendium of critical essays on sociobiology and its influence.[32] What makes this work particularly remarkable is that the authors do not stop short with the easy thesis that sociobiology is destructive of attempts to provide politically progressive environments—we have already encountered this type of criticism here, and indeed it has been a staple of the Left's analysis of contemporary science.

Rather, Lewontin, Rose, and Kamin also spend a great deal of time on the notion that sociobiology is too simplistic to do justice even to the animal kingdom. This holistic approach makes for a far-reaching work, because common sense would tell us that if the thesis does not hold for one part of the ecosystem, it does not hold for another. In addition, the authors present a sophisticated look at two of the important concepts underlying sociobiology and its emergence on the contemporary scene. They refer to these concepts as "reductionism" and "determinism"—crudely, the idea that wholes reduce to simpler parts that can be examined in and of themselves and the idea that, in some god's-eye science, everything can be predicted because everything is determined if only we could correctly understand science. (The latter belief is, in fact, a bit of an intellectual holdover from the positivists.)

With regard to the first point made above, the general inapplicability of sociobiological theses to forms of life, the authors write:

> But this [sociobiology's inapplicability to humans] is not because it has developed a theory applicable only to non-human animals; the method and theory are fundamentally flawed whether applied to the United States or Britain today, or to a population of savanna-dwelling baboons or Siamese fighting fish. There is no mystical and unbridgeable gulf between the forces that shape the societies of other organisms; biology is indeed relevant to the human condition, although the form and extent of its relevance is far less obvious than the pretensions of biological determinism imply.[33]

Lewontin, Rose, and Kamin are trying to say that the notion that nature stops at birth for humans and that culture then intervenes or takes over does not make much more sense if repackaged in some way that would seem acceptable for the nonhuman world—no culture and all nature. They claim that there is a "constant and active interpenetration of the organism with its environment"[34] and that the dichotomies that underlie much of what passes for current work in biology are untenable. A more sophisticated outlook, the authors maintain, would save us from the sorts of overly simplistic views that put the "organism" here and the "environment" out there.

In the same way, Lewontin, Rose, and Kamin provide an overview of the concept of intelligence that ties the truncated and abbreviated notion of "intelligence" available to us from its use in psychometric circles to the eugenics movement of the early part of the twentieth century. Although this story, which I discussed previously, is somewhat shopworn by now, the authors are careful to delineate precisely what kinds of narrowness informed the thought of some of the early investigators in this area and how it is tied to other concerns.

As I mentioned earlier, Binet himself had a rather mild and harmless concept of the use to which his original test could be put: He thought that it might aid in tracking the progress of children who were to undergo what would now be called "remedial" programs in French schools, programs that had already designated these particular children as somewhat behind for their age level.[35] But these ideas quickly took on a life of their own once they fell into other hands, and it is these other hands that did the most damage. The authors report:

> The translators and importers of Binet's test, both in the United States and in England, tended to share a common ideology, one dramatically at variance with Binet's. They asserted that the intelligence test measured an innate and unchangeable quantity, fixed by genetic inheritance. When Binet died prematurely in 1911, the Galtonian eugenicists took clear control of the mental-testing movement in the English-speaking countries and carried their determinist principles even further. The differences in measured intelligence not just between individuals but between social classes and races were now asserted to be of genetic origin.[36]

As Lewontin and the others assert, those who favored the introduction of these tests in the United States and Great Britain were not shy about their motives—Lewis Terman in 1916 is quoted by Lewontin as having stated that a lack of intelligence is "very common among Spanish-Indian and Mexican families of the Southwest and also among negroes. Their dullness seems to be racial, or at least inherent in the family stocks from which they come."[37] This comes from the individual who is probably most closely associated with the development of IQ testing in the United States and whose longitudinal study of intelligence is widely cited.

As the authors note, in any kind of leftist analysis the interests of those in power are served by these ideas. But, more importantly, it is also necessary to state what may not be quite as obvious: The "research" that led to these conclusions was paradigmatic of research of its time and of research in the social sciences. It is not just the early psychometricians or the early developmental or cognitive psychologists who are at fault here; it is the path of science itself, a path that leads to the kinds of analyses that produce evidence supporting established and entrenched hypotheses. Even if there were some other explanation for the rise in popularity of intelligence tests and the connections they are designed to make, the fact that these tests serve the interests of those in the better-off group is crucial. Lewontin, Rose, and Kamin also report, as an aside, that early U.S. Army beta testing (a precursor to today's IQ testing) asked immigrants to discover what was wrong with a picture that showed a tennis court with missing equipment. The fact that very few immigrants in turn-of-the-century America could ever even have seen a tennis court seems never to have entered anyone's mind.

Lewontin, Rose, and Kamin are equally harsh on what might be termed the "mental illness industry." Noting once again that a certain view or hypothesis tends to produce its own confirming evidence, the authors claim that the search for a biological cause for such (as they contend) ill-defined disorders as schizophrenia frequently leads to slapdash research based on everything from patients' blood to their urine.[38] Here the authors note that the old organic/functional distinction for mental illness, now largely outmoded, may have had some use. With the older way of categorizing phenomena, unless actual lesions were present or unless there was some known biological agent that had produced the syndrome—such as, for example, the third stage of syphilis—it was assumed that the "illness" was the result of some type of trauma that, ideally, could be explained in Freudian or semi-Freudian fashion. This approach may have had its defects (and those who accuse Freud of doing great damage to research in this area will be happy to assert that it had grave defects), but the one merit that it did possess was that it saved researchers from trying to find the "cause" of the apparently etiologically unrelated host of disorders categorized as schizophrenia.

The authors state:

> The diagnosis and treatment of schizophrenia are paradigms of the determinist mode of thinking, for this is the mental disorder on which more biochemical and genetic research has been lavished than any other, *the* one in which claims to have discovered the cause in a particular molecule or gene have been made most extensively. It is now so widely believed that psychiatry has proved the disorder to be biological that if the case fails here, where it is strongest, it must be even weaker elsewhere.[39]

As the authors go on to note, the assiduous attempts to find an early biological connection to schizophrenia led researchers to try every conceivable route to this conjectured linkage. The first attempts at finding differences in, say, the blood or urine of schizophrenics did not bear fruit, for it quickly became apparent that the "differences turned out to be artifactual; nonschizophrenic hospitalized patients showed similar differences from the normal. The differences were eventually traced to the effects of long periods of eating poor hospital diets, or to the chemical-breakdown products of drugs that had been administered to the patients."[40] Lewontin, Rose, and Kamin are saying, of course, that these differences were eventually explained in the cases in which it became obvious that there was no causal connection. But what about other cases? The reader is left with the inference—surely intentional on the part of the authors—that similar types of errors may still be occurring in mental illness and schizophrenia research and that the desire to produce a "biological" answer is leading those engaged in such research seriously astray.

This pushes the authors toward noting that mental illness, as R. D. Laing and Foucault both have claimed, is largely a societal construction consisting to a great extent of a set of names for various behaviors that others find offensive or dangerous.[41]

Lewontin, Rose, and Kamin are at their best in exposing the multiple links of schizophrenia research to other, frankly capitalistic endeavors, one of which is the pharmaceutical industry. To be fair, it is not at all unusual for drug companies to be heavily involved in medical research; given the cost of contemporary research and the scarcity of funding, one could not reasonably expect otherwise. But research on schizophrenia and other conditions that are usually classified as mental disorders suffers from two trends, at least one of which is a holdover from the nineteenth century, that adversely affect the results of the efforts.

The first difficulty with schizophrenia research, as alluded to earlier, is that there is a tendency to simplify and a real desire to gather together under one rubric phenomena that may not have a straightforward etiological relationship. Although, as the authors admit, some farsighted researchers "doubt whether schizophrenia is a single entity at all,"[42] there is also a pronounced trend toward clustering or grouping a variety of symptoms together. The authors relate this to earlier work on mind-brain relationships:

> The idea of a single disease of schizophrenia may be a hangover from the nineteenth-century definition of madness—so-called dementia praecox—which preceded it. The diagnosis of schizophrenia in a patient with a given set of symptoms can vary between doctor and doctor and culture and culture. . . . Comparisons of figures from different countries have shown that the most frequent use of the diagnosis of schizophrenia occurs in the United States and the Soviet Union.[43]

The search for a single entity drives research-related activity in one direction, while the drug industry pushes it in another. Not, of course, that pharmaceutical interventions have been less than extremely helpful in the management of psychoses—but, again, the drug industry has its own particular ends. As Lewontin, Rose, and Kamin claim: "Substances intended to cure one problem generate another, and the growth in such iat-rogenic [medically induced] disorders is serious and disturbing."[44] One can sense a spiral here; each iatrogenic disorder itself must be treated, which calls for still further pharmaceutical intervention, yielding another set of problems, and so forth.

The rush to try to find a "gene" for schizophrenia might not be so pro-nounced were it not for the fact that research much earlier in the century, involving twins, seemed to indicate a strong genetic component. Lewon-tin, Rose, and Kamin provide careful documentation of this research, and although Kallmann, one of the earliest researchers, was Jewish, it seems that much of his research, carried out in Germany in the 1930s, was origi-nally done under the auspices of Nazi-related groups and activities.[45]

A good deal of what we find when we examine schizophrenia, the re-search surrounding it, the variety of conditions that fall under its rubric, and so forth, matches the problems and stratagems involved in other ge-netics-related research. Lewontin, Rose, and Kamin are driven to con-struct a critique of this research because they know how dangerous such oversimplification can be—for a variety of politically charged reasons, the results of such research almost always negatively affect the poor, persons of color, and those groups most in need of protection. Yet, inevitably, powerful government agencies and funders of such research almost never have a constituency where such individuals are present in any-where near the numbers that make up their percentage of the population. As the authors suggest, it is crucial to present a strong critique of the mo-tives behind such research and to make the case for eliminating the worst tendencies of the research.

The Death and Destruction of Nature

In my attempt to articulate both the feminist and radical critiques and to find, where possible, the intersections between them, it is important to look at the work of those who have viewed the process historically. Car-olyn Merchant, in her very extensively cited *The Death of Nature*, provides us with a framework for understanding why theorists as disparate as Slocum, Bleier, and Lewontin can all agree on the masculinist structure of science and on the extent to which scientific activities have been detri-mental to the persons most in need of benefit.[46]

Merchant tells us that nature is female and reminds us of the split be-tween culture and nature. So much we already know, and if this were the full conceptual story then relatively little light would be shed. But more importantly, Merchant reminds us that there is more than one "female" or "feminine" side to nature, and reacquainting ourselves with the variation here goes a long way toward explaining why in contemporary science studies we want to hearken to the fact that nature has been exploited and raped by science at the same time that we instinctively feel that nature is in some sense our salvation.

The rise of science during the sixteenth and seventeenth centuries was, according to Merchant, accompanied by a changing view of organicity and human relationships to it:

> While the organic framework was for many centuries sufficiently integrative to override commercial development and technological innovation, the acceleration of such changes throughout western Europe during the sixteenth and seventeenth centuries began to undermine the organic unity of cosmos and society. Because the needs and purposes of society as a whole were changing with the commercial revolution, the values associated with the organic view of nature were no longer applicable; hence the plausibility of the conceptual framework itself was slowly, but continuously, being threatened.[47]

Part of the change was manifested in a turn toward the recognition that nature could be unruly. Although the fecundity of nature had in the past always provided a point of departure for theorizing about nature as feminine, in the late Renaissance a turn toward nature as Bacchanalian began to take place. In this turn, the identification of woman with nature also changed, and the emphasis on women as witches and nature as the progenitor of their wild forces became commonplace. As Merchant notes, this emphasis coincides with the beginnings of the scientific revolution and is strongly related to the desire to control that which is deemed to be uncontrollable—a wish also related, of course, to the yearning for mastery over capitalist markets and their expansion into "wild" new territories. Thus a reemphasis on the darker side of nature occurs at a time when the power of women ebbs, partially because society itself loses its organic moorings.

It is interesting to note that one of the series of twists and turns that occurs in this portrayal of nature as destructive is connected with the categorization of women and things female as "witchlike." This demonization of the feminine allowed theorists room in which to attempt to construct remedies, and at the same time reinforced the notion that there was something that had to be controlled.[48] Merchant is explicit about the relationship:

> The image of nature that became important in the early modern period was that of a disorderly and chaotic realm to be subdued and controlled. . . . Concurrently, the old organic order of nature in the cosmos, society, and self was symbolically giving way to disorder through discoveries of the "new science," the social upheavals of the Reformation, and the release of people's animal and sexual passions.[49]

As soon as social change and its concomitant disruptive force became evident, there had to be a reconceptualization of the natural in order to allow for a view of nature that would admit of dominance. One might be tempted to say, given the direction in which many Renaissance and post-Renaissance thinkers were headed, that the more dangerous the better: At least it is the case that this rubric of danger provided the theorists with some of their most formidable ammunition. Merchant notes that "[l]ike wild chaotic nature, women needed to be subdued and kept in their place";[50] one of the ways in which they could be kept in place was to accuse them of unbridled lust and then try them for witchcraft. The combination of the breakdown of the authority of the Church, the rise of science, the contact with non-European cultures, and a degree of technological change, albeit at a slow pace, resulted in the kind of view of nature that allowed for the composition of the *Malleus Maleficarum*.[51]

Science would soon be able to exert at least minimal control over nature, but the desire to increase this control and mastery did not give way. The death of nature is, then, the rise of science—it is the birth of modernist culture and the modernist themes of alienation, angst, and loss of the organic. In our time, this loss has manifested itself in the further commodification of science and in a culture so reliant upon technology that many persons living in developed countries have never experienced firsthand the kinds of phenomena that until a hundred years ago would have been part and parcel of human life on this earth.

Merchant's work has the virtue of reminding us simultaneously of the power of feminine imagery and the history of its connection with science and the scientific enterprise. The radical critics of science have, especially in citing Marx and Marxist theory, frequently reminded us of former times when the desire to master nature was not so great, or at least not manifested in such overt and blatant ways. But if it is true that the radical critics have been farsighted in noting the ways in which our dominance of nature has increased our tendencies toward technological destruction, it is also true that they have, perhaps unwittingly, pointed the way in other directions. As Carolyn Merchant herself notes, there are numerous interpretations of the feminine and nature throughout Western culture, and they can be used for a variety of purposes. Maybe part of what is necessary for future theorizing is the stance that sees nature as Arcadia—the "benevolent, peaceful, and rustic,"[52] to be lived with rather than controlled.

If the radical critics have one thing in common, it is a concern for the manner in which science has been conducted and for the fact that science seems to have ineradicable ties with capitalist economics. Rose, Graham, Bleier, Lewontin, and other radical theorists are all explicit about this concern, and it is implicit in the work of the other critics as well. Because capitalist economies are market driven, science becomes the tool of forces so impure that the kind of conception of purity adumbrated by the positivists does not really bear on the question. More importantly, perhaps, developed countries have bound the economic needs of their markets to the power structure already in place. Thus white male privilege is buttressed at a time when moral concerns would instead argue that the needs of the Third World should outweigh all other demands.

Although the radical critics are frequently overtly propelled by Marxist concerns, sheer humanism is part of the motivating force behind the writing of, say, Bleier or even of Lewontin and his colleagues, especially when one recalls the extent to which the kind of science under criticism has managed to leave out or devalue vast numbers of the population. The authors of *Not in Our Genes* are against much of what passes for intelligence testing, not only because it represents a kind of operationalism gone wild but also because the results of the testing leave out millions of children from the kinds of programs that enable other children to "get ahead."

The feminist and radical critics agree most obviously in areas like reproduction and concern for the environment—merging in a kind of "ecofeminism"—but they also share, historically, the path delineated by Carolyn Merchant, an intellectual path of European history that simultaneously glorifies and devalues both nature and woman. That which is virginal is attractive, but that which includes female sexuality is also uncontrollable, and the uncontrollable must be tamed. Virgins can turn into witches, and the pastoral into the demonic.

There is relatively little in the work of the radical critics that was not at least hinted at in the work of nineteenth-century thinkers, who understood that the rise of the bourgeoisie signaled the demise of the "natural." Nevertheless, as Graham has remarked, the new critics have the advantage of writing at a time when science has never been so entrenched and powerful, never so much a part of government and other institutions. This bringing to the fore of the critics' important points at this particular time provides an exciting juncture for feminist, holistic, and other views of science and reminds us how far science studies has come since the earlier work in philosophy and history of science, which was more descriptive than critical. The new departments of science studies at major universities attest to the importance of the endeavor and to its timeliness. The interdisciplinary nature of the work draws on all that I have demarcated here and in some cases adds dimensions that I have not addressed, such as French theory and poststructuralism.

Although poststructuralist theory might be thought to forward the radical project insofar as an overall critique of Western culture is concerned, it seems salient to note in closing that a strong counterargument to this claim can be made. As we saw when examining Haraway's arguments, the lack of epistemic privilege of any one position seems to indicate that no set of data can be valorized over another, thus giving every possible set of data, or every interpretation, an equal voice. Although at first blush this may seem to be a progressive move, it is not progressive when we take into account what we are trying to accomplish by viewing science radically in the first place, and what the fruits of such an endeavor might be.

As indicated earlier, we view science with a radical perspective because we want to be able to use some of the results of science for different sorts of purposes—purposes that might aid women, persons of color, and others who, in the past, may have been denied such benefits or denied them disproportionately. Although it is no doubt the case that no "god's-eye view" of Haraway's primates and their behavior is available to humans—the Complete Account not being one to which finite minds have access—it is also most likely the case that there will be some sets of observations that are less contaminated than others. Using the terms that Haraway herself originally employed for analysis, some observers will only minimally interfere with the situation, will observe silently, will make every effort to see to it that they are not noticed by the animals, and so forth. This is qualitatively different from the cases cited by Haraway of observers who intended to provoke aggression among the male primates or to alter observed behavior.

The point of this example is simply this: The radical critique avails us nothing if it does not move science in a certain direction. Abandoning science or casting science out only means that whatever might be the results of scientific enterprise will not be available to many or, worse still, will become further entrenched in the power structure. This, surely, is not the point of the critique. The goal of the critique of science currently under way is to alter the face of science.

8

Naturalizing
Scientific
Justification

The last two chapters have focused on the voices of criticism of science as an enterprise, and in delineating the positions associated with feminism and radicalism I have not had the opportunity to recapitulate some of the philosophy of science that led up to it. To reiterate, a great deal of work in philosophy of science—and history and sociology of science as well—that immediately preceded the development of these lines of criticism had already been pushed in a certain direction. As I indicated in Chapters 4 and 5, the turn away from positivist and positivist-oriented views had led to an emphasis on weltanschauungen views and on a certain kind of sociology of science.

Having said so much, the reader might well wonder if we are left with only criticism and without a proactive stance on what, if anything, science can accomplish at the end of the twentieth century. Some of the new work, if taken seriously and allied with other developments that may not at first seem applicable, may indeed lead the way to the development of a notion of scientific justification that is less logicized and more in tune with the way in which science is actually done, but that avoids the pitfalls of the kind of outspoken relativism that we associate with the work of Bruno Latour, Donna Haraway, and the postmodernist voice in general.

To return to work that I examined two chapters back, some of this effort in feminist theory is simultaneously critical of science and of philosophy of science up to that point but is unable to articulate a more forward position. Both Lynn Hankinson Nelson and Helen Longino are unwilling to "throw out the baby with the bathwater,"[1] to devalue the entire scientific enterprise, simply because of the fact that so much of what has been done is androcentric, logicistic, or insensitive to the needs of those exploited by capitalist consumerism.

Nelson, in particular, is drawing on W. V. O. Quine's own method of naturalization in her work in epistemology and philosophy of science to which I alluded earlier. As I noted, it is not the case that Nelson has no standards for justification—rather, her standards are those of a community of knowers, relying on the data of their senses and articulating agreements and disagreements as opposed to, for example, the individuated standard of the positivist cognizer whose ultimate epistemic criterion is the incorrigible data of the senses.

A number of moves in contemporary philosophy of science have attempted to be sensitive to this naturalistic turn, with varying degrees of success.[2] Part of the task of this chapter will be to set out some of these attempts, and it will become obvious that a number of views that have been labeled "naturalized" are probably not. (This applies in particular to some work in what has been labeled the "new realism.") The instrumentalist debate is also important here, for the instrumentalist is not wedded to the type of theory of reference that, in general, has developed a view of science resembling the Received View in its logicized rigor.

In order to develop the notions that will be employed in this chapter, I will first provide an overview of the contemporary work done in a few different fields. Naturalized epistemology *simpliciter,* although it is of crucial importance for those feminist theorists who, like Nelson, would like to develop an epistemology that relies on less than logicized notions, has not been examined in any depth in this work, and we need at least a cursory overview before proceeding. This will be followed by a brief recapitulation of the work of those feminist theorists who are the least relativist and the most comfortable with some sort of notion of empirical justification, and then a short summation of what is now being called "naturalization" in philosophy of science. Because the work of theorists such as Richard Boyd and Bas van Fraassen, who have been of paramount importance in the realist/instrumentalist controversy, has been deemed by many to be relevant to this debate, their work also will be examined.

The salience of a notion of justification for a feminist philosophy of science cannot be overestimated because, as I concluded at the end of the previous chapter, without such a notion claims are placed on all fours with each other, undermining the attempts of those whose voices have not yet been heard to develop a stance. Although we cannot develop a theory of justification in the old sense to cover all cases (indeed, as the critics have charged, this was one of the defects of such theorizing), we can attempt to develop a theory that will be serviceable in a number of intellectual contexts and that will forward the project at hand. Though no single theory may be worthy of an encomium or extended praise, attempts to develop such a theory are praiseworthy in and of themselves because they encourage the development of broadly applicable theories in general.

Naturalized epistemology, particularly in its post-Quinean interpretations, draws on work from contemporary cognitive science and the social sciences in general in order to try to see what cognizers actually do and how their work might be relevant to epistemic theory, especially epistemic justification theory. Here we can see the greatest point of variation between the older, more traditional, quasi-positivist theorizing and the new thinking: In the old theorizing, as I posited in earlier chapters, it really did not matter if what was set down bore any conceivable relationship to the practice of cognizers or, indeed, scientists. Since the point was to develop a logic of justification, no relationship need be claimed. But later awareness of the fact that the theory itself did not hold together, along with the fact that virtually no science seemed to even minimally mirror such a theory, undercut the Received View and its offshoots and led to the large and somewhat amorphous body of theorizing that I have examined here.

The practice of justifying knowledge claims is, then, something that can be modeled along the lines already employed by a number of thinkers whose work I have examined to mimic the practice of justifying claims in the specific context of scientific theories. Whether or not the "old" epistemology has anything to offer is a bit like asking whether the old philosophy of science has anything to offer—at this point, they are both of historical interest.

Naturalized Epistemology and Justification

Naturalized epistemology not only provides us with a handle on how agents actually cognize; it provides us with new notions that might be consonant with the general project of justification, including scientific justification.[3] If it is true, as Kornblith and others have argued, that agents are in some sense hardwired, particularly at an early age, to pick up on the social features of their surroundings and to make the requisite inferences, it is also true that this kind of material has never been emphasized in traditional, normative epistemology, and it is normative epistemology, with its complex history in the twentieth century, that has intersected heavily with philosophy of science.

How might it be possible to construct an overview of justification that meshes with what we know about contemporary cognition but that is not necessarily as relativistic as, for example, some of the work that I cited in Chapter 5? If we think of justification as a social process—and this is particularly true in the case of scientific claims—then we will have a point of departure for further theorizing. Conversational models might be invoked here, capturing as they do the "top-down" flavor of the process of justification, and there are several types of current work in the social sciences (such as work in sociolinguistics and social psychology, to name but two areas) that might be used in devising such a model.

Does this mean that we can obtain a view of justification that will be airtight? Of course not—agents err, and a naturalized epistemology will take this fact into consideration. The logic of justification of the Received View was constructed to provide a framework for incorrigibility, and nevertheless incorrigibility and its components have now been severely undercut. But epistemic warrant is not out of the question; some views might be more justified than others, and the view that is most justified is then warranted. This type of work can and should be done, and any model of justification derived from this work will have the virtue of at least being instantiable, which is more than can be said for many of the classical models.

Lately, a number of philosophers of science have indulged in what is referred to in the literature as "naturalized" philosophy of science. Whether or not this label really fits the work that is being forwarded is another question.[4] Naturalized philosophy of science presumably would still be at least minimally interested in the concept of empirical justification but would avoid the defects of the Received View to which I have already alluded on a number of occasions. Part and parcel of the difficulty of spelling out the notion of such a philosophy of science will have to do with theory of reference, and it will be part of the task of this chapter to show how theory of reference is an important and frequently overlooked topic in philosophy of science.

If naturalized epistemology relies largely on recent work in cognition, there is still another area of endeavor that is relevant to this discussion, and that is social epistemology. This work will have at least a small intersection with Continental theory.

When we think of the circumstances under which justification normally occurs (ordinary epistemic justification, not necessarily the justification of scientific claims), we can rest assured of the fact that agents do not usually engage in the procedure of epistemic justification unless their claims have been challenged. That is, many or even most knowledge claims in ordinary or mundane contexts go unchallenged precisely because they are "obvious," empirically uncontested, and so forth.[5] My claim to my five-year-old cousin that we are looking at a cow in a pasture is unlikely to require justification unless there is something about the context itself that might necessitate epistemic support—and, although such a situation is conceivable, it is a much less frequent occurrence than the normative epistemologists, with their false barns and conniving twins, would have us believe.[6]

Nevertheless, some knowledge claims and beliefs are, of course, challenged. It may be the case that, for reasons unknown to me, my neighbor has decided to raise a rare gaur on his farm, and I and my preschooler are not looking at a cow at all but at a statistically unusual type of ox. My claim that the incessant ringing of the doorbell on Halloween is only the neighborhood children trick-or-treating may not be challenged until someone points out to me that it is really a not-so-nice prankster of the adult variety checking to see whether people are home for the purpose of committing a break-in. In any case, if a belief or knowledge claim is challenged, the process of justification then ensues. Almost always, it is a verbal process, and because it is a verbal process it can be modeled not only on what we now know from the cognitive sciences, and cognitive psychology in particular, but on material from sociology, sociolinguistics, anthropology, and so forth.

The point is that justification as a process requires a naturalized model; furthermore, if a naturalized model can be the basis for epistemic justification of the usual type, it can also be the basis for the process of scientific justification. In fact, if the work of some of the social-science theorists discussed earlier has any bearing, these sorts of justificatory endeavors may have more in common than some seem to believe. Most importantly, it is not the logic of justification that is important here—not only was such logic provided at an earlier point in time, but as we saw there is general agreement that such logic does nothing to provide a model that will in any way mesh with the actual practice of science. What is required, presumably, is something like the logic of discovery or, even more aptly, the pattern of discovery and/or the pattern of justification. It is here that some of the feminist epistemologists and philosophers of science whose work I have cited are on the right track, when they write of communities of knowers and when they eschew the model of the lone knower, lone cognizer, or lone justifier.

Communities and Feminist Theory

In several previous sections I reiterated crucial elements of the feminist critique, but among those elements one is paramount for purposes of articulating another sort of theory of justification, and that is the notion of a community of knowers.[7]

Whatever the merits or defects of an incorrigibility theory of epistemic justification, other theories invoked by the classically minded normative epistemologists usually had similar disadvantages; that is, they were concocted on the basis of the concept of one individual (paradigmatically male) attempting to confront the phenomenal world and to justify the knowledge claims and/or beliefs that he might develop with respect to it. Classical coherentism, then, was no more user friendly in this regard than foundationalism—the problems associated with the standard version of coherentism have to do with the size of the justificatory sets and so forth.[8] The coherentist was still an individual cognizer who, without giving any single claim special epistemic status, tried to justify or warrant other claims.

But the concept of justification as a community-based process has two paramount strong points. One is that it frees us from the tedious and problematic debates between such theories as foundationalism and coherentism, since both of these theories, as I have just indicated, are highly individualized. One could envision socialized versions of these theories, but, particularly in the case of foundationalism, such a version would be meaningless since the focus of epistemic privilege has traditionally been the incorrigible or strongly warranted sense datum of one percipient. The second strong point of the community-based approach is that it virtually demands advertence to certain material in the social sciences, cognitive sciences, and areas of cognition in general that has come to the fore since the 1960s. We now have so much more information about cognitive processes of social interaction, sociolinguistic phenomena, perception in general, and so forth that although the classical theories were seldom if ever formulated with allusion to such material, a lack of reference to this material in newer theories would constitute a lacuna indeed.[9]

Finally, the notion of a community of inquirers or knowers saves, at least to some extent, the concept of empirical justification and works to move the debate away from the most relativistic areas. In describing the work of Haraway or Latour, for example, it has been clear, as I have indicated, that the lack of any kind of established epistemic criteria leaves the potential knower in a dangerous position because it places all knowledge claims on all fours with each other, privileging none.[10] The danger of this position, as was made clear earlier, is that if one believes that the fruits of science should be distributed on a fairly equitable basis, then any type of claim based on past disadvantages would need some sort of substantiation, and the extremely relativistic views do not allow for that. Again, the concept of a community of knowers does go some way toward alleviating the strain associated with such a position.

Part of the appeal of this concept is that we experience little difficulty in envisioning how the process of justification would work. In the Third World, women's lives are enmeshed in everyday needs, and frequently women are solely or largely responsible for obtaining food, water, shelter, and other necessities. We know that if there is a drought in a village in India or Bangladesh, speculation is an unlikely source of information about where to obtain food or water. Rather, we can readily imagine that someone (very likely a woman) who has found a well or a source of food will tell someone else, and so forth. She could, of course, err. The well may be dry—she may have been mistaken in what she thought she saw. What appears to be food may not be food, or it may not be edible. But such mistakes, based on information obtained from the senses, are readily rectified in a community of knowers. We can imagine that they most frequently would be rectified by dialogue and by allusion to evidence. Occasionally, correction may take place without the need for speaking.

But the point is that an empirical model of confirmation is exactly that which best fits our contention that ordinary justification occurs in contexts of epistemic challenge, and it is an empirical model that admits of input (in fact, virtually requires input) from many different sources. People working alone may take longer to find out that they have erred, and it is even possible, in unusual circumstances, that the mistake may never be revealed or acknowledged. Communities of knowers not only are models for the kind of cooperative activities in which women are somewhat more likely to engage, based on Chodorowian theory, but they also are effective models for the adjudication of disputes. Here we cannot say that all knowledge claims are on a par with each other—thirsty human beings will readily be able to tell, in most instances, what does and what does not constitute a water source.

The notion that such claims themselves are subject to a sort of politicization is not disputed—it is merely that there is more than politicization that is up for grabs here. It is one thing to claim that we cannot privilege one take on the primates; it is another to say that we cannot privilege one set of claims about a water source. The communitarian epistemic model helps us out greatly in this regard.

In the following sections I will examine work that is currently associated with naturalization in philosophy of science, and in the later sections I will go on to present a theory developed within the confines of the work done here. The point, presumably, is to allow for a view of science that is sensitive to the needs of all persons on the face of the earth.

The New Realism

Much of the work in recent philosophy of science that might be regarded as more rigorous and less relativistic falls under the rubric of the "new realism."[11]

The original idea here, more optimistic than some that we have been exposed to, was that the success of science required explanation and that a realist account of scientific terms was necessary to provide such an explanation. The thinking goes that there is indeed a path to science and that that path is upward bound: We know more than the ancients. Unlike a theorist such as Latour, the new realists assume that there is such a thing as confirmation and that it is far from a slapdash and accidental process.

The difficulty with the new realism, as we shall soon see, is that it is frequently tied to a stringent notion of reference. Whether or not such a notion of reference can be countenanced is a debatable point, and a point for the realists that requires much explanation.

In addition, there is a question of more than historical interest about what precisely the relationship is between the new realism and more positivistic views. As I indicated earlier, one strain of positivism appears to favor an instrumentalist approach because some of the early positivists, Moritz Schlick in particular, had been seen as favoring a bare-bones phenomenalistic outlook that did not tie sense-data to any underlying structure.[12] Indeed, to attempt to posit an underlying structure would be, of course, to go beyond the data. On the other hand, the notion that science is an explanatory project and other, more Quinean notions to the effect that it is impossible to force a cognitive split between the phenomena and the nascent attempts to categorize them seem to push even positivism in a direction that is more realist. I will examine this conundrum in more detail shortly, but in the meantime it is important to note that, especially for the newer varieties of realism, arguments as to their ties to positivism can move in both directions. Perhaps more important than the historical material is the notion that what is now being referred to as realism is one of the more stringent and philosophically rigorous views to develop in quite some time, and is a view that, in its rigor, is markedly at variance with the trend toward weltanschauungen views that was prevalent at an earlier time. Needless to say, this new realism is also wildly at variance with many of the views demarcated as science studies, and its attempts to tie terms to their referents demand a correspondentist view that is now, according to some, out of style and out of date.

In any case, to return to the explication, the notion is that the success of science, both predictive and explanatory, requires key terms used in scientific contexts to refer.[13] Science could not have achieved what it has without such reference. The realist thinker Boyd writes:

> There must operate some principle of "matching" or continuity between the theoretical vocabularies of different accepted theories. . . . What we will eventually claim is that these principles operate to guarantee that the referents of the same theoretical terms occurring in two different theories (in the same subject area) should be the same. . . . This claim cannot, of course, be made from a metaphysically neutral position on the status of theoretical terms in scientific theories.[14]

Here we get into the area that is most interesting for contemporary realist theories—the one that, if fully developed, yields the most interesting positions for the notion of developing a wider view of justification. For if the realist view is sound, then it is unlikely that the slippage between language and reality that the Continental (and many non-Continental) theorists posit actually occurs, and it would indicate that there is a need for a tight theory of reference, something along the lines of Kripkean causal reference.[15] As has been noted in the literature, this kind of view is about as far as one can get from most of what is extant in contemporary science studies.

More importantly, the notion of justification in the realist view is then not only empirical but, again, tied to a philosophy of language that would allow for most or all of the referents used in discourse in a justificatory context to refer—without such "go through," nothing yielding epistemic warrant or justification would have been said.

At this point it might be instructive to ask what has driven so many contemporary theorists to write of the problematized status of reference, thus driving a wedge between language and the world and making views such as those of the new realists look implausible in their entirety, and not just in part.

Part of the difficulty has been the transfusion into the more technical areas of Anglo-American philosophy of material taken from French and other Continental theory that is essentially literary. The work of Derrida, Lacan, and Foucault—and here I speak in general terms, without allusion to any particular work or doctrine—has emphasized the failure of language to hook up to the world and has also, interestingly enough, emphasized the androcentricity of the very process of hookup, thus undermining attempts to make such matching look like an interesting, tenable, or worthwhile endeavor. French feminist theorists such as Hélène Cixous, Luce Irigaray, and Julia Kristeva have also written in this regard; Irigaray has theorized about the acquisition of language as part of the project of male growth and development (à la Nancy Chodorow, Dorothy Dinnerstein, and the psychoanalytic thinkers), a pursuit that she labels the "bobbin game."[16] Like many such thinkers, Irigaray sees a phallocratic enterprise of establishing dominance over items by labeling them vocally, an enterprise that she hypothesizes begins with the male infant (Freud's prototypical male infant) calling for his mother.

One might naively wonder why so much of this theory, which is clearly aimed in a more literary than technical direction, has infused contemporary American philosophy. Although a large number of journal articles are still being written and published as if no such infusion had occurred, a glance at the dialogue and discourse across university campuses today indicates the overwhelming importance of contemporary Continental theory and the tremendous, if vague, impact that it has had.

Having said so much, it can be seen, then, that there are two lines of argument that militate against the kind of reference that the realists require to make their vision work. The first line of argument is itself technical and, as I have indicated, relies on work in theory of reference and other areas of philosophy of science. But the second line of argument alludes to the work of the French theorists, and if this more metaphorical line is purchased it is indeed difficult to refute because it is by no means clear what would constitute an adequate refutation.

In any case, realism asks us to think about whether terms refer; if so, how they refer; and under what circumstances we might obtain "confirmation" of this. (Notice that there is a dangerous circularity here.) Is it possible to obtain a view of science as some kind of progressive apparatus without positing a hard view of reference? The instrumentalists, or "strict empiricists" as they are currently called, believe that it is.

Strict Empiricism and Justification

What is deemed to be "instrumentalism" is a view that refuses to posit anything beyond the phenomena actually known through the senses.[17] In other words, one can think of a set of contentions about the phenomena as an "inference ticket" that allows one to make predictions based on the evidence, but that does not allow one to posit entities behind the phenomena or to look for the kinds of causal explanations of the phenomena that the existence of the entities usually provokes.

This kind of strict empiricism is currently associated with the work of Bas Van Fraassen, and insofar as such work can be labeled, the labeling is appropriate and just, for it is an empiricism that posits nothing and asks us to borrow nothing. Van Fraassen has actually gone so far as to claim that the realist exhibits a "touching faith";[18] even where it is obvious that one might be drawn toward taking a realist stance, the instrumentalist refuses to do so.

Justification, qua process, is thus somewhat simplified for the instrumentalist, and it is this portion of the original Received View that has probably attracted most of the attention in the literature. Justification would require only matching phenomena or matching accounts of the phenomena; since no entities are posited, no theory of reference (at least none that requires a causal connection) need be invoked, so the kinds of problems associated with the realist views are obviated or avoided altogether.

Here the model of justification to which I alluded earlier—the model associated with ordinary epistemic justification, not necessarily justification occurring in a scientific context—can be helpful to us, because if the scientist looks only at the phenomena, then some bare description of the phenomena, passed on to someone else, may be precisely the sort of claim that is challenged; this claim would then be justified in terms again alluding to no more than the phenomena in question, and so forth. This kind of process, as indicated earlier, could be modeled conversationally; one could allude to many strands from the contemporary social sciences in order to obtain a more precise model.

Part of the motivation behind the strict empiricist's parsimoniousness is a desire to avoid metaphysical commitments. The original work done in the sciences by the ancients and even the early moderns was aimed in the right direction in one regard: These thinkers understood that one could not really theorize about the nature of things without some underlying ontology. As theorists adopted the style of thinking associated with the twentieth century, it became increasingly clear that the only type of metaphysics that really made any sense was a monistic materialism, and yet it was the very growth of science itself that made the establishment and articulation of such a materialism a difficult project.

Instrumentalism avoids these conundrums by refusing to take an interest in any material substratum underlying the phenomena. Insofar as this latter type of theorizing is normally pinned to explanation (and to success, as we saw in the last section), Van Fraassen's refusal to engage in it amounts to a refusal to buy the project. Here is his commentary on the related project, evolutionary epistemology:

> But the "pure case" of evolutionary epistemology apparently runs like this: We need methods of forecasting if we are to plan and hence if we are to survive at all. The methods we have been following are the methods of the most successful organisms on earth, namely, us. So they clearly have survival value. It remains only to show how, specifically, each feature of that methodology (as described by some account X, say, a list that includes inference to the best explanation) contributes to our fitness for survival. As Popper apparently first said, that is epistemology for dinosaurs.[19]

The humor here is warranted from a theoretical standpoint if we remember that the ad hoc nature of the construction is a reflection on the type of project under investigation. Rather than asking if we can genuinely call ourselves "successful" (except, perhaps, in a reproductive sense), the project assumes that we can—a clear instance of question begging—and then proceeds retroactively to try to reconstruct the epistemological underpinnings of the success without further speculative questioning.

It is this type of theorizing that the instrumentalist, or strict empiricist, will not buy. Nothing in strict empiricism requires that we provide an overview of what "real" entities are, of how we got as far as we did, so to speak, or of what the relationship between these two intellectual enterprises is. Rather, we can continue to make predictions, which may themselves have survival value, simply by saving the phenomena. As Van Fraassen also says, the realist is looking for a level of correspondence that amounts to something like the following: "[I]f the theoretical structure enjoys adequatio a rem, then hypotheses exploiting and building on that structure can be expected to do well."[20]

As was pointed out earlier, one benefit of the instrumentalist view is that it alters our conceptions of justification, particularly in a scientific context, to a relatively simple model that parallels or mimics nonscientific justification in that both rely on a phenomenal account and do not proceed any further. In this sense scientific justification does, in fact, merge a bit with some of the lines of criticism that I examined in previous chapters, for if realist explanations drop out and if strict empiricism is employed, criticisms like Haraway's, or even Latour's, become more relevant.

It might well be the case, then, that there are a number of stories and that it will be difficult to privilege any one story. Difficult, one is tempted to reply, but not impossible. The privileging of the various stories, as was argued earlier, will presumably have something to do with whether or not one story represents evidence that is less contaminated, evidence that is obtained under certain conditions, and so forth. No metaphysical commitments toward the reality underlying the primates and our observations of them are necessary, in the case of examples constructed like Haraway's, for us to be able to say that some sets of observations of the primates are less tainted, less contaminated, less turned to political purposes than others.

In fact, we can make use of the notion of politicization that is employed by the theorists who focus on these claims to make something of a move in another direction. If, for example, we can determine that original observations of the primates made during the 1920s were driven by wildly overt political considerations, it might then be possible to make the claim that the considerations employed today are less overt and, in that sense, less politicized.

Thus strict empiricism, by asking us to focus on the phenomena, enables us to see our way clear to an account of things that, particularly in a conversational model, would allow us to develop a theory of justification. It is interesting to recapitulate some of the material to which I alluded in Chapters 2 and 3 of this work, where I discussed the importance of a phenomenal account for the original Received View. As I indicated, the status of such an account is up for grabs, with commentators divided over whether or not the Received View can be said to be more realist or more instrumentalist.[21] It is worth remarking upon this point of controversy one more time, since it illuminates other portions of the current contretemps between the realists and the instrumentalists.

To remind us of the relevance of this issue, Joia Lewis writes:

His [Schlick's] early criticisms of positivism, particularly the fact that it ignored the significance of the logical and conceptual in favor of the immedi-

ately experienced, became the issues that he then had to deal with.
. . . Schlick identified intuition specifically with the act of sensing, with the
fleeting moment before the one who is sensing has become consciously
aware of what it is one is sensing. . . . Besides this strict identification of intuition with the act of sensing, Schlick also identified intuition more generally
with any philosophy that was "anti-science" in attitude.[22]

Lewis's point, as mentioned before, is that Schlick has partially misunderstood the positivist attitudes as formulated by Ernst Mach, but in any
case the articulation is intriguing. The identification with the "act of sensing" tells us that any phenomenal account has its strengths and weaknesses. The strength of such an account is that it saves us from looking for
unknown and/or hypostatized entities; the weakness of such an account
is that it can never purport to give us causal explanations or, indeed, any
explanations.

The realist wants to beef up such an account with some other kind of
reification that will allow certain theoretical work to be done; the instrumentalist will have none of this. But, as I have claimed earlier, the realist
account entangles us in problems of reference and difficulties involving
how terms connect with the phenomenal world. Thus any theory of justification tied to such an account will have similar problems; at a certain
point, one would like to know how the linguistic hookup will be made.
Taking all of these items into consideration, a strict empiricism begins to
look more promising, especially since "saving the phenomena" is what
science was supposed to have been about all along.

Thus a project like Haraway's, or the one described by Haraway in
Simians, Cyborgs and Women, looks different depending on which view of
science one posits the experimenter as holding. With a more instrumentalist view, it might be possible to concoct a theory of justification that
asks us to provide only a phenomenal account and that does not rely on
underlying causal mechanisms. If such an account is then given, it tends
to allow for the notion that some purely phenomenal descriptions are, in
fact, more consistent with the phenomena, thus undercutting the notion
that all accounts are equally politically motivated and are thus on a par
with each other.

Concerns in Philosophy of Mind

Recent work in philosophy of mind, however recondite it might seem
from the standpoint of work now being done in philosophy of science
simpliciter, gives us reason to think that a number of directions consistent
with contemporary science can be delineated. This work would not be so

relevant were it not for the fact that a great many of the most vexing and perplexing questions surrounding philosophy of science involve the social sciences and the status of human-related sciences within the vast scope of the scientific enterprise.

Philosophy of mind in current terms tries to give us a handle on how we might theorize about human intentions and endeavors.[23] When introductory material having to do with questions in philosophy of mind is set out, theorists almost always seem to feel the need to write of such hallowed topics in the Western philosophical tradition as Cartesianism, responses to it, and so forth. Presumably those with some training in philosophy of science will recognize that the decline of Cartesianism occurred long ago.

More germane to contemporary theorizing is the rise of the computational model of mind and its offshoots, such as connectionism and neural networks.[24] The influence of this model has meant that, for the first time, genuine quantitative work could be done on how, for example, human beings process the complex information needed to perform relatively simple tasks like typing.[25] The ramifications for certain work in philosophy of science—although seldom clearly elucidated—are enormous. No matter which of the contemporary models is used, new work in modeling promises that gaps can be filled, so to speak, in a number of issues that affect at least the social sciences, if not the sciences as a whole.

Eliminative materialism, as articulated by Patricia Smith Churchland and Paul Churchland, holds out the promise that what we think of as folk psychological terms (the intentional terms commonly in use in ordinary language such as "hope," "desire," and so forth) will be deemed useless in the future, and that reductive accounts of these states can be given.[26] The somewhat odd consequence of such a position is that it would give one, if one were so inclined, the impetus to believe in the future of a project much like the former positivist project—the unification of the sciences. In any case, there is little question that a number of moves are being made in the neurosciences that are promising from this or similar points of view. There is also the work of Gerald Edelman, the Nobelist whose strictly biological research actually intersects with specifically philosophical questions in some of his published writings.[27]

A great deal of what is being done now in philosophy of mind has to do with trying to become clear on the notion of "consciousness." No matter how much work is done biologically or with respect to connectionist models, it seems that a problem remains with respect to how we can account for a phenomenal sensation of consciousness within the framework of an account of the mental that actually has scientific and theoretical strength.

Daniel Dennett's work in *The Intentional Stance* gives us a way of looking at the mental that, although not neurologically based, may still be useful for the purposes of science. Dennett's major point is that folk psychological terms are useful for their predictive value.[28] In other words, we would like to be able to predict Marie's future actions—simply for the purposes of simplifying our encounters with her—and the knowledge that she wishes that she owned a large house may be helpful in making those predictions. The notion of the folk psychological, then, cuts both ways: Eliminative materialism holds out the promise that the folk psychological can ultimately be dispensed with in favor of some other reductionist account that would be more "scientific." On the other hand, it does not take much ingenuity to determine that folk psychological terms became part of human languages because they already had predictive value.

Thus one replacement—that is, the reductive replacement—is helpful only if we insist on the possibility of a level of precision here that we had not encountered before. Without such insistence, we can already argue that we do indeed have language that gives us a handle on the possibility of predictions, or of meaningful talk about human behavior. Folk psychological terms may be nonnomological, but they trigger a wide variety of responses in most human languages, and it is here that some knowledge of sociolinguistics may be helpful in developing an overview of what it is that the folk psychological does.

As indicated earlier in this section, the split between those who hold the more reductionist position in philosophy of mind and those who do not is similar to the divisions that I have spent a great deal of time explicating in this work. Reductionism in philosophy of mind does indeed remind us of the early positivist project, whereas acceptance of some level of intentionality as signaled by the folk psychological is akin to the positions of those in philosophy of science who have been willing to settle for something less than Complete Accountism, including, of course, most of those whose views I have examined under the rubric "weltanschauungen views." Larry Laudan has written: "I propose that the rationality and progressiveness of a theory are most closely linked—not with its confirmation or its falsification—but rather with its *problem solving effectiveness.*"[29]

Here we have the kind of stance that mirrors a great deal of the debate (on the anti- or nonreductionist side) in contemporary philosophy of mind. It may be neither necessary nor desirable to attempt a Complete Account version of the mental, regardless of whether the account is neurophysiological, connectionist, or something else altogether. Instead, we may be better off admitting that a great deal of what we need with respect to intentionality and the mental is already provided in the formulations of natural language. This kind of attitude saves the intentionality inherent in folk psychological terms without committing us to a larger program.

A Naturalized Theory of Justification

Having examined a number of lines of argument, we are now in a position to begin to develop a notion of naturalized justification and to show how this might be related to au courant philosophy of science.

Most of what has been done in contemporary epistemic justification theory elides the notion that justification, as I indicated before, occurs in a recognizable context and usually does not occur at all unless a challenge is posed to someone who is making a knowledge claim. All of what we have gleaned from the foregoing, including the feminist account of communities of knowers, the notion of naturalization itself, and what I have been able to recover from a recounting of the realist/instrumentalist debates and the controversies in philosophy of mind, assures us that it is possible to construct a distilled theoretical view of justification while relying on intentionality and empiricism, without trying to posit any of the views that make arcane accounts of reference, for example, necessary components of a theory.

A knowledge claim is made in a context, and in many contexts the knower's senses can provide sufficient warrant for the claim. But in other contexts the claim may be challenged—and the notion that the challenge usually comes from without provides us with our first hint that communities are involved. For although the first process of justification may be dyadic, inevitably parts of what is said (or gestured) by that dyad will be repeated to other persons; and dyads, triads, and so forth eventually make up an epistemic community.

Just as community standards will prevail in most instances (and just as those standards will differ from group to group, although most of them will be empirically based), it will also be the case that a community's ways of speaking and modes of communicating will have a great deal to do with what counts as justified in a given context. Oral traditions, for example, will allow for standards that may be different from those employed by members of communities that possess written languages; interestingly enough, much has been written on this topic by a number of feminist theorists, and women of color who come from communities with oral traditions have been instrumental in imposing precision on the meaning of such a tradition.[30]

Thus a number of strands of research from the social sciences may be of help in developing such a theory. But, in its crudest terms, justification in a given context consists of a challenge to an agent, the agent's attempting to meet that challenge with at least one instance of what would constitute a justification, and acquiescence or closure on the part of the challenger. In other words, the challenger curtails the attempt to obtain justification just precisely because the challenger regards the agent's response as adequate.

Now the history of thinking about science in the twentieth century, which I have recapitulated at some length here, might lead us to believe that what counts as justification in everyday circumstances has little or nothing to do with the process of scientific justification. But this coheres only if one sees the process of science as having some epistemically pristine quality that almost all observers—regardless of their stance on the prospects of empiricism—now agree it does not have.

If science is a human endeavor conducted in social circumstances, then what can we posit for it as an account of justification? A theory of justification pertaining to science and scientific activity would, we can hypothesize, very much resemble the skeletal elements of a general theory of justification. Again, except for mathematically oriented theorizing (which, presumably, does not require anything in the nature of empirical justification), scientific activity is simply one particular, possibly more carefully performed, instance of the activity I have just described—general empirical confirmation.

Two examples may help to clarify the nature of these issues. In the first example, I return to material drawn from Haraway's description of the work of the primatologists, reexamining the material with an eye toward what might count as a "better" description. Haraway was concerned that in some cases the daughters, as she had it, went out of their way to obtain confirming evidence for Washburn-related hypotheses by engaging in activities with the primates that might provoke aggression, by selective reporting, and so on. But we can speculate that there might be conditions approaching an ideal for human observation: The primates might not be aware that they are being observed, there might be a complete absence of intervention and provocation, everything that does take place might be recorded (perhaps on videotape), and so forth. Although this "story" does not constitute a "god's-eye view," it *can* claim to be free of the blatant elements of manipulation and distortion that Haraway was able to identify in the work of some of the researchers. Therefore, those who might be interested in or inclined to challenge the results of the research would be able to participate in the social process of confirmation and justification, based on the evidence at hand—a process that is paradigmatically empirical and on which there could presumably be some social agreement.

A second story might involve applied physics and laser technology. It might be hypothesized that a new use could be found for existing technology, and lab work might be done. Again, nothing in the human realm can constitute a divine overview, but if appropriate care is taken with gauges and instruments, and if the results are repeatable and replicable, then the social process of confirmation can point us in a certain direction. This case of the laser research is either simpler or more complex than the case involving the primates, depending on one's point of view, since it is clear that much of the technology involved in measuring laser beams and their applications is an extension of the human eye and hence still involves empirical principles, although the shortcomings of such principles can be ameliorated with technology.

Science, then, occurs in a social frame, as do most human endeavors. If one were asked to articulate very bluntly the major difference between a scientific and a nonscientific endeavor, the response may not concern the questions asked so much as the care taken in formulating the answers. Both ordinary situations and scientific situations almost always involve the empirical.[31] It is not that one is "more" empirical than the other; rather, the difference frequently amounts to a greater care taken in empiricism. If this is the hallmark of scientific thinking, then we need to be still more precise about how to formulate a theory of justification to accommodate it.

Sociolinguistics and Justification

Much that has transpired in naturalized epistemology (and that has been used to at least minimally address justification) involves cognitive processes. But this blithe acceptance of the notion that a cognitive account is the only type of account drawn from contemporary theory that might be helpful ignores work done in linguistics and sociolinguistics. The work of Erving Goffman and William Labov, for example, different as it may be, is extremely helpful in getting clear on the social circumstances that surround a process such as justification—which is, after all, a speech act process—and on the sociolinguistic cues that accompany it.

In preceding sections I have written of this process as largely a verbal encounter, and I have directed notions of intentionality and empirical justification toward it. The polarizing effects of certain types of discourse now prevalent in science studies obscure the very real fact that work already exists in the social sciences that can assist us in modeling speech acts and situations surrounding them.

Although Erving Goffman is in some senses more a sociologist of language than a sociolinguist, his work is helpful in establishing norms for public encounters.[32] Goffman points out in many of his works that much of what transpires between individuals, particularly in situations of dyadic encounter, is driven by what he refers to as "face saving strategies."[33] We have, for example, an entire repertoire of such responses— laughter, fixed smiles, turned glances—that allow us to deflect attention from ourselves in embarrassing situations and that are part of our cultural heritage (although such responses do, of course, vary from culture to culture). The importance of work like Goffman's is its acknowledgment that social processes of justification amount to more than mere agreement on empirical data or mere acquiescence on the part of one who has challenged the knowledge claim of another. It is here that some of Latour's commentary in *Science in Action* actually is most accurate: If, as Latour wants us to believe, the "finding" that DNA is a double helix is very reliant on the verbally expressed desire of a number of scientists to have an easy double-helix shape to work with, one can imagine that the circumstances surrounding the expression of such desires are also important. In other words, as the popular culture teaches us, body language counts. Gestures are an important part of our repertoire (the knowledge claim maker who does not have quite enough evidence may exhibit face-saving strategies when challenged, thus indicating embarrassment), as are the questions with tag endings, the curt responses in what sociolinguists refer to as adjacency pairs, and the myriad other small cues that make up our communicative lives.

We can glean insights like these not only from Goffman's work but also from the work of theorists such as Labov or even Deborah Tannen, whose popular work is now very familiar. Since social class markers are also important in communication—and since, as the feminist theorists have reminded us, social class has been one of the determinants in keeping many out of the enterprise of science—any work in sociolinguistics that aids us in dealing with the notion of social class can prove extremely helpful.

Some of Labov's early work on social class differences among New Yorkers and also among residents of Martha's Vineyard indicates that people are so attuned to relevant social class differences that "lower class" speakers may frequently alter their manner of speech in the presence of those whose speech patterns are markedly of a higher social class.[34] This is more important than it might superficially seem—the desire to imitate speech patterns can lead to the desire to imitate beliefs, to replicate the content of what is said, and so forth. Thus any kind of account of the social process of justification must also consider these factors—the process can be modeled not only on the individualistic level of the cognizers involved but also on the level of speech acts, on microscopic information relating to the sociolinguistic components of such acts, and so forth. The popular work of Deborah Tannen derives directly from her academic work, all of which moves us in this same direction. That the well-known phenomenon of following statements with the tag ending "isn't it?" is associated with female speakers indicates not only that women tend to be unsure of their status and even hesitant with regard to their opinions but also that listeners may misinterpret this hesitation as an inability to produce evidence for an opinion, as a genuine uncertainty about the epistemic status of an opinion, and so forth. It is indisputable that this simple phenomenon may have something to do with the success of women in science, since it is too naive to assume that every woman who is trained scientifically has learned once and for all to divest herself of these markers of female speech patterns.

Thus any kind of overview of justification as a naturalizable process indicates to us that many of the current controversies in philosophy of science, philosophy of mind, epistemology, and even philosophy of language are relevant to the structure of such a theory of justification, but perhaps only if we develop the ability to see the forest for the trees. As I previously indicated, parts of the realist/instrumentalist controversy, if considered from the realist perspective, would seem to indicate that theory of justification intended to do work in the sciences would have to incorporate a theory of reference for scientific terms, would have to give some account of how the terms do in fact refer, and so forth. But this is precisely why we want to utilize the areas referred to in such controversies only insofar as they are helpful in trying to create a theory of justification that works in social situations.

The notion that scientists form a community and that communities of knowers are the ultimate epistemic arbiters, referred to repeatedly throughout this work, is one that pushes us in the direction of a conversational model of justification that saves the notion of empirical justification while simultaneously providing a base for some of the insights furnished by the weltanschauungen views. We need a theory that enables us to grapple with the concept, left over from the Received View, that there is such a thing as the context of discovery, without necessarily divorcing that concept from the context of justification. In short, we need a theoretical view that helps us accommodate the at least partially adequate notions, taken from Haraway and Latour, that justification is political, without abandoning the realist insight that science does indeed have some successes (and even some instances of progress) that we must also be able to account for.

Toward a Scientific Theory of Epistemic Justification

A theory of epistemic justification that would be relevant to the sciences must encompass the conversational model that I alluded to in the previous section and must also encompass elements of stringent empiricism. That is, if we are to give science its due, so to speak, and further any notion of scientific activity that goes above and beyond the extremely relativistic concepts that derive from science studies and the post-weltanschauungen views, we must develop a notion of justification that adequately accommodates the concept of empiricism.

Thus our model for ordinary justification relies on a kind of simplistic, everyday empiricism that helps us manage our lives—we might think of it as a more sophisticated version of Hume's original "out-through-the-door-and-not-the-window." But surely science requires something more. The "something more" here can come from two sources. First, it stems partly from the notion of a community of knowers, the same notion that I have indicated has its contemporary roots in feminist theory. Constant checking and feedback from a variety of sources promote empirical confirmation and make it less likely that purely political motives will prevail, although there may be exceptional cases where this kind of checking does not actually take place. (Recent accounts in the press indicate that this lack of checking and feedback is more common than some of us would like to believe.) A second source of strength for the concept of a theory of epistemic justification sufficiently hardy for the sciences comes from the notion of the tool as an extension and further precision of the eye. In other words, particularly in the hard sciences, comparatively little will be accomplished with unaided human sight, which was the basis for most work in seventeenth- and eighteenth-century science. Contemporary work will almost always require tools, and this is also true in the social sciences to a greater extent than may be immediately obvious.

These two sources of strength—the concept of a community of knowers and the concept of human senses aided by technology and tools—add greatly to our notion that epistemic justification is largely conversational and communicative and that previous models of such justification, derived originally from Cartesian accounts of solitary knowers, do not do justice to the context of discovery for science. Thus, in a more contemporary account, the context of discovery and the context of justification merge, and what we now know about scientific activity more or less precludes the kind of a priori theorizing about scientific logic in which the positivists were originally engaged.

Whether or not science can withstand the challenge of science studies is, in a certain sense, a moot question. However painful the charges of those who see feminist and radical critiques of science as silly or perverse, the kernel of accuracy in their responses is that many or most practicing scientists probably have not been affected by these areas of criticism.

To recapitulate, then, a sketch of a theory of justification for science revolves around a core notion of conversational (or at least communicative) endeavors that may be thought of as involving at least two persons from the start. The person who is the knowledge claim maker, when challenged by someone else, will issue a string of justifiers in order to bolster that knowledge claim.[35] In a scientific context, this notion of justification is strengthened by the repetition of the challenges and responses by a community of knowers, all of whom presumably engaged in similar or like investigations and many of whom with firsthand knowledge of the material. In addition, particularly in the hard sciences, there would be many ways of reinforcing sensory data to enable firmer conclusions than would be available to one using only the unaided senses. Finally, our knowledge of the social sciences could, over the long run, help us refine such models by allusion not only to branches of cognitive science but also to such areas as sociology of language and sociolinguistics, which indicate that a great deal of what we call "communication" is either nonverbal or relies on aspects of the verbal that are themselves not communicative of content, such as accent and intonation.

The tensions inherent in our discussion of science, broadly construed, revolve around two areas, and the dialogue tends to shift rapidly back and forth between these two poles without articulating a middle ground. The older tradition asks us to think of an idealized science and to ask ourselves what a theory of justification would look like in ideal circumstances—that this type of theorizing is embedded in the Western tradition is an obvious fact. Although those who wrote in the tradition of the Vienna Circle, as we saw in earlier chapters, never claimed that their material was in any way descriptive, many now *do* claim that this lack of descriptive validity indicates that positivistic theorizing fails to illuminate science.

The second pole, manifested most obviously by the views and the social-science work that came subsequently, has no interest in the logic of justification and may in fact see the process of "justification" as a hodgepodge of accidental strokes of luck, power plays, political maneuvers, and everyday chitchat. The difficulty with this view is that it so thoroughly undermines the claims of science to greater rigor that it reduces scientific activity to a status somewhere below a fifth grader's earnest efforts with a chemistry set.

The middle ground here would seem to be that, although we can no longer require or rely exclusively on a logic of justification, we need theories of justification that do indeed accept the existence of empirical confirmation and that at least partially shade off into an area of independence from purely political concerns. The relevant phrase here is "shade off"— in many cases, these theories may not shade off. But we must not fail to acknowledge that the very reason we can criticize research on the primates, for example, is that Haraway is presenting us with cases that fail to adhere to an ideal of research that we already possess. What needs to be acknowledged is that there will be at least a few real-world cases that will come closer to this ideal than others.

A great deal has been written recently about how the "decline of the Western narrative" is related to a number of points that, apparently, are supposed to somehow involve current science studies. To be fair, we can see at least a partial relationship in the work of the theorists whose writings I examined in Chapter 5, and we can also see how this work itself would advance other research in the same direction. (In fact, one might be tempted to say that this relationship forms a "hermeneutic circle.") But whether or not one cares to press the relationship between science studies and other work that is done in the humanities and social sciences, it can also be argued that a close analysis of the situation yields an outcome slightly different from what one might expect to come from postmodernism.

Empiricism is a way of examining our surroundings that we employ in our everyday life. Although, as indicated earlier, there may be a few individuals who make great use of the nonempirical in most of their activities, this would entail an exceptional set of circumstances and would still not prevent these individuals from making empirical judgments about how, for example, to open the elevator door in case of emergency. Thus the current work proclaiming the decline of empiricism, or its lack of import, is more metaphorical than anything else—it may well be the case (as has been indicated by a great deal of the work that I have examined here) that science has lost prestige in the developed countries, particularly since the 1960s, but this does not mean that our examinations of science have yielded the conclusion, as Harding phrased it, that we should "throw out the baby with the bathwater."[36] If it means anything at all, it is perhaps that we should take a sharper look at how science came to be in this predicament and how the embattled aspects of science might be resuscitated.

Asking ourselves these questions may reveal some surprising answers. As I argued earlier, we do indeed have standards about how research should be conducted, and we also carry in our minds ideals of what research should be; although these ideals may not be achievable, something close to them probably is achievable since our images of the research that is currently under way in a variety of fields already stem from older images of human activity that we have internalized over the years.

To ask science to try to approach at least some of these ideals is, then, not to ask the impossible. And in articulating and setting out these ideals, we come much closer to developing an overview of science that is actually of some use. Although such an overview eschews the emphasis on the hyperidealized logicism of the positivists, it does carry its own set of standards. What we need to do is come to some degree of clarity about how these standards are implemented and what their uses might be.

Part Four

Conclusion

9

Concluding Comments

Given the truism that scientists and those who actually practice science have little or no interest in science studies or philosophy of science, it is not clear what the overall cultural impact of science studies amounts to. One might be tempted to say that it amounts to very little—except perhaps to further the aims of some literature courses—were it not for the fact that works like *Higher Superstition,* authored by scientists (in this case, Paul Gross and Norman Levitt), demonstrate that it apparently does have some impact.

At the least sophisticated level, it might well be the case that one of the main results of the current alliance of radical and feminist critique in science has been an opening up of science programs, in some cases with stated aims, in a sort of affirmative action. These changes should not be seen as merely temporary; if they last for any reasonable length of time, they will have added greatly to the number of women and persons of color who are scientists, and this will be no small accomplishment.

Science studies and the contemporary emphasis on sociology of science might be looked at in another way. It often happens that a certain line of critique focuses on its subject in such a way that we feel compelled to go back for a second look. Because the Received View has taken such a beating, and because the phrase "positivism" is frequently bandied about without any understanding of what the positivist project originally involved, many who work in history, philosophy, and sociology of science are now more sensitive to what was originally constitutive of the positivist position, and in a sense a small retrieval has occurred. The logic of justification was, as we have seen here, no minor enterprise. The attempt to construct such a logic, whatever its original impetus, was laudatory in the sense that it provided a framework for an idealized type of epistemic justification. The fact that this was never consistent with the practice of science was acknowledged from the outset, as has been repeated here many times.

In this chapter I plan to recapitulate briefly some of the more obvious effects of the critiques that I have examined in previous chapters, and then devote some time to the future of science studies. Stated crudely, science studies either does or does not make a difference. If it does make a difference, we have to become clear on what that difference is.

From Positivism to the Weltanschauungen Views

As we saw in the early chapters of this work, positivism was no mere creed or formula. Despite the numerous contemporary misuses of the term, the doctrine promulgated by members of the Vienna Circle was noteworthy for its reliance on the rigid epistemology that I examined with respect to the correspondence rules.[1] These rules, despite the rigorous foundationalism that they embody, would not be so noteworthy as a formalization of the logic of justification were they not tied together by biconditionals—as I noted earlier, the biconditional formulation of the rules allowed each statement in the language of observation to be interpreted in terms of a statement in the language of theory.

It is this aspect of positivism that forms its heart, and in a sense this is the aspect that became the most controversial. W. V. O. Quine and others later cast doubt on the extent to which we could ever formulate statements of observation that could, antecedently, be purely demarcated from statements of theory, and this line of argument did much to dismiss the remaining influence of positivism at the time that Quine was writing, the 1960s.

But the other important historical consequence of the Received View lies in its connections to the attempt to move notions of space and time away from a metaphysics that was at best quasi-Hegelian. Both work in logic itself, initiated by Gottlob Frege toward the end of the nineteenth century, and work in physics indicated a level of precision that had not been available to previous philosophical attempts to deal with the concepts of space and time. Kantian analyses of these concepts, for example, labeled them "pure forms of intuition." But this kind of labeling did not assist in the development of a metaphysical view that would be consonant with the new work done in physics. This new work demanded new levels of conciseness and precision, and this kind of precision could be purchased, in a sense, by employing Russellian logical atomism, or something like it, for the formulation of statements in the language of observation. Thus, as we observed when examining Otto Neurath's material, "red here now" was the sort of statement that could be formulated in the predicate logic and (according to the Vienna Circle) that could serve as a paradigmatic statement of observation.

Thus two lines of argument—one having to do with the theory/observation distinction and one having to do with epistemic foundationalism—began to undermine the status of positivism. As recounted earlier, Austinian objections to foundationalism were articulated in just these terms, since J. L. Austin was largely replying to A. J. Ayer's *Language, Truth and Logic* and since Ayer's work directly acknowledged its debt to the Vienna Circle. In his work, Austin reminds the reader that any statement about qualia—however hedged, and cast in whatever first-person language—could potentially be rebutted. This undercutting argument also did great damage to the Received View, since it was clear that the import of epistemic foundationalism for the view was large.

The move toward the weltanschauungen views was fueled, then, partly as a response to the perceived defects of positivism and partly as a move forward to try to provide a view of science that was more in tune with the context of discovery. For if positivism was a response to the work in physics in the early part of the twentieth century, then moves against science in the culture at large might be thought of as an outgrowth of World War II and its aftermath. The desire to find out how science "really is" no doubt stems at least partly from the notion that the purity of science was a specious concept, and one that was destructive in many ways.

If we step back for a moment from philosophy of science and use some of the material that we now have from science studies (and that I have investigated here) to try to come to grips with the rise in popularity of work like Thomas Kuhn's, we can see that this work was itself reflective of general cultural trends. The chaotic aftermath of the war meant that a general interest in historicism became somewhat politicized; therefore, any interest in the history of science was bound to reflect notions of the power structure of science.

It is this interest in the progress of science, along with the specific criticisms of more transparent technical areas, that led to the emergence of views like those of Kuhn and Imre Lakatos. But what is also remarkable about these stances is that they gave rise to still another set of twists and turns that might be deemed more relativistic. For if it is accurate to say that science was never pure, then any type of analysis that could be applied to one level of science could be applied to another. Thus we see something like a path or progression to science studies as it currently stands.

The Move Toward Philosophy of the Social Sciences

The work of David Bloor, Peter Winch, and to some extent even Bruno Latour can be seen, then, as attempts to get clear on what a more precise (and sociologically accurate) account of the relationship between scientific epistemology and social structures might actually be. These thinkers feel free to undercut any notion of an epistemology that has alabaster pristineness, because they are able to establish absolutely no point at which epistemology precedes the social. This line of argument might be thought, in its own way, to be an offshoot of Quine—acknowledging that concepts are irrevocably tied to language and that language is indisputably in the sphere of the social does not build a case for anything that is epistemically foundational.

Nevertheless, the three thinkers mentioned above pushed this stand further than ever before. As Bloor himself says: "However, a more naturalistic approach would simply take the facts as they are and invent a theory to explain them."[2] Viewing science as a series of exchanges, like virtually any other social phenomenon of the contemporary world, Bloor is unable to find an area of scientific expertise or endeavor that is not affected by politics, power struggles, and exchange commodification. Focusing on individual scientists' motivations for achievement goes a long way toward denying the existence of a realm that is free from petty disputes and that has the protected status of a Cartesian chamber. Winch uses a similar line—the separation of the epistemological from the social has always been an artificial one, and nothing in contemporary philosophy (especially since Wittgenstein) encourages us to believe that we can continue to draw such spurious divisions.

Here we can see not only the rise in importance of the social but also the decline in importance of the notion of confirmation. The idea that some phenomena can be confirmed more or less independently of our antecedent beliefs (and more or less independently of our desires) loses a great deal of its impetus here. It is from this point an easy leap to Latour's *Science in Action*—Latour is not interested in claims that it is possible to "confirm" or "disconfirm" the status of DNA as a double helix. What he is interested in is the networks of power and authority that push us in the direction of claiming that DNA is a double helix once it has already been claimed that such a conclusion would be "neat," "elegant," or scientifically appealing.

To be more specific, what Latour relates is another, more sophisticated version of our gut-level reaction to much scientific research: We are tempted to say, without knowing much about the situation, that the desire to find confirmation frequently produces confirmation, and indeed budding scientists are usually warned by their mentors against this very phenomenon. But the fact that one has been warned, or that one is aware of the phenomenon on some level, is not enough to ensure that the phenomenon does not occur. Thus what Latour is implicitly saying is that the wish-fulfillment style of "confirmation" may indeed be the most statistically frequent; even more importantly, he seems to be saying that we have no adequate criteria for distinguishing between "genuine" confirmation and confirmation of this other sort. How can we be sure that the desire to replicate someone's experimental results on the genetic splicing material in laboratory mice does not, in fact, lead to a misinterpretation of results?[3] It is especially difficult to obtain certainty here if, as so often happens, the particular research reported was done without others in the room and with no other method of verification than the researcher's written notes.

All of the descriptive work in history and philosophy of science moved during the 1960s and 1970s in one direction. This work encouraged us to see science as the flawed practice of fallible human beings rather than as an endeavor best examined through the guise of the logic of justification or through the lens of an incorrigibly foundationalist epistemology. That new epicycles were placed on this descriptive work has been apparent since the 1980s with the waves of feminist and radical criticism that I have examined, and we can trace an obvious path between the social-sciences way of viewing science as a whole and these other, more politically pronounced critiques.

The Radical Critiques in Toto

Part of what gives these critiques their impact is that, taken together, they undermine virtually all that is constitutive of the practice of contemporary science, even when science is viewed in the Kuhnian or Lakatosian ways that I described earlier. Androcentrism is apparent throughout science and science-related activity, and views that are not positivistic are only slightly, if at all, less masculinist or androcentric than views that are. The radical critique, while hitting science from another angle, ties into the feminist criticisms because both lines attack masculinist and class-related bias.[4]

It might be worthwhile to recapitulate briefly the origins of such bias. As mentioned earlier, all intellectual endeavor in the Western tradition ultimately has its roots in the kind of endeavor envisioned by Plato and Aristotle: intellectual inquiry performed by upper-class privileged males under conditions of leisure, where the leisure is made possible (particularly in Aristotle's view) by the labor of impoverished people, people held in slavery, or women. One might not think that material from the ancients could prove so powerful in setting the stage for a contemporary outlook were it not for the fact that it is transparently obvious that this very tradition reaches down into our century. The structure of American colleges and universities—and of European universities also—until very recently reflected these hallowed if unarticulated beliefs about who is and is not fit to participate in intellectual pursuits.

The radical critique is as strong as it is because it reminds us not only of this structure but also of how this particular set of social circumstances is tied into the economic structure. Here, as I indicated before, Marxist lines of argument become powerful: Not only is intellectual enterprise in the hands of powerful white males but they themselves are the purveyors of the very bourgeois culture that stands to benefit most from science and that directs its operations. Writing in the nineteenth century, at the height of bourgeois power, Marx noted how such social institutions as marriage—however idealized they might seem—reflected the need for primogeniture, inherited power and wealth, and enforced domesticity. Engels, in his "Preface to *The Condition of the Working Class in England*," noted the extent to which colonialism was trying to create new markets and predicted that what we now refer to as the Third World would become the dumping ground for First World products once exploitation had begun.[5]

The two critiques taken together might be thought of as radically feminist or as gender radical. In any case, regardless of the difficulty of determining a label that does justice to the merger of these two lines of argument, they are indeed provocative. As we have seen, Donna Haraway's work alone exemplifies their combination, since she sees the lack of privileging as one source for making a statement about the aims of science.

What a theorist such as Haraway wants to posit as lack of epistemic privilege can be seen as a response to the androcentric and bourgeois privileging of a certain sort of stance. In other words, we can consider something that, on the one hand, might appear to be straightforward, such as the articulated version of the Received View with its correspondence rules, and we can consider the critiques of it. The feminist critique would ask us to remember that the Complete Accountism inherent in such a view (the Unity of Science thesis, for example) is the product of ramified male personality development and exhibits the signs of stylistic aggression that Evelyn Fox Keller, for one, mentions in her work. The Marxist, or politically radical, critique would ask us to remember that the privilege of seeing things in this Complete Accounts view also stems from economic and social privilege and is unlikely to be available as a psychological distancing device to those who do not come from a certain level of bourgeois background.

Thus it is accurate to say that these two critiques reinforce each other, and it is also accurate to say that what can be gleaned from one critique could, at least in principle, be gleaned from the other, particularly since it is clear that Marx and Engels, for example, anticipated much of what would later become the feminist critique in their "Origin of Family, Private Property and the State."[6] There have been, however, still other turns that led to the outgrowth of what we now refer to as science studies. Although I have alluded to the history of science qua discipline here, I have not analyzed what it is, precisely, that history of science as a specialty has brought to science studies on the whole.

The Importance of History of Science

The journals *Isis* and *Science in Context*, the growth in the number of academic institutions offering HPS (History and Philosophy of Science) programs, and the general historicizing of many disciplines, including literary disciplines, all signal the importance of history and historical aspects of various academic endeavors.

The history-of-science approach has been still one more relativizing aspect of science studies, and one that does double duty, so to speak, because as it relativizes it provides at least a minimally accurate factual base from which to structure such relativism. A number of recent pieces have addressed specific problems—whether, for example, some of the concepts used in Aristotle's *Physics* and *On Generation* actually do or do not prefigure the use of such concepts in later science, and so forth. Inevitably, the upshot of such studies is to add still further impetus to the consideration of the social and political factors that underlie "discoveries," scientific hypothesis construction, and so forth. Just as the work of Stephen Greenblatt on Renaissance England has led to a better understanding of Shakespeare since it helps us fill in the blanks with regard to Shakespeare's missing allusions, work in the history of science furthers many of the same aims supported by the radical critiques (and, for that matter, by at least some of what was promulgated by the weltanschauungen views).

Historical work certainly tends to undercut many of the more rigid realisms and does a great deal to undermine the notion of continuity or stability of referent. If, as we have seen, the realist position may be characterized as holding that "existing theories provide approximate knowledge . . . of the unobservable structures which underlie observable phenomena,"[7] and if that position may be linked to the maintenance of a certain sort of reference, then work in the history of science can do a great deal to dissuade us from such claims. Here the historian Michael Wolff comments on the move between Copernican and Newtonian mechanics: "Thus there is good reason to say that the so-called Copernican revolution was brought to a close only by Newtonian mechanics, which provided an adequate explanation for the motions of the earth. . . . [But] it is obvious that the concepts of inertia and gravitation have an exact equivalence neither in Copernicus' theory nor in the theory of his contemporaries."[8]

Thus the relativizing effect of historical inquiry becomes apparent when attempts to create a spurious continuity are found not to bear fruit or when attempts to show that science has been on a unified and progressive course from day one, so to speak, are found not to hold up. History of science has burgeoned as an area of inquiry not only because of the new emphasis on things historical but because these kinds of studies can help us clarify and resolve other, more philosophical and sociological issues in science. The conservative, logic-of-justification views with which we were concerned in the opening chapters perhaps tried to find linkages in previous scientific work where none existed. To be able to now do actual research that shows that the attempts to make such linkages were and are meretricious forwards our understanding both of science and of its practitioners.

Finally, one last linkup between history of science *simpliciter* and the sorts of views we have been examining here comes from the radical critique. If Marxist criticisms of bourgeois society tend to articulate the ways in which science is part of the large enterprise of capitalist exploitation and domination, then these types of criticisms can be made at virtually every step of the way for the history of science, at least since its emergence from the Middle Ages. Sixteenth- and seventeenth-century growth in the sciences can be seen, for example, as allied to expanding markets and progressing European notions of how to secure further markets. The advances in science during the nineteenth and twentieth centuries can be directly linked to notions of domination and colonial exploitation, even if in some cases the linkages fail to be immediately obvious. History of science here can give us factual accounts that reinforce, at least to some degree, the more interpretive accounts that we obtain from the radical critique. Interestingly enough, some of the material comes together in ways that might not be expected. Primatology derives much of its early impetus from the explorations in East Africa, in particular, by European entrepreneurs in pursuit of land or in other ways involved in the exploitation of colonial markets.

If all of the foregoing pushes us in a certain direction, it must be toward the articulation of what might count as the skeleton of a more progressive theory of justification for science. I have already discussed at length the notion that science, as a justificatory process, proceeds by social communication, in the same way that all of our other justificatory processes do. It is time now to be more explicit about this process.

Justification and Science

Combining a number of lines of thought from all of our inquiries, we can see that a view of justification that is less centered on the logic of decision and that is simultaneously aware of the social nature of the process of justification is one that can be useful as a model for the sciences today. Such a model is of necessity communitarian. Borrowing from the insights of such feminist theorists as Lynn Hankinson Nelson and Helen Longino, we can see that justification begins perhaps in dyadic inquiry, moving on and spilling over into other dyads, triads, and larger groups.

More importantly, many strands of inquiry from what we term "naturalized epistemology" can help us pave the way for a theoretical overview. Not only is it the case that the cognitive portion of the process of justification could be modeled (and this could be either an individualistic or at least a dyadic model), but perhaps more importantly sociolinguistic information and theory taken from sociology of language and the sociology of everyday life aid us in developing a conversational model of justification. Such a model captures a great deal of the type of insight we can glean from thinkers as diverse as Bloor and Latour without sacrificing the notion of empirical confirmation.

We are all coworkers in the process of epistemic justification, and in the sciences the only distinctions that are made—distinctions to which the radical critics are, of course, quite sensitive—have to do with the training and status of the investigators. Nevertheless, in principle many persons (perhaps virtually all persons) could potentially engage in some kind of scientific activity, and the insight that the confirmational process for such activity is not significantly different from what it is in an everyday context is a valuable one that should not be lost.

Tersely, then, our model matches the brevity of some of Latour's boxed caricatures in *Science in Action* without reducing the notion of confirmation to a sort of partylike wishful thinking taking place in the scientific arena on a regular basis.[9] But whereas Latour seems to think that what counts as confirmation is more or less repetition of the desired result— "DNA has the form of a double helix"—what is probably a more accurate model is that the repetition takes place with respect to social recognition of what counts as evidence. In other words, conversationally based models of the social process of confirmation involve:

(a) a stated claim, with perhaps some allusion to evidence for the claim;
(b) a challenge or inquiry from another about the claim or the evidence for it;
(c) a repetition of the claim, this time with citation of evidence or, in certain circumstances, actual physical production of the evidence; and
(d) iterations of the above throughout a number of social channels.

The importance of the model is twofold. First, since it is conversational, it increases our awareness of the social nature of confirmation and does so in a way that allows us to see that a great deal of what we count as confirmation or justification is brought to the fore by dyadic interaction. Second, the model forwards a notion of empirical evidence. Unlike the more relativistic models, it does not presume that all stories are on a par with each other. Some stories will count precisely because, under social conditions, they have repeatedly been confirmed or justified. This does not mean, of course, that they could then match some "god's-eye view" of justification, that that justification could be set down in a manner that would accord with some canons of confirmation, or that some other ideal has been met.

But this, surely, is precisely the insight that we should have been able to obtain from the work of the weltanschauungen theorists and those in the social sciences who were first concerned to move us, as investigators of science, away from the logic of justification. The difficulty with an ideal that can rarely or never be instantiated is that it remains just that—an ideal. It is not so much the case that what the positivists wrote with respect to correspondence rules fails to cohere or does not make sense as it is the case that there are strong reasons (and philosophical reasons, at that) for thinking that no actual instance of the matchup that the correspondence rules ask for can actually be found.

It is the latter area that is the cause for concern in the theorizing immediately following World War II and in the work done since then. In a sense, all work in the sciences is prescriptive, because we can look at the work done by members of the Vienna Circle as a set of "oughts" about what science should or should not do. Even if it is the case that we can find comparatively few examples of the logic of confirmation at work in real-world confirmation, for instance, perhaps we should think of these logical models as areas for which we should aim.

But the difficulty with the sorts of views of science that I examined in Chapters 2 and 3 is that they are not, in general, instantiable. One cannot find "pure" instances of science, and it is not realistic to think that the enterprise of science—since it involves human investigators and not robots—could proceed in this manner. Because of the notion that prescription is recommendation, it could be argued (and, indeed, has been argued by proponents of the other views I have examined here) that there is little point in pursuing projects that cannot be instantiated.

Thus science needs to be given a philosophical overview that is consonant with the functioning of scientists. In rounding out this project, it is fruitful to think in terms of comparison. Work being done in the sciences today can be viewed in more traditional terms or along the lines of the critiques that I have examined here. The contemporary controversy over the possibility of life on Mars, recently reported extensively in the media, is but one example.[10] It is interesting to note that the desire to believe in this case is overwhelming, despite the fact that the organisms described in the press, if indeed such organisms exist, would be comparable to the lowest forms of life found on Earth during the course of the planet's earlier evolution. I will now examine differing responses to contemporary areas of scientific research along the lines of the three broad categorizations scrutinized in this work.

Responses to Contemporary Research

The recent "life on Mars" controversy is but one example of how the media, interacting with other social forces, create a situation that then becomes a sort of intellectual fait accompli. An overview of the situation in the October 1996 issue of *Scientific American* indicates that this is not the first time that alleged meteoric evidence of life on Mars has surfaced.[11] More importantly, the summary article indicates that there are strong reasons for believing that the apparent organic origin of the anomalous findings in the meteorite is just that—apparent—and that the findings can be accounted for in an inorganic way.[12]

Leaving aside for the moment the tendency to want to believe—and its relationship to many other contemporary sociological phenomena, such as the decline of formal religion, the rising interest in the occult, and so forth—a number of responses to the time, money, and attention invested in the research are possible. David S. McKay of NASA and eight colleagues extensively investigated meteorite ALH84001 (and others as well) with electron microscopy, and other researchers from other institutions have been drawn into the fray. Traditional research is here concerned with alternative hypotheses and with the notion that there must be some way to account for the "tiny, teardrop-shaped crystals of magnetite and iron sulfide" without accepting the hypothesis that they are bacterial residue.[13] But what of the lines of critique that I have brought to bear on other issues? Although so far the media have not, in general, used these arguments on this particular question, one could imagine their doing so.

The feminist critique, in particular, might find at least two points of focus in the "life on Mars" controversy. Aside from the obvious "desire to believe" that I have just discussed, another blatant point of response is that the issue smacks of Complete Accountism. In other words, not only is finding life on Mars, were such a finding to be documented beyond contention, interesting from the point of view of what it says about conditions on earth, but it is also interesting from the larger point of view of what it says about life-in-general-and-its-place-in-the-universe. The same *Scientific American* article that carries the disclaimers about the importance of the evidence also quotes Stanley Miller of the University of California at San Diego as saying: "My impression is that bacterial life exists on planets around one in ten stars, maybe more."[14] One goal, then, of finalizing the Martian life debate is to come to definitive conclusions about life in the universe on the whole. We know so little about galaxies other than our own that it is not clear what possible conclusions could be drawn from such a small arena, yet it is obvious from the tone of the comments in the media that it is in just these terms that most of the scientists involved in the dispute are thinking.

Another version of what feminist theorists might well label the masculinist or androcentric Complete Accountism of the project can be found on a smaller scale in the construction of the evidence in the meteorite itself. As we saw in the material cited with respect to the "teardrop-shaped" structures, there is more than one way to interpret the evidence, and it is tendentious to insist that the evidence is biological.

This tendentiousness is, of course, part of the androcentric stylistic aggression that we have seen in other arenas of scientific endeavor. In a sense, of course, any argument will be forced—part of what it means to build a case or a line of argument is to push a point of view, and this may mean that we may have to push a point of view where it will not go. But in this particular instance the counterarguments are strong; there are already developed lines of argument that can account for the evidence in other, nonbiological ways. Only a strong desire to believe—an aggressive desire to make the evidence conform to one's favorite hypothesis—can explain the pronounced and somewhat forced stance of those who insist on interpreting the evidence biologically. Like so many other contemporary enterprises in science, this issue smacks of the aggressive and masculinist theorizing on which much of the theoretical structure of the sciences is built.

A radical critic of science must surely be more than annoyed at the amount of time and money spent supporting the rather dubious claim that the given meteorite presents evidence of "life" on Mars. Some of the lines of argument here are obvious, and so to repeat them here does no real service to the radical stance; one can say that the money could have been spent on more useful work, and so forth. But the most poignant linkup here, it appears, occurs with the feminist material just adduced. It is not merely that the project is expensive and time consuming; it is that the project is expensive and time consuming in ways that show us what science is all about and that reveal in rather startling ways the ego-investments of those involved. Desire to interpret the evidence in one way is one thing; expenditure (of time or money) is another. It is the unification of these desires and expenditures that recalls, on a small scale, boundless past wastage from the vast sums spent on the buildup of nuclear armaments to the staggering waste of time and resources on products such as coolants for refrigerators and the exploitation of the environment in national parks and elsewhere for financial purposes.

Thus the radical critique intersects with the feminist critique in ways that are profoundly revelatory. In addition to the foregoing, the radical critic will notice the inevitable attempts at commodification that we can visualize as springing from the Mars research, almost without regard to the ultimate "success" of the contentions involved. Although commodification has not, as near as can be determined, yet occurred, it is perhaps an inevitable by-product of any highly publicized line of scientific research in a capitalist society. One can imagine a number of products and publications that might be related to life on Mars; there is undoubtedly (somewhere) a "Life on Mars" World Wide Web page on the internet, and so forth. The original Marxist stance that markets must be found above and beyond the so-called home markets can have few more obvious successes in the way of prognostication than what has occurred since the 1970s.[15] Markets have expanded to Third World countries, and the merger of the newly created international mania for certain products with the developing technologies and remnant cultures of such areas has led to the rise of postmodern youth who adhere nationalistically to portions of the local culture while wearing Madonna T-shirts. The scientific equivalents to this, of course, are the various waves of publicity (much of it unwarranted) surrounding everything from cold fusion to lines of research in cancer. These research lines themselves then become commodified, and the researchers associated with them media stars.

How does a quest such as the search to confirm the existence of interplanetary life look to those who are more traditionally minded with respect to the sciences? The short answer is that it appears to be science as usual. Because of the wave of government-funded scientific activity that arose subsequent to World War II, and because of the intrusion of the media into the sciences—an intrusion that is, at this point, decades old—there is little reason to believe that those who are engaged in science on an everyday basis and who cannot step back from it, as it were, would see the "life on Mars" blitz as anything other than business as usual. Seen from a statistically average perspective, the battle between the two competing evidential camps is nothing more than the usual scientific debate about whose evidence has the upper hand. After all, even though it is clear (as I have just indicated and as Sears contends) that there are strong arguments favoring the nonbiological origins hypothesis, there are also strong arguments that support the opposing hypothesis. In other words, a plausible and coherent position can be created on either side. Furthermore, the kinds of critical analyses that might be made by feminist critics, radical critics, or any other critics are simply beside the point to most working scientists and to those who noncritically support their efforts. After all, there is no reason to believe that the "life on Mars" scenario is any more or less spurious than a number of other scenarios that have been played out in the press in the past few decades, including all of the contretemps surrounding infertility work, the human genome project, and so on.

In other words, the weaknesses of the intellectual structure of the situation, as perceived by one point of view, are strengths insofar as the articulation of another stance is concerned. Why should it not be the case that we, as human beings, can spend a great deal of effort trying to answer questions about extraterrestrial life—questions, after all, that hearken back to the sorts of grandiose queries that inform philosophy originally and at its base? And why should it not be the case that, given that technology and the media work hand in hand, so to speak, the rise in power of both over a period of time gives rise to other phenomena, including a barrage of overpublicity with regard to certain scientific projects?

A given debate such as that concerning extraterrestrial life on planets in our own solar system is the debate about science writ small. Each conundrum within the public area of inquiry mirrors and reflects other paradoxes that we have already uncovered in the questions currently being asked about science itself. Whether or not it makes sense to think of science as an enterprise that can be subject to coherent criticism generated by those who stand outside the enterprise depends, of course, on what point of view one originally holds about science itself. Those who are antecedently inclined to believe in the sanctity of science will have a great deal of trouble concluding that anyone not specifically trained in the sciences will have anything to say about science itself. Those who are inclined to believe that the pretensions of science are just that—pretensions—will experience incredulity at the notion that science is not an enterprise like any other, on an equal footing with our attempts to find out how to get our car started in the morning and how to get information on what transpired at the latest Middle East peace conference.

What We Can Conclude

It is difficult, during an age in which almost everything that can be said about contemporary culture smacks of the "postmodern," to say anything about science that seems to valorize it as an enterprise without sounding irretrievably old-fashioned. But if anything can be learned from our excursion into the contemporary admixture of philosophies of science and feminist theories, it is that there is no position that is the obvious position, and no one way out of the debate, which presents itself as clear and concisely formulated.

The criticisms that were originally broached against the rigorous doctrines of positivism and the Vienna Circle, some as far back as the 1940s and 1950s, were made because it was clear even then that there was a descriptive component to work in the sciences that should have been set out and was not. In other words, it was obvious that a logic of justification alone is not enough to give us some kind of overview of science.

As frequently happens when we apply a corrective, the pendulum swings in the other direction, and this is exactly what happened with the weltanschauungen positions and with the work done in sociology of science and science studies that—as we saw in the writings of Bloor, for instance—gives no credit to empirical content devoid of political or social motivation. The combination of this direction in sociology, philosophy, and history of science with the feminist and radical critiques has meant that, according to some, science as an enterprise has lost all credibility. Understandably, many practicing scientists are appalled by this turn of intellectual events, and a backlash against this characterization has occurred, revealing itself not only in the Gross and Levitt work cited earlier but also in the response to the recent Sokal hoax.[16]

If there is any coherent response to be made to this contretemps that is not itself intrinsically question begging, it probably revolves around the notion, articulated here in several places, that the same principles of empirical confirmation that we use to get through our everyday lives are indeed the principles that can guide some kind of account of justification in science, and these principles need not be arcane. The notion, now popular in many intellectual circles in which the participants have training primarily in literature or the humanities, that empiricism is the "same as" positivism, is a dangerous one and is at least partly responsible for a number of areas of weakness in contemporary dialogue.

As we have seen, the positivist project was a specific one, and the setting out of a logic of justification was a project that had its place in its time. At a relatively early point in the proceedings, a number of commentators became aware of the fact that the correspondence rules, based as they were on an epistemology of incorrigibility, were conceptually weak, and the Quinean criticisms of the separation of observation and theory that did, indeed, motivate a large part of the formulation of the correspondence rules also helped to undo them. None of this meant, however, that a relatively bland and workaday notion of empirical confirmation had to be discarded. Indeed, it is empirical confirmation that Quine is trying to put forward as a basis for epistemology in his well-known essay "Epistemology Naturalized."[17]

Having said so much, we must remind ourselves of a point that has been made throughout this text. Without some kind of notion of empirical confirmation, claims to have had any kind of experience—including an experience of victimization—cannot be confirmed. The contemporary efforts on the part of many reactionary political forces to delegitimize a great deal of what has transpired in the history of various minority groups should disabuse us of any notions we may have that confirmation is not important. To cite but one example, the move toward denial of the Holocaust is not merely a move toward the denial of a fundamental part of Jewish history; it is a move toward denial of similar sorts of claims made by many groups. One could claim, for example, that some of the cruelty that we associate with slavery never occurred, or has been exaggerated; or one could claim that the Cherokee "Trail of Tears" experience is largely myth and fantastical reconstruction.

In order to forward notions of progress, we need to be clear about what has actually taken place. In other words, we need to know what victimization, if any, certain groups experienced, what took place during the periods of alleged mistreatment, and so forth.

Speaking more broadly still, it is also important for the sake of one's notion of history to be able to document, at least to some minimal extent, what did and did not happen. Now that the concepts of the "death of history" and of historiography as itself mythmaking have become popular, it is especially important to try to resuscitate at least minimal notions of empirical confirmation.[18] This is why it is also urgent, from the standpoint of feminism, to try to build on those theories that offer at least some connection to the tradition of women engaged in the world. As I have asserted repeatedly in this work, it is the male tradition of ratiocinative speculation that is rigidly androcentric and masculinist, and it is also this tradition that excludes women and in fact (certainly insofar as the ancients were concerned) devalues the role of women.[19] Although it might well be claimed that, at least until the nineteenth century, there is virtually no tradition that valorizes women and female roles, some traditions leave fewer loopholes than others, and the tradition that culminates in rationalist thought is perhaps the most androcentric of all.

We might also inquire how a more empirically oriented tradition has given rise to the expression of feminist concerns. One articulation of such a stance has been put forward by the American pragmatist tradition, and the long line of women thinkers associated with this tradition (including, of course, Jane Addams) is a spectacularly rich one and well worth further investigation.[20] Pragmatism, in particular, might be thought to be a home to women and to women theorists because it is a line of thought that is concerned to reintegrate theorizing and the living of life itself.

The pragmatists originally asked us to divorce ourselves from the tradition of a priori speculation that had been the hallmark of philosophy up to that point, and they were quite right to do so. As has been repeatedly argued here, it is that tradition, with its distanced and detached voice, that has denied the experience of so many and that has, indeed, failed to be consonant with the experience of most human beings. If we have learned anything from the science wars, it is that, despite poststructuralist denials, some claims seem to bear more confirmation than others, and the experiences of some can help us confirm or disconfirm a number of claims that might be made.

Philosophies of science and feminist theories intersect at precisely those points where we might wish for a clearer notion of confirmation. Philosophy of science originally pushed us in the direction of a logic of justification; feminist theory reminds us that no logic of justification can be detached from its origins and that no justificatory stance has the pristine quality that some purport to have. The interweaving of feminist theory, philosophy of science, sociology of science, and science studies in general has indeed been fructifying for the enterprise of science as a whole. The future of science seems to rest on some notion of accountability. It is perhaps the strongest contribution of feminist theorizing to philosophy of science that, with its reliance on the notion of women's lived experience, it asks for accountability and refuses to do without it.

Notes

Chapter One

1. For an overview of much of this recent work, see the writings of Steve Fuller, especially *Social Epistemology* (Bloomington: Indiana University Press, 1988).

2. Hilary Rose and Steven Rose, eds., *The Political Economy of Science* (New York: Holmes and Meier, 1976).

3. See Oswald Hanfling, ed., *Essential Readings in Logical Positivism* (New York: Basil Blackwell, 1981).

4. Bertrand Russell, "The Philosophy of Logical Atomism," in *Bertrand Russell: Logic and Knowledge*, ed. Robert C. Marsh (New York: G. P. Putnam's Sons, 1971), pp. 175–282.

5. Joia Lewis, "Schlick's Critique of Positivism," in *PSA 1988*, vol. 1 (East Lansing, MI: Proceedings of the PSA, 1989), pp. 110–118.

6. A fine overview of these intellectual moves is provided in Frederick Suppe, *The Structure of Scientific Theories* (Urbana: University of Illinois Press, 1977).

7. See Suppe, *Structure*.

8. Kuhn's work was originally published as part of the International Encyclopedia of Unified Science. Thomas Kuhn, *The Structure of Scientific Revolutions* (Chicago: University of Chicago Press, 1962).

9. See esp. Norwood Hanson, *Patterns of Discovery* (New York: Cambridge University Press, 1967).

10. See the work of Richard Boyd, esp. "Scientific Realism and Naturalistic Epistemology," in *PSA 1980*, vol. 2 (East Lansing, MI: Proceedings of the PSA, 1981).

11. Jane Duran, "Causal Reference and Epistemic Justification," *Philosophy of Science* 55, no. 2 (Summer 1988), 272–279.

12. A fine feminist articulation of these problems is Helen Longino, *Science as Social Practice* (Princeton: Princeton University Press, 1990).

13. Evelyn Fox Keller, *Reflections on Gender and Science* (New Haven: Yale University Press, 1985).

14. Evelyn Fox Keller, "Love and Sex in Plato's Epistemology," in *Reflections on Gender and Science* (New Haven: Yale University Press, 1985).

15. See Susan Bordo, *The Flight to Objectivity* (Albany: State University of New York Press, 1981).

16. Thomas Nagel, *Mortal Questions* (New York: Oxford University Press, 1985).

17. See note 12 above.

18. See any number of pieces published in the 1990s in the journal *Science, Technology and Value.*

19. Richard J. Herrnstein, *The Bell Curve* (New York: Free Press, 1994). A group of sociologists at the University of California at Berkeley is in the process of publishing responses (forthcoming).

20. See Suppe, *Structure,* for an overview of this controversy.

21. Boyd, "Scientific Realism."

22. See Bas Van Fraassen, *The Scientific Image* (Oxford: Oxford University Press, Clarendon Press, 1981).

23. See note 5 above.

24. See note 22 above.

25. As of this writing, the work that is being most frequently cited seems to be Bruno Latour, *Science in Action* (Cambridge: Harvard University Press, 1987).

26. Ibid.

27. See also Steve Fuller, *Philosophy of Science and Its Discontents* (Boulder: Westview Press, 1991).

28. See any one of a number of Baudrillard's translated works.

29. Fuller, *Social Epistemology,* devotes an entire chapter to this problem.

30. Fuller, *Social Epistemology,* pp. 100–102.

31. Ibid., p. 104.

32. Ibid., p. 105.

33. Ibid.

34. Mitchell G. Ash, "Historicizing Mind Science: Discourse, Practice, Subjectivity," *Science in Context* 5 (Autumn 1992), 193–197.

Chapter Two

1. See any of a number of interesting essays in James Chandler, Arnold I. Davidson, and Harry Harootunian, eds., *Questions of Evidence* (Chicago: University of Chicago Press, 1994).

2. For a fine source of accounts of positivism and responses to it, see Frederick Suppe, *The Structure of Scientific Theories* (Urbana: University of Illinois Press, 1977).

3. J. L. Austin, *Sense and Sensibilia* (Oxford: Oxford University Press, 1964), pp. 111–116. Austin's work contains lengthy arguments on this material.

4. Although this question may not have been addressed straightforwardly in the feminist literature, questions related to it have been. See, for example, Helen Longino, *Science as Social Practice* (Princeton: Princeton University Press, 1990).

5. Joia Lewis, "Schlick's Critique of Positivism," in *PSA 1988,* vol. 1 (East Lansing, MI: Proceedings of the PSA, 1989), pp. 110–118.

6. Moritz Schlick, "The Boundaries of Scientific and Philosophical Concept-Formation," in *Philosophical Papers,* vol. 1 (Dordrecht, Netherlands: Reidel, 1979), pp. 25–40.

7. Ibid., p. 31.

8. Schlick employs an interesting example here; it is the case of the move from pitch to frequency: "But once we have done this, and so learnt, for example, to

speak quantitatively of frequency instead of alluding to qualitative differences of pitch, the return from the realm of numbers to that of qualities is finally barred to us" (Schlick, "Boundaries," p. 31).

9. For the arguments with respect to the divorce of the purely phenomenal from the conceptual, see any of a number of essays in W. V. O. Quine, *From a Logical Point of View* (Cambridge: Harvard University Press, 1953).

10. Moritz Schlick, "Critical or Empirical Interpretation of Modern Physics?" in *Philosophical Papers*, vol. 1 (Dordrecht, Netherlands: Reidel, 1979), p. 325.

11. Ibid.

12. J. Alberto Coffa, "Carnap's *Sprachansauung* Circa 1932," in *PSA 1976* (East Lansing, MI: Proceedings of the PSA, 1977), pp. 219, 222.

13. Lindley Darden, "The Heritage of Logical Positivism: A Reassessment," in *PSA 1976* (East Lansing: Proceedings of the PSA, 1977), p. 247.

14. Ibid., p. 254.

15. Suppe, *Structure*, pp. 30, 34.

16. Mark Pastin, "Modest Foundationalism and Self-Warrant," in *Essays on Knowledge and Justification*, ed. George S. Pappas and Marshall Swain (Ithaca: Cornell University Press, 1978).

17. Neurath's well-known essay "Protocol Sentences" (in *Essential Readings in Logical Positivism*, ed. Oswald Hanfling [New York: Basil Blackwell, 1981]) contains some points of dispute with the early Carnap on this score, but it is clear that Neurath's sentences must, if they are to receive epistemic support, ultimately run in a direction closer to Carnap's original formulation.

18. Part of the distinction here has to do with whether or not the terms will be those of "everyday physical objects" or whether they will already, in the sentences, be somewhat phenomenally reduced.

19. For a concise but readable exposition of what precisely these formulations amount to, see Suppe, *Structure*, pp. 16–17.

20. See, for example, Herbert Feigl, "The Origin and Spirit of Logical Positivism," in *The Legacy of Logical Positivism*, ed. Herbert Feigl (Baltimore: Johns Hopkins University Press, 1969), p. 17.

21. "Self-justifying" is a term associated with the work of Roderick Chisholm. See his *Perception* (Ithaca: Cornell University Press, 1967).

22. Neurath, "Protocol Sentences," p. 164.

23. Suppe, *Structure*, pp. 8–10.

24. Ibid., p. 10.

25. Suppe specifically notes that the Received View may be thought of as "the inductive method of doing science advocated by Bacon [1620]," in *Structure*, p. 15 n. 30.

26. For the notion of generality, see Suppe, *Structure*, p. 14 n. 26.

27. Suppe, *Structure*, pp. 16–17.

28. Ibid., p. 12.

29. Oswald Hanfling, introduction to *Essential Readings in Logical Positivism* (New York: Basil Blackwell, 1981), pp. 6–7.

30. Hanfling characterizes this as "the idea of analysis into 'elementary propositions'" (Hanfling, introduction to *Essential Readings*, p. 6).

31. Hanfling, introduction to *Essential Readings*, p. 15. Hanfling terms unity and the concomitant reduction a "major objective."

32. Ayer's work is, of course, the source for much of this view.

33. Michael Scriven, "Logical Positivism and the Behavioral Sciences," in *The Legacy of Logical Positivism*, ed. Herbert Feigl (Baltimore: Johns Hopkins University Press, 1969), pp. 195–209.

34. Ibid., p. 201.

35. Ibid., pp. 203–205.

36. Hanfling, introduction to *Essential Readings*, p. 23.

37. Schlick was, of course, the author of a book-length work entitled *The Place of Value in a World of Facts* (Englewood Cliffs, NJ: Prentice-Hall, 1965).

38. Rudolf Carnap, "Logical Foundations of the Unity of Science," in *Essential Readings in Logical Positivism*, ed. Oswald Hanfling (New York: Basil Blackwell, 1981), pp. 112–129. This essay was originally published in the *International Encyclopedia of Unified Science* (Chicago: University of Chicago Press, 1938).

39. Carnap, "Logical Foundations," p. 128.

40. Ibid., passim.

41. Ibid., p. 128.

42. This phrase is specifically cited by Keller in her *Reflections on Gender and Science* (New Haven: Yale University Press, 1985).

43. Suppe, *Structure*, passim.

44. N. J. Block and Gerald Dworkin, "IQ: Heritability and Inequality, Part 1," *Philosophy and Public Affairs* 3 (Summer 1974), 331–409.

45. Susan Bordo, *The Flight to Objectivity* (Albany: State University of New York Press, 1987).

46. Feigl, "Origin and Spirit."

Chapter Three

1. Carl Hempel, *Aspects of Scientific Explanation* (New York: Free Press, 1965).

2. Carl Hempel, in *Twenty Questions*, ed. Robert Solomon (New York: Macmillan, 1992), p. 78.

3. Hempel, in *Twenty Questions*, p. 293.

4. Ibid.

5. See N. J. Block and Gerald Dworkin, "IQ: Heritability and Inequality, Part 1," *Philosophy and Public Affairs* 3 (Summer 1974), passim.

6. Carl Hempel, "A Logical Appraisal of Operationism," in *Aspects of Scientific Explanation* (New York: Free Press, 1965), p. 123.

7. Block and Dworkin, "IQ," passim.

8. Hempel, *Aspects*, p. 125.

9. Ibid., p. 129.

10. This term is Hempel's; see *Aspects*, p. 130.

11. Hempel, *Aspects*, p. 131.

12. Block and Dworkin, "IQ," p. 337.

13. Ibid., p. 337.

14. The latter counterargument is in a cleverly worded footnote (Block and Dworkin, "IQ," p. 337 n. 14).

15. Block and Dworkin, "IQ," p. 338.

16. The German-language edition of *Logik der Vorschung* was originally published in 1935.

17. Frederick Suppe, *The Structure of Scientific Theories* (Urbana: University of Illinois Press, 1977), p. 167.

18. Ibid.

19. Moritz Schlick, *The Place of Value in a World of Fact* (Englewood Cliffs, NJ: Prentice-Hall, 1965).

20. Carl Hempel, "Science and Human Values," in *Aspects of Scientific Explanation* (New York: Free Press, 1965), p. 87.

21. Ibid., p. 96.

22. Paul Feyerabend, "Problems of Empiricism," in *Beyond the Edge of Certainty*, ed. R. Colodny (Englewood Cliffs, NJ: Prentice-Hall, l965), p. 212.

23. Paul Feyerabend, "Explanation, Reduction, and Empiricism," in *Minnesota Studies in the Philosophy of Science*, vol. 3, ed. Herbert Feigl and Grover Maxwell (Minneapolis: University of Minnesota Press, 1962), p. 29.

24. Paul Hoyningen-Huene, *Reconstructing Scientific Revolutions: Kuhn's Philosophy of Science*, the International Encyclopedia of Unified Science (Chicago: University of Chicago Press, 1962).

25. See, for example, the citations Hoyningen-Huene has made to scholarly commentary on the use of the term "paradigm" in Kuhn (Hoyningen-Huene, *Reconstructing*, p. 132).

26. Suppe, *Structure*, p. 218.

27. Hoyningen-Huene, *Reconstructing*, pp. 132–133.

28. Dudley Shapere, "Notes Toward a Post-Positivist Interpretation of Science," in *The Legacy of Logical Positivism*, ed. Herbert Feigl (Baltimore: Johns Hopkins University Press, 1969), pp. 118–119.

29. This is the actual wording to which Shapere refers; see "Post-Positivist Interpretation," p. 119.

30. Shapere, "Post-Positivist Interpretation," p. 119.

31. Feyerabend, "Problems of Empiricism," pp. 148–149.

32. Ibid., pp. 147–148.

33. Ibid., p. 149.

34. Morris R. Cohen and Ernest Nagel, *An Introduction to Logic and Scientific Method* (New York: Harcourt, Brace & Co., 1934), pp. 391–392, 394.

35. Nicholas Rescher, "The Ethical Dimension of Scientific Research," in *Beyond the Edge of Certainty*, ed. R. Colodny (Englewood Cliffs, NJ: Prentice-Hall, l965), p. 275.

36. Evelyn Fox Keller, *Reflections on Gender and Science* (New Haven: Yale University Press, 1985), pp. 229–230.

37. It is for this reason that, in her chapter on Plato (*Reflections*, pp. 21–32), Keller refers to the marriage of male minds desired by Plato in *Symposium* as the "union of kindred essences," and their offspring (as Plato himself notes) as strands of theory in the world of ideas. The enterprise of early-twentieth-century physics, particularly as seen in positivist theory as developed by Neurath, might be thought of as a perfect exemplar of such offspring.

38. See note 34 above.

39. See J. L. Austin, *Sense and Sensibilia* (Oxford: Oxford University Press, 1964), passim.

40. In Chapter 2, we looked at "Otto now joy" as such a statement.

41. See Mark Pastin, "Modest Foundationalism and Self–Warrant," in *Essays on Knowledge and Justification*, ed. George S. Pappas and Marshall Swain (Ithaca: Cornell University Press, 1978).

42. Particularly valuable is Kornblith's anthology, recently reissued in a second edition (Hilary Kornblith, *Naturalizing Epistemology* [Cambridge: Bradford of MIT Press, 1994]).

43. Ann Garry, "A Minimally Decent Philosophical Method?" *Hypatia* 10 (Summer 1995), 7–30.

44. The work of the PDP theorists alone has been instrumental in this regard.

45. Bertrand Russell, "The Philosophy of Logical Atomism," in *Bertrand Russell: Logic and Knowledge*, ed. Robert C. Marsh (New York: G. P. Putnam's Sons, 1971), pp. 175–282.

Chapter Four

1. Thomas Kuhn, *The Structure of Scientific Revolutions*, the International Encyclopedia of Unified Science (Chicago: University of Chicago Press, 1962).

2. Paul Hoyningen-Huene, *Reconstructing Scientific Revolutions: Kuhn's Philosophy of Science* (Chicago: University of Chicago Press, 1992).

3. Kuhn, *Structure*, pp. 35–42.

4. Ibid., pp. 36–37.

5. Ibid., p. 37.

6. Ibid., p. 62.

7. The citation for the original literature on this experiment is given in Kuhn's text as J. S. Bruner and Leo Postman, "On the Perception of Incongruity: a Paradigm," *Journal of Personality* 18 (1949), 206–223 (Kuhn, *Structure*, p. 63 n).

8. Kuhn, *Structure*, p. 64.

9. Ibid., p. 63.

10. Ibid., pp. 66–67.

11. Kuhn notes that theory change demands "large-scale paradigm destruction" (*Structure*, p. 67).

12. Kuhn, *Structure*, p. 69.

13. Sandra Harding, *The Science Question in Feminism* (Ithaca: Cornell University Press, 1986), p. 200.

14. Ibid., pp. 207–215.

15. Ibid., pp. 210–211.

16. Ibid., p. 213.

17. The phrase occurs in chapter 9, "Problems with Post-Kuhnian Stories," pp. 216–242.

18. Mary B. Hesse, *Models and Analogies in Science* (Notre Dame, IN: University of Notre Dame Press, 1966).

19. Ibid., p. 157.

20. Ibid., p. 159.

21. Ibid., p. 168.

22. Ibid., p. 167.

23. Imre Lakatos, "Falsification and the Methodology of Scientific Research Programmes," in *Criticism and the Growth of Knowledge* (New York: Cambridge University Press, 1984), pp. 91–196.

24. Ibid., pp. 177–178.

25. Ibid., p. 137.

26. Ibid., p. 135.

27. This particular piece by Lakatos does contain many historical examples that cannot be recapitulated here.

28. Stephen Toulmin, "Does the Distinction Between Normal and Revolutionary Science Hold Water?" in Imre Lakatos and Alan Musgrave, eds., p. 41.

29. Ibid., p. 44.

30. Ibid., p. 43.

31. J. W. N. Watkins, "Against 'Normal Science,'" in Imre Lakatos and Alan Musgrave, eds., pp. 25–37.

32. Ibid., p. 27.

33. Ibid., p. 30.

34. Norwood Hanson, *Patterns of Discovery* (New York: Cambridge University Press, 1967), pp. 4–30.

35. Ibid., pp. 4–5.

36. Ibid., p. 5.

37. Ibid., p. 22.

38. An interesting and easily readable overview of the alterations of belief systems is available in Walter Truett Anderson, *Reality Isn't What It Used to Be* (New York: Harper & Row, 1992).

39. Geoffrey Gorham, "The Concept of Truth in Feminist Sciences," *Hypatia* 10 (Summer 1995), 100.

40. Hilary Rose and Steven Rose, eds., *The Political Economy of Science* (New York: Holmes and Meier, 1976).

41. Ibid., pp. 14, 19.

Chapter Five

1. For an overview of the Mannheimian project, see John Harms, "Mannheim's Sociology of Knowledge and the Interpretation of *Weltanschauungen*," *Social Science Journal* 21 (1984), 33–49.

2. See Hilary Kornblith, *Naturalizing Epistemology* (Cambridge: Bradford of MIT Press, 1985).

3. Steve Fuller, "The Elusiveness of Consensus in Science," in *PSA 1986* (East Lansing, MI: Proceedings of the PSA, 1987), p. 107.

4. Ibid., passim.

5. Ibid., pp. 114–115.

6. Andre Gorz, "On the Class Character of Science and Scientists," in *The Political Economy of Science,* ed. Hilary Rose and Steven Rose (New York: Holmes and Meier, 1976).

7. Ibid., p. 60.

8. Steve Fuller, *Social Epistemology* (Bloomington: Indiana University Press, 1988), p. 13.

9. Ibid., p. 5.

10. Interestingly enough, one of the main examples employed in the dialogue as a counter to the second proposed definition of knowledge is that of a "jury having hearsay evidence."

11. Fuller, *Social Epistemology*, pp. 5–6.

12. David A. Bloor, *Knowledge and Social Imagery* (London: Routledge and Kegan Paul, 1976).

13. Ibid., p. 18.

14. Ibid., p. 65.

15. See the chapter entitled "A Naturalistic Approach to Mathematics" (Bloor, *Knowledge*, pp. 74–94).

16. Bloor, *Knowledge*, p. 76.

17. Peter Winch, *The Idea of a Social Science* (London: Routledge and Kegan Paul, 1958).

18. Ibid., pp. 40–41, 42.

19. Ibid., pp. 112–113.

20. Ibid., p. 133.

21. Ibid.

22. Jon Elster, *Explaining Technical Change* (Cambridge: Cambridge University Press, 1983).

23. Ibid., p. 92.

24. Jon Elster, ed., *The Multiple Self* (Cambridge: Cambridge University Press, 1986).

25. Ibid., pp. 98, 101.

26. Bruno Latour, *Science in Action* (Cambridge: Harvard University Press, 1987).

27. Latour, *Science*, p. 15.

28. See, for example, popularizations of science by such writers as Walter Truett Anderson.

29. One thinks, for example, of recent meetings of the Philosophy of Science Association.

30. Paul R. Gross and Norman Levitt, *Higher Superstition* (Baltimore: Johns Hopkins University Press, 1994).

31. Two such positive citations address the work of Marc Bloch and Gar Alperovitz (Gross and Levitt, *Higher Superstition*, p. 69).

32. Gross and Levitt, *Higher Superstition*, p. 60.

33. The authors do, indeed, at least allude to such theory when they state, for example, that "Keller's position rests upon unsupported speculations about psychosexual developmental differences between men and women" (Gross and Levitt, *Higher Superstition*, p. 142).

34. Gross and Levitt, *Higher Superstition*, p. 112.

35. Ibid., p. 142.

36. Ibid., p. 110.

37. Ibid., p. 113. The piece in question, "Toward a Feminist Algebra," is cited by Gross and Levitt as authored by Mary Anne Campbell and Randall K. Campbell-Wright and originally read as a paper at a meeting of the Mathematical Association of America (Gross and Levitt, *Higher Superstition*, p. 272 n. 7).

Chapter Six

1. A powerful collection of her own writings is *Simians, Cyborgs and Women* (New York: Routledge and Kegan Paul, 1991).

2. Ibid., p. 90.

3. Ibid., p. 91.

4. In fact, at one point she calls the stories "ordinary good scientific practice" (Haraway, *Simians*, p. 108).

5. Haraway, *Simians*, p. 97. For example, Haraway says with respect to DeVore (a student of Washburn's): "DeVore also experimentally provoked the male-male dominance interactions that had to be seen to signify central meanings, called observations."

6. Ibid., pp. 99–100.

7. Sandra Harding, *Whose Science? Whose Knowledge?* (Ithaca: Cornell University Press, 1991), pp. 222–223.

8. Ibid., pp. 226–227.

9. Ibid., pp. 51–76.

10. Ibid., p. 54.

11. Indeed, Harding writes: "Most critics of science-as-usual hold that political struggle is a necessary part of learning how to criticize the dominant conceptual schemes from the standpoint of women's activities" (*Whose Science?* p. 71).

12. Harding, *Whose Science?* p. 74.

13. Ibid., p. 75.

14. Lynn Hankinson Nelson, *Who Knows: From Quine to a Feminist Empiricism* (Philadelphia: Temple University Press, 1991). This term and terms like it are found throughout chapter 1 (pp. 20–42).

15. Ibid., p. 20. At one point she says, "In an important sense, just about everyone is an empiricist."

16. Ibid., p. 7.

17. Ruth Hubbard, *Profitable Promises: Essays on Women, Science, and Health* (Monroe, ME: Common Courage Press, 1995).

18. Ibid., p. 193.

19. In an essay titled "Transparent Women, Visible Genes, and New Conceptions of Disease," Hubbard writes: "It is an enormous waste of talent and resources to try to foresee the potential health hazards that lurk in the genes of each of us" (*Profitable Promises*, p. 64).

20. Hubbard, *Profitable Promises*, p. 107.

21. Ibid., pp. 109–110.

22. Kathleen Lennon and Margaret Whitford, eds., *Knowing the Difference: Feminist Perspectives in Epistemology* (London: Routledge and Kegan Paul, 1994).

23. The Rawls citation is given as John Rawls, "Outline of a Decision Procedure for Ethics," *Philosophical Review* 60, no. 2 (April 1951), 177–197.

24. Janna Thompson, in *Knowing the Difference: Feminist Perspectives in Epistemology*, ed. Kathleen Lennon and Margaret Whitford (London: Routledge and Kegan Paul, 1994), pp. 226, 228.

25. Diana Sartori, "Women's Authority in Science," in *Knowing the Difference: Feminist Perspectives in Epistemology*, ed. Kathleen Lennon and Margaret Whitford (London: Routledge and Kegan Paul, 1994), pp. 110–121.

26. Sartori refers to this authority through male community as "refracted through the father's eye," and notes that "[f]emale authority is the only thing that can authorize a woman to escape the image 'refracted through the father's eye'" (Sartori, "Women's Authority," p. 114).

27. Sartori, "Women's Authority," pp. 114–115.

28. Evelyn Fox Keller, *Reflections on Gender and Science* (New Haven: Yale University Press, 1985), p. 182.

29. Maura Fricker, "Knowledge as Construct: Theorizing the Role of Gender in Knowledge," in *Knowing the Difference: Feminist Perspectives in Epistemology*, ed. Kathleen Lennon and Margaret Whitford (London: Routledge and Kegan Paul, 1994), pp. 96–109.

30. Fricker, "Knowledge as Construct," p. 99.

31. Anna Yeatman, in *Knowing the Difference: Feminist Perspectives in Epistemology*, ed. Kathleen Lennon and Margaret Whitford (London: Routledge and Kegan Paul, 1994), p. 189.

32. Helen Longino, *Science as Social Practice* (Princeton: Princeton University Press, 1990), p. 68.

33. Ibid., p. 64.

34. Ibid., pp. 87–88.

35. Ibid., p. 83.

36. Longino notes, with respect to this importance, "They [the press] treat Nobel prize winning scientists as experts on topics far beyond their special competence, thereby creating a new priesthood."

37. Longino, *Science*, pp. 165–166.

38. Sandra Harding, *The Science Question in Feminism* (Ithaca: Cornell University Press, 1986).

39. Patricia Hill Collins, *Black Feminist Thought* (Boulder: Westview Press, 1990).

Chapter Seven

1. See Hilary Rose and Steven Rose, eds., *The Political Economy of Science* (New York: Holmes and Meier, 1976), chap. 1.

2. Hilary Rose and Steven Rose, "The Problematic Inheritance: Marx and Engels on the Natural Sciences," in *The Political Economy of Science*, ed. Hilary Rose and Steven Rose (New York: Holmes and Meier, 1976), p. 3.

3. Giovanni Ciccotti, Marcello Cini, and Michelangelo de Maria, "The Production of Science in Advanced Capitalist Society," in *The Political Economy of Science*, ed. Hilary Rose and Steven Rose (New York: Holmes and Meier, 1976), p. 33.

4. Regina Markell Morantz-Sanchez, *Sympathy and Science* (Oxford: Oxford University Press, 1985), pp. 352, 355.

5. Hilary Rose and Jalna Hanmer, "Women's Liberation: Reproduction and the Technological Fix," in *The Political Economy of Science*, ed. Hilary Rose and Steven Rose (New York: Holmes and Meier, 1976), p. 149.

6. The birth of the baby Louise Brown, conceived by this method, was widely publicized in 1978.

7. Rose and Hanmer, "Women's Liberation," pp. 152–153.

8. Morantz-Sanchez, *Sympathy*, p. 293.

9. Anja Hiddinga and Stuart Blume, "Technology, Science, and Obstetric Practice: The Origins and Transformation of Cephalopelvimetry," *Science, Technology and Human Values* 17 (Spring 1992), 163.

10. Gina Corea, *The Mother Machine* (New York: Pantheon, 1985).

11. Gina Corea, quoted in Hiddinga and Blume, "Technology, Science, and Obstetric Practice," 156.

12. Susan Hornig, "Gender Differences in Response to News About Science and Technology," *Science, Technology and Human Values* 17 (Fall 1992), 532.

13. Hornig, "Gender Differences," 536.

14. Loren Graham, *Between Science and Values* (New York: Columbia University Press, 1981).

15. Ibid., pp. 291–318.

16. Ibid., pp. 295–296.

17. Ibid., p. 301.

18. Ibid., pp. 301–302.

19. Ibid., p. 313.

20. Ibid., pp. 303–304.

21. Sally Slocum, "Woman the Gatherer: Male Bias in Anthropology," in *Toward an Anthropology of Women*, ed. Rayna Reiter (New York: Monthly Review Press, 1975).

22. As Slocum puts it in her commentary on this line of thought, "Modern humans have become so accustomed to the thought of tools and weapons that it is easy for us to imagine the first manlike creature who picked up a stone or club" ("Woman the Gatherer," p. 45).

23. Slocum, "Woman the Gatherer," p. 46.

24. Ibid., p. 45.

25. Ibid., p. 47.

26. Ibid., p. 49.

27. Ruth Bleier, *Science and Gender* (New York: Pergamon Press, 1984), p. 195.

28. Ibid., p. 195.

29. Ibid., p. 194.

30. Ibid., p. 4.

31. Ibid., pp. 9–10.

32. Richard C. Lewontin, Steven Rose, and Leon J. Kamin, *Not in Our Genes* (New York: Pantheon, 1984).

33. Ibid., p. 10.

34. Ibid., p. 12.

35. Ibid., p. 84.

36. Ibid., p. 85.

37. Ibid., p. 86.

38. See Richard C. Lewontin, Steven Rose, and Leon J. Kamin, "Schizophrenia: The Clash of Determinisms," in *Not in Our Genes* (New York: Pantheon, 1984), pp. 191–232.

39. Lewontin, Rose, and Kamin, *Not in Our Genes*, p. 200.

40. Ibid., p. 203.
41. Ibid., p. 200.
42. Ibid.
43. Ibid.
44. Ibid., p. 204.
45. Ibid., p. 208.
46. Carolyn Merchant, *The Death of Nature* (New York: Harper & Row, 1980).
47. Ibid., p. 5.
48. See, in particular, the chapter entitled "Nature and Disorder: Women as Witches," in Carolyn Merchant, *The Death of Nature* (New York: Harper & Row, 1980), pp. 127–148.
49. Merchant, *Death*, p. 128.
50. Ibid., p. 132.
51. Ibid., p. 134.
52. Ibid., p. 6.

Chapter Eight

1. This phrase is used by Sandra Harding in *The Science Question in Feminism* (Ithaca: Cornell University Press, 1986).
2. See Hilary Kornblith, *Naturalizing Epistemology* (Cambridge: Bradford of MIT Press, 1994).
3. See Hilary Kornblith, "Some Social Features of Cognition," *Synthese* 73 (1987), 27–41.
4. The work of Richard Boyd is often cited in this context. But see, for example, the theory of reference implicit in his "Scientific Realism and Naturalistic Epistemology," in *PSA 1980*, vol. 2 (East Lansing, MI: Proceedings of the PSA, 1981).
5. Jane Duran, "Intentionality and Epistemology," *The Monist* 68 (1986), 620–626.
6. Such examples are a staple of the kind of literature that was produced in American epistemology during the last two decades, especially the 1970s. Much of this literature was written in response to the Gettier examples.
7. This notion has been associated very strongly with the work of Lynn Hankinson Nelson, *Who Knows: From Quine to a Feminist Empiricism* (Philadelphia: Temple University Press, 1991).
8. See James Cornman, "Foundational vs. Nonfoundational Theories of Empirical Justification," in *Essays on Knowledge and Justification*, ed. George S. Pappas and Marshall Swain (Ithaca: Cornell University Press, 1978).
9. To be sure, there is always the possibility of naturalizing some of the more classical theories in ways that do not use the notion of a community, but that is not my aim here.
10. I have especially alluded to this problem in discussions of the work of Haraway.
11. See note 4 above.
12. See Joia Lewis, "Schlick's Critique of Positivism," in *PSA 1988*, vol. 1 (East Lansing, MI: Proceedings of the PSA, 1989), pp. 110–118.
13. Boyd, "Scientific Realism," passim.
14. Ibid.

15. Jane Duran, "Explanation and Reference," *Metaphilosophy* 27, no 3(1996), 302–310.

16. Luce Irigaray, "Le Sujet de la Science: Est-il Sexué?" trans. Carol Mastrangelo Bové, *Hypatia* 2 (1987), 85.

17. Bas Van Fraassen, *The Scientific Image* (Oxford: Clarendon of Oxford University Press, 1981).

18. Bas Van Fraassen, in *Images of Science*, ed. Paul M. Churchland and Clifford A. Hooker (Chicago: University of Chicago Press, 1985), p. 260.

19. Ibid.

20. Ibid., p. 283.

21. See Lewis, "Schlick's Critique."

22. Ibid., pp. 110, 110–111, 111.

23. "Intentionalism" is a term that has most of its contemporary usage in philosophy of mind.

24. A good, popular overview of this material can be found in Pamela McCorduck, *Machines Who Think* (San Francisco: W. W. Freeman, 1983).

25. Most of the classic material with respect to this work is found in James McClelland and Donald Rumelhart, *Parallel Distributed Processing*, 2 vols. (Cambridge: MIT Press, 1985).

26. The single best exposition of this material is probably Patricia Smith Churchland, *Neurophilosophy* (Cambridge: MIT Press, 1985).

27. See Gerald Edelman, *The Remembered Present* (New York: Basic Books, 1984).

28. Daniel Dennett, *The Intentional Stance* (Cambridge: Bradford of MIT Press, 1984).

29. Larry Laudan, *Progress and Its Problems* (Berkeley: University of California Press, 1977), p. 5.

30. For a twist on this topic from the Native American perspective, see, for example, Paula Gunn Allen, *The Sacred Hoop* (Berkeley: University of California Press, 1978).

31. There are, of course, "ordinary" situations—such as those involving religious speculation—that are not primarily empirical. Encounters with such situations are, however, statistically rare for most individuals on a day-to-day basis.

32. His classic *Behavior in Public Places* (New York: Random House, 1965) is very helpful in this regard.

33. Goffman, *Behavior*.

34. William Labov, *Patterns of Language* (Philadelphia: Temple University Press, 1967).

35. As I have set out the precise elements of this model in a number of previous works, I will not do so again here. The latest to describe this model is Jane Duran, *Knowledge in Context* (Lanham, MD: Rowman and Littlefield, 1994).

36. Harding, *Science Question*.

Chapter Nine

1. See Frederick Suppe, *The Structure of Scientific Theories* (Urbana: University of Illinois Press, 1977).

2. David A. Bloor, *Knowledge and Social Imagery* (London: Routledge and Kegan Paul, 1976).

3. The recent David Baltimore controversy, widely discussed in the popular press, is a good example of this phenomenon.

4. For a feminist argument on how these notions tie together, see Elizabeth Spelman, *Inessential Woman* (Boston: Beacon Press, 1987).

5. Friedrich Engels, "Preface to *The Condition of the Working Class in England*," in *Karl Marx and Friedrich Engels: Selected Works*, vol. 2 (Moscow: Foreign Languages Publishing House, 1962), p. 416.

6. Karl Marx and Friedrich Engels, "Origin of Family, Private Property and the State," in *Karl Marx and Friedrich Engels: Selected Works*, vol. 1 (Moscow: Foreign Languages Publishing House, 1962).

7. Richard Boyd, in *Images of Science*, ed. Paul M. Churchland and Clifford A. Hooker (Chicago: University of Chicago Press, 1985), p. 14.

8. Michael Wolff, "Impetus Mechanics as a Physical Argument for Copernicanism: Copernicus, Benedetti, Galileo," *Science in Context* 1, 216.

9. See Bruno Latour, *Science in Action* (Cambridge: Harvard University Press, 1987), chap. 1.

10. This story was reported extensively as this chapter was being written, in August and September 1996.

11. News and Analysis, In Focus section, "Bugs in the Data?" *Scientific American*, October 1996, 20.

12. Responding to the biological origins hypothesis, *Scientific American* quotes Derek Sears, a specialist in meteoritics, as saying: "There are nonbiological interpretations of [NASA's David S.] McKay's data that are much more likely" (News and Analysis, "Bugs," 20).

13. News and Analysis, "Bugs," 22.

14. Ibid.

15. See note 5 above.

16. See Paul R. Gross and Norman Levitt, *Higher Superstition* (Baltimore: Johns Hopkins University Press, 1994). The Sokal hoax has prompted wide discussion, including pieces in *Lingua Franca* and *The New York Review*.

17. W. V. O. Quine, "Epistemology Naturalized," in *Naturalizing Epistemology*, ed. Hilary Kornblith (Cambridge: Bradford of MIT Press, 1994).

18. Hayden White, for instance, is a historian whose work may be read in this manner.

19. For an especially clear account of the role of misogyny in much of what has passed for political philosophizing, see Diana Coole, *Women in Political Theory* (Sussex, UK: Harvester Press, 1993).

20. See the work of Charlene Haddock Seigfried for an account of women in the pragmatist tradition.

Index